SUBWAY NICKELS

A SURVEY

OF

NEW YORK CITY'S TRANSIT PROBLEM

SUBMITTED TO

HON. JOHN F. HYLAN
MAYOR OF THE CITY OF NEW YORK

AND

BOARD OF ESTIMATE AND APPORTIONMENT
OF THE CITY OF NEW YORK

By

HARRY A. GORDON
Special Corporation Counsel

JANUARY 29, 1925

"I HAVE vigorously opposed the Transit Commission's efforts to put into effect transit plans, similar to those foisted upon the people under the dual contracts, that will tie the City of New York for generations to the traction corporations now operating the City-owned subways.

"Over ten years have passed; the money has been invested; the business has been more prosperous than was ever contemplated; the subways are more packed than was ever expected; more nickels are coming in than could possibly have been calculated, but the net result is that the City has not received one cent interest.

"The City regards that as a poor business investment for the people and I regard those with whom the City has that investment as not good partners; and my point of view is that if the City is to continue in the same line of business, it certainly does not want to continue with the same partners, where it can expect the same results—in other words, more money and no return. . . . . .

"My position in this matter is, that as the business representative of the City of New York, it would be folly to put more money in an enterprise with partners who have promised a return which they have never made."

Hon. JOHN F. HYLAN,
Mayor.

CONTENTS

CHAPTER I

Introduction

Hon. John F. Hylan,
Mayor of the City of New York,

and

The Board of Estimate and Apportionment
of The City of New York.

Honorable Sirs:

As Special Counsel retained to present the charges for the removal of the Transit Commissioners, I hereby submit this report:

THE TRANSIT PROBLEM

The importance of the Transit problem to the public and to the Government of the City of New York which has invested $300,000,000 in the unfortunate partnership with the traction corporations operating in the City of New York, and the recent investigation by the Moreland Commissioner, is the reason for this extended presentation and analysis of the situation. The magnitude of the problem and the vital interests of the city require, that once and for all, a complete and exhaustive statement of the situation shall be presented.

The city's strait reduced to its final and ultimate terms is two-fold: *First,* the miserably inadequate ser-

---

Note.—Italics are the writer's. All references, except where otherwise indicated, are to names of witnesses and to pages of stenographer's minutes of the hearings before the Hon. John V. McAvoy, Commissioner under the Moreland Act, held Dec. 15, 1924–Jan. 8, 1925.

vice rendered by the two traction companies, which between themselves and with the connivance of those who are still the Transit Commissioners of the State of New York, have seized the traction monopoly of the city. The I. R. T. holds in the hollow of its hand the traveling public of Manhattan and the Bronx, and the B.-M. T., a holding company organized to evade direct responsibility for its conduct, is in substantial control of the transit situation in the Boroughs of Brooklyn and Queens; and, *Second,* the unprecedented growth of the city necessitates the building of new and more subways and transportation facilities such as buses, which the development of the automobile has made possible, desirable and necessary.

THE CITY'S DILEMMA

One would suppose that the Government of the State of New York would not treat the City of New York as a satrapy or as a subjugated province, and would at least afford to the citizens of our City an opportunity to create organs of administration and government to control the destinies of the City, as they affect this all important problem of transportation. Unfortunately the contrary is the fact. The City of New York never had, and has not now, the right or authority to say a word as to the adequacy of the service rendered by the traction corporations. The City of New York never had any power to initiate new routes or new subways.

Unbelievable as it may seem the City of New York with its $300,000,000 investment is chained, to a partnership with the traction companies through the betrayal of the City's interests, by the outrageous Dual Contracts of 1913. The climax of the iniquity was reached when, under the Transit Act of 1921, enacted during the administration of Governor Miller, the "leading spirit" in this indefensible betrayal of the City was clothed with the great authority of the Empire State, to continue in the capacity of an alleged "regulator of service" to be rendered by these corporations and as an "initiator of new subways." The Transit Commissioners aim at but one purpose—forever to compel the City to remain in bondage to these traction corporations, as their partner—to pay all the losses and share in no profits.

When the Transit Commission was created, the office of the Transit Construction Commissioner held by John H. Delaney, was abolished. The Transit Commission succeeded to the regulatory powers of the then only Public Service Commissioner Barrett, First District, and also to the construction powers exercised by the then Transit Construction Commissioner Delaney.

It should be clearly borne in mind, particularly because of attempts of the Transit Commissioners, to confuse the issue and shift the blame, that the sole *power to initiate construction and provide for new subways from the time the Transit Commission came into office in April,* 1921 *until July* 1, 1924, *when the present Board of Transportation was appointed, was vested exclusively in this State Transit Commission.* Throughout the seven years of the present administration repeated but unsuccessful efforts were made to secure from the legislature such power for the City. The City has a right to make suggestions for new subways to the Transit Commission. The Mayor presented a comprehensive program for rapid transit construction, as early as September 6, 1922, which the Transit Commission has ignored.

The excuse for the creation of the Transit Commission is written in the law which created it. The

Legislature took cognizance of an "emergency" which existed in the transit situation in the City of New York. Ostensibly the Transit Commission was created to give relief to the public from the emergency. Nothing has been done to give that relief, either by requiring the traction companies to give, on the existing lines, the kind of service that the contracts with the city and the law require, or by the construction of new subways. Its principal concern has been the financial rehabilitation of the traction companies.

The members of the Transit Commission are all glib-tongued garrulous orators. One would hardly expect that from Commissioner O'Ryan, a General with previous military training. No one will deny that all that was said by these gentlemen could be very succinctly stated in at most seventy-five pages of testimony.

Mr. Leroy T. Harkness apparently is the business manager of the Commission. He had charge of its records and accounts, and supervision over the reports and accounts of the railroad companies, and of the determinations of cost made by the Chief Engineer. He was the employment agent of the Transit Commission and a lecturer and writer on increased fares for traction companies.

Commissioner O'Ryan is outstandingly the author of the famous "Readjustment Plan" of the Transit Commission, for the so-called unification of our transit lines, the financial rehabilitation of forty traction companies, and purchase for the city of a thousand franchises and obsolete surface car lines. He superintended the reorganization of the Interborough and New York Railways Company, and it is to him that we should be thankful for destroying his colleagues' alibi based on the lack of shop and yard facilities, as we shall see.

Commissioner McAneny, the Chairman of the Commission is apparently its master mind. He is the expert who gave the kind of service that we got on our rapid transit lines. To him was left the difficult task of explaining the unexplainable, and well did he carry this burden. Too bad this silver-tongued gentleman, who can talk endlessly, and with his perfect command of words, conceal any thought and confuse any issue, did not live in the ancient days of the Greeks. How well he might have functioned as the Dean of the School for Mental Gymnastics, described by Aristophanes in "The Clouds." How plausible are his proofs that wrong is right!

I am wondering whether Governor Miller in appointing these gentlemen had in mind that all that was required to relieve the emergency in our transit situation was lip service. Judging from the record, their activities since their appointment, have been only in that direction, and in the preparation of words and figures in attempted justification for their inaction.

THE LIMIT OF ENDURANCE REACHED

CHARGES AGAINST THE TRANSIT COMMISSION

All the protestations of Mayor Hylan against the intolerable conditions on our transit lines and against the outrageous treatment of the City by the Legislature, all the appeals of the city administration to the State Legislature for relief from this impossible situation, have been unheeded. When the hope for relief from a hostile legislature was seen to be in vain, the Board of Estimate and Apportionment decided to appeal to the Governor of the State of New York for the only relief which lay within his power. Accordingly, on May

7th, 1923, a resolution was adopted by the Board of Estimate and Apportionment as follows:

> "Whereas, The Transit Commission * * * has failed to afford proper relief to the citizens of New York in the way of proper and adequate transportation facilities and has accomplished nothing of substantial or constructive nature, although it had held office for a period of almost two years, at an unwarranted cost to the taxpayers and at the expense of health, comfort and convenience of the traveling public, and
>
> "Whereas, In the opinion of this Board, the interest of the city would be best served by the termination of the Commission, be it
>
> "Resolved, By the Board of Estimate and Apportionment that the Corporation Counsel be requested to advise the Board whether the members of the present Transit Commission can be removed from office, and if so, what steps should be taken to bring about such removal."

I was retained to finally formulate the charges for the removal of the Transit Commissioners and to collect and present the evidence in support thereof. On October 14, 1924, the proposed charges were read before the Board of Estimate and Apportionment and on October 24, 1924, a resolution was adopted, voting the charges and their submission to the Governor. Much has been said, although entirely immaterial to the inquiry, as to differences between the original draft as read, and the charges finally adopted. I am responsible for those changes. A comparison will disclose that the modifications were in the main, in verbiage only; that not a single allegation of fact was withdrawn, that the changes were made to conform them to the form of charges, rather than of an indictment. A copy of the charges is attached, marked Exhibit "A."

Section 4 of the Public Service Commission law provides that the Governor may remove the Transit Commissioners upon charges, after a trial upon ten days' notice. The charges lie on the Governor's table. On November 29, 1924, his Excellency, the Governor, appointed the Honorable John V. McAvoy, one of the Justices of the Supreme Court, New York County, a Commissioner, under Section 8 of the Executive Law, called the Moreland Act, to make an investigation into the affairs and management of the Transit Commission.

HEARING BEFORE COMMISSIONER MC AVOY

At the outset of the hearings before Commissioner McAvoy, the City of New York was represented by Hon. George P. Nicholson, Corporation Counsel, Mr. Edgar J. Kohler, Assistant Corporation Counsel, Mr. Max D. Steuer and myself, as Special Counsel, and Mr. Louis Lande, Special Assistant Counsel. From the beginning, the representatives of the City stated their position, that because the investigation was the result of charges, filed by the Board of Estimate against the Transit Commissioners, that the Board of Estimate be allowed to make proof of the charges, and that the City's counsel be permitted to examine its witnesses and cross-examine the Transit Commissioners and their witnesses. *The Moreland Commissioner ruled that counsel for the City would not be permitted to call, examine or cross-examine witnesses.* Upon the grounds stated by Mr. Steuer, that no useful purpose could be served by him, in sitting and listening, and that he had not been retained for that purpose, and upon the additional ground which I assigned, and in which Mr. Nicholson concurred, that "right of cross-examination of witnesses was an inherent right under our Anglo-Saxon Jurisprudence in connection with any proceeding where there is a hearing on any controversy"—the City's representatives withdrew their appearance on the second day of the hearings, and did not further participate, save that when Mayor Hylan testified I was present and suggested to Mr. Henry L. Sherman, the counsel designated by Commissioner McAvoy, certain inquiries (p. 251-253).

Hearings before Commissioner McAvoy commenced on December 15, 1924, and were held on fifteen days. Twenty-seven hundred and twenty-three pages of testimony were taken, three hundred and twenty exhibits were received.

The witnesses were the three Transit Commissioners, Mr. Philip Mathews, the Chief Executive Officer of the Transit Commission; Mr. Willam C. Menden, the President of the B.-M. T.; Mr. Frank Hedley, the President of the I. R. T.; Mr. James S. Doyle, Mr. Hedley's assistant; Mr. George Keegan, another of Mr, Hedley's assistants;; Mr. S. Herbert Wolfe, an accountant engaged by Commissioner McAvoy; Mr. Robert Ridgway, the Chief Engineer of the Board of Transportation, formerly Chief Engineer of the Transit Commission; the Mayor, the Comptroller, Margaret Quirk, Mary Collins Rooney, C. L. Hutzelman, John S. Coppola, complaining citizens. Although Mr. Henry L. Sherman, Counsel to the Commissioner, stated: "I stand ready at any time to receive from the Counsel of the Board of Estimate and Apportionment, or from anyone else, evidence which may be deemed pertinent to this inquiry so that it may be presented to you for consideration, so that all the questions relating thereto may be propounded to any witness who may be called, that relates not only to the general scope of the investigation but also to the charges preferred by the Board of Estimate and Apportionment, which up to this time, as your Honor is aware, has been before us" (p. 254). Apparently the policy of the investigation was subsequently changed.

This is evident from the fact that at the close of Mayor Hylan's testimony, I suggested that an inquiry be conducted into an alleged expenditure of nearly six million five hundred thousand dollars, as an incident of the reorganization of the B.-M. T., and on January 7, 1925 I also caused to be delivered to Mr. Sherman, a communication, a copy of which I am annexing, Exhibit "B," in which I suggested further subjects for examination. Reference to the receipt of this communication will be found on page 507 of the record. My suggestions have been ignored, and the evidence which I have sought will not be found in the record.

An examination of the stenographer's minutes will disclose that at least 90 per cent. of the testimony elicited, consists of a statement, restatement and endless repetition of a mass, of what is now ancient history in the transit situation, and practically all of which is contained in public records. The archives of the Transit Commission and its predecessors, were raked and their contents dumped into the record. Lengthy communications were prepared, after notice of the charges, between the Transit Commission and the traction companies containing nothing probative, and only self-serving declarations, and their united arraignment of the City Administration, and attempts to cast the blame for our present intolerable transit situation upon the Mayor and were freely admitted in evidence. This is not intended as a criticism of Commissioner McAvoy. There was no one to object to the admission of this irrelevant evidence. His counsel stated that he was anxous that the Transit Commissioners have the fullest opportunity to present their views and the Transit Commissioners took that full opportunity. It became a self-exculpating proceeding for the Transit Commissioners. Notwithstanding this unlimited latitude, as I shall indicate, they convicted themselves, not only of the charges which the Board of Estimate made against them, but of grossest indifference to the interest of the traveling public and proved themselves concerned solely as benefactors of the traction companies.

It would be purposeless further to comment upon the manner and method of the investigation conducted by Mr. Sherman. The citizens of the City of New York who have followed from day to day the developments of this hearing, have formed their own opinion of this futile and fruitless investigation. But for good or evil, the transit problem is still with us, after the presentation of nearly three thousand pages of so-called testimony and truck loads of exhibits.

What is this problem? I shall endeavor to give what I hope, will be an adequate picture of the plight of the City, in regard to rapid transit. The following pages will tell their own story. Undisputed and uncontradicted facts and admissions of the Transit Commissioners themselves will reveal the shocking situation and will show that the strong language used in these introductory pages are restrained under-statements of an appalling situation.

CHAPTER II

The Background

HISTORY OF RAPID TRANSIT—DUAL CONTRACTS
INVESTMENT—OPERATIONS—FIVE-CENT FARE

The rapid transit system of the City of New York, all boroughs except Richmond, which is not yet physically embraced in the system, consists of the four elevated lines in Manhattan and Bronx (Second, Third, Sixth and Ninth Avenues), owned by the Manhattan Railway Company and leased to the Interborough Rapid Transit Company, with extensions and additions made since 1913; the old elevated lines of the B. R. T. system in Brooklyn, as these existed in 1913, extensions and additional tracking added since; and the subway and elevated lines constructed under what have come to be known, as Contracts 1, 2, 3 and 4, the first three with the Interborough Rapid Transit Company and the last, with the New York Municipal Railway Company, a subsidiary of the old B. R. T., whose rights have now passed to the New York Rapid Transit Corporation, a subsidiary of the B.-M. T.

Contracts Nos. 1 and 2 were made with the railroad companies by the Board of Rapid Transit Railroad Commissioners, and Contracts 3 and 4 by the Public Service Commission of the First District, both acting for and on behalf of the City of New York.

Contract No. 1 was made on February 21, 1900, and has been supplemented by agreement dated April 15, 1915. Under it there was constructed the subway from Van Cortlandt Park to 42nd Street on the west, thence across 42nd Street to Grand Central Station, thence south along Fourth Avenue to City Hall; also the subway from Bronx Park to 110th Street and Lenox Avenue, thence westerly connecting with the westerly line at about 96th Street and Broadway. Under this contract the city paid the entire cost of construction and the company the cost of equipment. This subway, together with that which was constructed under Contract No. 2 was leased to the company for periods respectively of fifty and thirty-five years, with certain privileges of renewal to the railroad company, which are no longer effective, because of the merger of these contracts in Contract No. 3.

Contract No. 2 was made July 21, 1902, and modified January 31, 1914. Under it was constructed the subway from City Hall under the East River and into Brooklyn to Atlantic Avenue.

The investment of the City under Contracts 1 and 2, as determined in 1921, is $62,767,713, and of the company $43,398,479, a total of $106,166,192.

The subway under Contract No. 1 commenced operation in 1904 and under Contract No. 2, between 1906 and 1908. *Between* 1908 *and* 1913 *no provision was made for the construction of any new subways in the city.*

On March 19, 1913, the so-called dual contracts, No. 3 and No. 4, the former with the I. R. T., in Manhattan, and the latter with the subsidiary of the B. R. T. in Brooklyn, were made. The contracts provide that they shall be completed and the new subways be in operation by January 1, 1917. *In other words, the new subways, and the elevated extensions and third tracking provided for by the so-called related certificates accompanying the dual contracts, and all equipment and facil-*

ities, including repair and inspection shops and storage yards were required to be fully completed by January 1, 1917.

The "Related Certificates" were in the nature of supplementary contracts executed simultaneously with the dual subway contracts, and made provision for the extension and third tracking of the existing elevated lines in Manhattan, Bronx and Brooklyn.

The present City administration came into office on January 1, 1918, and the greater part of the record before Commissioner McAvoy consists of an inquiry into the non-completion of the subway lines and facilities, under Contracts 3 and 4, and particularly with respect to the non-completion of certain additions to repair and inspection shops and storage barns, and not one word of comment is made upon, or criticism directed at the parties responsible for the non-fulfillment of these contracts before the present administration, except the testimony of Comptroller Craig, who brought to the attention of the Commissioner, that this delay in the completion of these contracts served to the great advantage of the railroads and detriment of the public, and that in 1915 and 1916 when the work should have been done, the cost of labor was cheaper than before the outbreak of the World War (p. 1891).

In this connection it should be borne in mind that on January 1, 1918, we were in the midst of the War, when steel fabrication was controlled and to all intents prohibited by the Federal Priorities Board, and that the three years following the cessation of hostilities, on November 11, 1918, brought kaleidoscopic changes of financial depression and inflation which did not lend themselves to a program of stable and progressive rapid transit construction.

Contract No. 3 provided for an extension of the old subway, by a continuation north of the easterly leg, from 42nd Street into the Bronx, adding the Jerome Ave. and Pelham Bay Park branches, and the continuation south, of the westerly leg, down 7th Avenue and under the East River in a new tunnel (Clark Street), the linking with the old line at Atlantic Avenue, thence proceeding along Flatbush Avenue to Prospect Park Plaza, and thence by Eastern Parkway as a subway so far as Buffalo Avenue, and then as an elevated line to New Lots Avenue, the Brownsville District of Brooklyn, with a branch from Eastern Parkway, from Nostrand to Flatbush Avenues.

It also provided for the so-called Queensboro line running originally from Times Square and later from 8th Avenue and 42d Street, under 42d Street and through the Steinway Tunnel. It also provided for the dual operation by the Interborough and the Brooklyn Company of two elevated lines from the Queensboro Plaza in Long Island City, one to Astoria and another to Corona.

As a result of these constructions the Z formation of subways, under Contracts 1 and 2, was converted into the H system by the addition of the Lexington Avenue Line to the north, on the easterly side, and the Seventh Avenue Line to the south, on the westerly side.

It provided also for the linking up of these subways with the elevated lines owned by the Manhattan Railway Company and leased to the Interborough and for the extension and additional tracking of those elevated lines. The cost of construction was paid by the city, with a contribution by the railroad company, which also paid the entire cost of equipment, and improvements to the elevated lines.

Under Contract No. 3 the investment of the company as of June 30, 1923, is $105,970,736, and of the city $93,362,704, a total of $199,333,440 besides $41,423,759 invested by the I. R. T. in extensions and additional tracking of the Manhattan "L" Line. Thus the total investment of the city under Contracts 1, 2 and 3 is $156,000,000 and of the company $150,000,000, besides its investment in "L" improvements. Their investments are roughly the same.

Under Contract No. 3 it is provided that after payment of operating expenses, there shall be first paid to the city interest and sinking fund charges on its investment of about $63,000,000 under Contracts 1 and 2, a total slightly in excess of 4 per cent per annum. During the year ending June 30, 1924 the city's return on this investment was $2,610,999 (p. 2175).

The Company then receives a so-called preferential of $6,335,000 which was stated to be the average profit realized by the I. R. T. from operation of the subways under Contracts 1 and 2 during the years 1910 and 1911.

This Contract No. 3, was negotiated between the Board of Estimate and Apportionment, acting through a Committee of which Mr. George McAneny, now Chairman of the Transit Commission, was Chairman, and the Public Service Commission of the First District and the Railroad Company. Leroy T. Harkness was Assistant Counsel to the Public Service Commission and drafted the contract. In other words, the agreement was, that, out of the first proceeds of operation of the combined subway system, the city receive slightly over 4 per cent. on its investment of $63,000,000 under Contracts 1 and 2 and that the railroad company receive $6,335,000 on its investment, under those same contracts, of under $46,000,000. The city receives a return of 4 per cent. on its investment, whereas the railroad company receives a return of about 14 per cent. on its investment.

This $6,335,000, it is claimed, respresents $3,157,000, the interest charges of the company, at 6 per cent. on the bonds of $52,615,000 which it issued to finance its investment under Contracts 1 and 2, and $3,178,000, a profit, on absolutely no investment. The $52,615,000 bonds represent at least $6,000,000 over the actual investment of the railroad company under Contracts 1 and 2.

Contract No. 4 and related certificates provided for the extension and additional tracking of certain of the Brooklyn elevated lines, the reconstruction and adaptation for rapid transit operation, of other specified elevated lines, and the construction of the following new city-owned lines—all to be operated as one system:

Broadway-Brooklyn-Fourth Avenue Line—Beginning at Queensboro Bridge Plaza, crossing the East River to 59th Street and Seventh Avenue, then south on Broadway, to Whitehall Street, under the East River via the Montague Street Tunnel, to DeKalb Avenue, then down Fourth Avenue to 86th Street. This line includes the Centre Street loop, running to the Municipal Building (constructed prior to 1913) and used for operation of trains, from Brooklyn over the Williamsburg and Manhattan Bridges; and the Nassau-Broad Street section, running from the Municipal Building in Manhattan and connecting with the Montague Street tunnel. Provision was also made for the joint operation with the I. R. T. of trains from the Queensboro Bridge Plaza of the lines, one to Corona and the other to Astoria, as previously indicated;

Culver Line, an elevated structure which connects with the Broadway-Fourth Avenue line at the 38th

Street cut, Brooklyn, and runs via Gravesend Avenue to Coney Island;

Fourteenth Street-Eastern Line, which begins at Sixth Avenue, Manhattan, and runs as a subway through Fourteenth Street under the East River to Williamsburg, and then as an elevated structure (so originally projected) to East New York.

Under this contract the company agreed to furnish the equipment, and to pay for the extensions, additional tracking, and the reconstruction of the existing lines, and to contribute towards the cost of construction of the city lines as follows: $13,500,000 (which includes $1,000,000 for easements), plus the cost of making the physical connection at Canal Street between the Centre Street loop and the main Broadway-Fourth Avenue line.

The investment of the city under Contract No. 4, as testified to, is $149,000,000, and of the company is $88,000,000. Of this sum only $46,177,000 was invested by the company in subway cost of construction and equipment and $41,823,000 in extension and improvements of its L lines (p. 2266).

Thus the total actual investments of the New York and Brooklyn companies in subways under all the contracts are, about $150,000,000 by the New York Company and $46,000,000 by the Brooklyn Company, a total of less than $200,000,000, and the City's investment is nearly $300,000,000.

Contract No. 4 provides that after payment of operating expenses and allowances for depreciation, the first charge on the profits, shall be a preferential of $3,500,000 claimed to have been the profit of the B. R. T. from operation of its elevated lines during the years 1910 and 1911. There is no *accurate* appraisal of the value of these old elevated lines and equipment. There is an appraisal by the Transit Commission as of June 30, 1921 which fixes the same at about $22,400,000. Undoubtedly $20,000,000 would be a very fair value. On that basis Contract No. 4 assures to the B.-M. T., by the guaranteed preferential, at least 17½ per cent. per annum on its investment in L lines. On that basis Contract No. 4 assures to the B.-M. T., by the guaranteed preferential, at least 17½ per cent. per annum on its investment in L lines.

Contracts Nos. 3 and 4 both provide, that, after payment of interest on the city's investment under Contracts 1 and 2 amounting to about $2,500,000 a year, and after the payment to the railroad companies of not only their preferentials of $6,335,000 to the I. R. T., and $3,500,000 to the B. M. T., there shall next be paid to the railroad companies, interest and sinking fund charges upon their investments under Contracts 3 and 4; that then only shall the city receive interest and sinking fund requirements on its investment, and that the balance shall be shared equally between the companies and the city. Of course the city only gets interest and only divides the profits after all deficits from prior years have been made good to the companies. With respect to the I. R. T., the deficits bear compound interest at the rate of five per cent per annum computed semi-annually.

The city, as indicated, has about $300,000,000 invested in these subways. Except for the interest on the $63,000,000 invested under Contracts 1 and 2, it has not to date received one single cent interest on its remaining $240,000,000 investment. The annual cost to the city in 1924 for interest on the bonds which it issued for this investment was $10,230,000 (p. 2177). This and prior deficits are included in the budget and have been paid by the taxpayers. To date the deficits from operation under Contract No. 3 (The Interborough) are as follows: due the city $44,702,831 (p. 2267); due the company $10,434,623, a total of $55,137,453 (p. 2293), and under Contract No. 4, due the city for period from August, 1920 to June 30, 1924, $25,851,790 (p. 2282) and due the company $15,623,318 (p. 2281) besides $18,000,000 due the city, for period prior to August, 1920, and included in cost of construction, a total of $59,478,108 deficits, under Contract No. 4, and a grand total of $114,600,000 deficits under Contracts 3 and 4.

And these are the contracts which McAneny boasts that he engineered, and Harkness brags that he drafted. The only redeeming aspect of the contracts, are that the city has the satisfaction of knowing that at least on paper, the city owns the subways and the equipment, and that on some remote day, the right to operate them will revert to the city, *and that the contract specifically limits the companies to charge a single fare of five cents with universal free transfers* (p. 2576) *and that besides under given conditions the city may "recapture" these lines—a word very well chosen.*

It is important that the provisions for "recapture" be clearly understood, because to "recapture" has definitely become the policy of the city, and has the approval of the citizens of the city as indicated at the polls in 1921 and of the people of the State as indicated by recent constitutional amendment legalizing municipal operation of our rapid transit lines.

Both Contracts Nos. 3 and 4 provide that the city may recapture the whole or parts of our subway system. Under Contract No. 3 the system is divided into four parts or sections and under Contract No. 4 into three sections. The sections under Contract No. 4 are classified as:

1. Broadway-Fourth Avenue Line,
2. Culver Line and
3. Fourteenth Street-Eastern Line.

Under Contract No. 3 the sections are as follows:

1. Steinway Tunnel Line,
2. Seventh Avenue-Lexington Avenue Line,
3. White Plains Road Line, and
4. Eastern Parkway Line.

Both contracts provide that the city may recapture the subways in toto, at any time after ten years after the commencement of operation of any part of the system, or may recapture any section at any time after ten years, after the commencement of the operation of any substantial operable part of that section (McAneny, p. 2583) and the right to recapture may be exercised upon one year's notice to the railroad company and the payment of the company's investment in the subway proposed to be recaptured, plus a maximum sum of 15 per cent. on such investment, which recapture price gradually diminishes until at the expiration of the terms of the leases of the railroad companies, which is about 49 years, the roads revert to the city without payment. These leases will expire in 1964 and 1962 under Contracts Nos. 3 and 4 respectively. Each year the recapture price with respect to the I. R. T. is reduced by $2,700,000 and with respect to the B.-M. T. by $1,300,000, a total annual reduction of $4,000,000 (McAneny, p. 2574).

The city's right to recapture in toto, the subway lines operated by the Brooklyn Company under Contract No. 4 accrued on August 4, 1923 so that the city may at any time reclaim that subway.

The city's right to recapture the entire subway system of the Interborough will accrue on June 22, 1925 (p. 2584, 2585).

The dates of accrual of the rights of the city to recapture sections only under Contract No. 4 with the Brooklyn Company are as follows:

Gravesend-Culver Line—March 16, 1929;
Broadway-4th Avenue Line—August 4, 1923;
Fourteenth Street-Eastern Line, which is not yet completed from Montrose Avenue—10 years from date of completion.

Under Contract No. 3 the dates of recapture of sections are as follows:

Steinway-Tunnel Line—June 22, 1925;
Seventh Avenue-Lexington Avenue Line—June 2, 1927;
White Plains Road Line—March 3, 1927;
Eastern Parkway Line—April 15, 1929.

It should be borne in mind that a recapture by the city of the subways in Manhattan and the Bronx under Contract No. 3, would leave to the railroad company the "Z" system, which is not recapturable under Contracts 1 and 2, namely the line from Van Cortlandt Park in the west, Bronx Park in the east, which runs down to 7th Avenue and 42d Street on the west, across 42d Street and down 4th Avenue to Atlantic Avenue, Brooklyn, and give the City the Clark Street tunnel, the 7th Avenue Line below 42d Street, the road in Brooklyn from the Clark Street tunnel and the Lexington Avenue Line above 42d Street, with branches in the Bronx. Accordingly, in order that it may have continuous trunk lines in Manhattan, the city is granted the privilege of exchanging, either the northerly or southerly leg in the "H" system, so that the city may on recapture, have either the Lexington Avenue Line with branches in the Bronx running through the old tunnel under the East River, or the westerly line from Van Cortlandt Park through the Clark Street tunnel and out into Brooklyn, upon appropriate adjustments of prices, on an earning basis.

As already indicated the investment of the B.-M. T. subsidiary under Contract No. 4 is $46,000,000. Not all of that represents real cost of construction or equipment. Included in that sum are high interest rates paid on the money which was borrowed for that construction and equipment, duplications, damages from delay, mistakes, and the penalties of extravagance. Undoubtedly under economic and businesslike management that construction and equipment would not have cost in excess of $30,000,000.

Be that as it may, the City must pay that alleged cost of construction and equipment, together with a bonus upon recapture. The cost to the City of recapturing the entire B.-M. T. subway system is $52,995,000 (McAneny, pp. 2588-2589) and of the I. R. T. subways $123,995,000.

If the downtown legs of the "H" in Manhattan are traded, so that the City will own the easterly line, there will be an additional $10,000,000 cost, or if the uptown legs are exchanged so that the City will own the westerly line, there will be an additional cost of $24,300,000, and taking into account additional equipment and improvement, the total cost to the City of recapturing all the subways under Contracts 3 and 4 will not be in excess of $200,000,000, according to the testimony of McAneny (p. 2589).

If the $275,000,000 proposed to be exempted from charge against the City's debt limit, is made available, the City will not only be able to recapture all of the subways, but will have at least $75,000,000 for use towards future construction.

Taking into account estimates given by the Comptroller before Commissioner McAvoy of amounts available from regular sources and conservative estimated increased real estate assessments, at least $175,000,000 besides this $75,000,000, a total of $250,000,000 will be available during 1925 and 1926 for subway construction (p. 2147), should this constitutional amendment be enacted, with corresponding amounts in subsequent years, during the course of the contemplated future construction of subways. There can be no question of the City's financial ability to carry forward its present subway construction program. It is true, as has been urged, that the constitutional amendment cannot be made effective until January 1, 1928, but with reasonable assurance of its passage, the City can readily regulate the letting of contracts, in accordance with its assured prospective borrowing capacity. Besides, the City can arrange to physically take possession of the recaptured lines contemporaneously with the commencement of operation of the new subways.

During the year ending June 30, 1924 there were carried by the I. R. T. 714,000,000 passengers, and by the B.-M. T. 600,000,000 passengers, an aggregate of 1,314,000,000 passengers or at the rate of about 4,000,000 a day. The population of the city is 6,000,000, of whom about 2,000,000 are children under 14. Thus the rapid transit lines of this city carry a very substantial part of the entire population, and their operation and particularly the limitation in the contracts to a five-cent fare may unquestionably be said, to insure to the benefit of the great majority of the people of the city, who as taxpayers pay the city's $10,000,000 deficit from subway investment. It was forcibly presented before Commissioner McAvoy that subway operation is a benefit, not only to the riders, but to all who own property or are engaged in business in territory served by our rapid transit lines.

The five-cent fare has become a settled municipal policy of the City. It was urged by the Comptroller before Commissioner McAvoy that it is a sound economic municipal policy that these deficits in the light of the benefits, which rapid transit confers upon the whole people of the city, be treated as legitimate expenses of the municipal government and are properly includible in the City's annual budgets.

It is unnecessary to concur in these views because in fact the City, in the last analysis is not mulcted by these deficits, but on the contrary, is financially benefited by our subways to the extent of many times the amount of these deficits. In the first place, the railroad companies pay in taxes and assessments nearly $10,000,000 annually (O'Ryan, pp. 2488-2489). Besides, since the commencement of subway operation, the city's assessment valuations have increased three billion dollars, of which at least two billion is due to the construction of our new subway lines, the income of which to the city is at least fifty million dollars a year (McAneny, pp. 2596-2597). The point is that the City can have these benefits but, instead of deficits, have profits from the municipal operation of its subways.

Much of the testimony before Commissioner McAvoy was directed to an inquiry as to the cause of these deficits. It was shown that repeated efforts were made since 1918 by the railroad companies to secure increased fares. There are carried on the transit lines of the City about 6,000,000 passengers daily. An increase to an eight-cent fare would spell an exaction from the traveling public of $180,000 per day or in excess of

$65,000,000 per annum and the huge sum of nearly $3,000,000,000 during the term of the leases. Mayor Hylan is blamed by the Transit Commissioners for stubbornly opposing and preventing this increase in fares.

It appears that early in the present administration, on January 10, 1919, the Board of Estimate and Apportionment declared its policy in opposition to any fare increases (p. 1992) that the Mayor has ever since carried forward that policy and that there have been no increases in fares and the companies have been held to their obligations under Contracts Nos. 3 and 4.

It is claimed that the deficits from operation under Contracts Nos. 3 and 4 are due to the impossibility to operate with financial success, our rapid transit lines, on a five-cent fare. As early as August of 1921 Harkness began agitating for increased fares in New York and read an article before the Public Utilities section of the American Bar Association in Cincinnati, in which he says:

> "The question naturally occurs, if most of the cities in the country have relieved their traction situation by increases in fare, why hasn't New York City done so? To those who have examined the situation superficially, a sufficient answer has been found in the hostility of the City administration. The City administration has been vigorously and bitterly opposing an increased fare."
>
> * * * * * * * * * *
>
> "To carry out such a plan of readjustment, the Commission is vested with the broadest powers to vary rates, including the power to vary rates fixed in municipal consents and contracts; to revise existing contracts and to make new ones, and to value and acquire railroad properties for and in the name

of the City. Provision is made for submitting plans and contracts to the local Board of Estimate and Apportionment, but if that Board finally refuses to approve, the ultimate power to carry the plan into effect is vested in the Commission" (Craig, p. 2112).

Notwithstanding that, on September 9, 1921, the Transit Commission made public its plan of readjustment, to which reference will be made later, under which a fare of at least eight and possibly ten cents would have been inevitable, the almost incredible situation is presented that at the conclusion of the hearings before Commissioner McAvoy, both Harkness and McAneny, and I understand also O'Ryan, in public statement made January 14, 1925, have finally unequivocally endorsed the Mayor's stand for a five-cent fare on existing lines as justifiable, on the basis of present operation.

The question naturally presents itself, why, under these circumstances, and in view of the fact that even the Transit Commissioners have finally committed themselves to the five-cent fare, there should have been this aggregate deficit of over $100,000,000 from operation of our subways. The answer is simple when consideration is given to the waste, extravagances, huge sums paid in swollen dividends on watered capitalization, receivership expenses, Wall Street syndicates and various committees, counsel and committees of stockholders and bondholders and fees of receivers and lawyers on reorganization.

The I. R. T. collected during the year ended 1924 over $38,000,000. The fact is that the I. R. T. during every single year without exception, commencing 1912, made a substantial profit from operation of its subway lines under Contracts 1, 2 and 3, after payment of all interest, maintenance and operating expenses, etc., the profits for the last three years being respectively as follows:

1924	$3,359,259.73
1923	2,002,854.04
1922	2,012,587.56

I am annexing hereto Exhibit "C" showing the results of operation of the Interborough Rapid Transit Company from 1912-1915 to 1924.

So too with respect to the B.-M. T. and its predecessor, the B. R. T., that company earned a profit from the operation of its subways under Contract No. 4 for every year, except 1920-1921 of the Receivership of the B.-M. T., when there was an extraordinary cost of operation due to strikes. Exhibit "D" hereto annexed, shows that during each year commencing 1915 and ending 1924, excepting 1920-1921, the Brooklyn Company earned such profit. The profits in 1924, 1923 and 1922 are respectively as follows:

1924	$2,492,982.43
1923	1,038,939.65
1922	1,106,623.12

The interest deductions include the interest on all of the obligations of the Brooklyn Company, including its watered bonds on the old elevated lines.

It is to be borne in mind that these are the company's figures, that none of the items of expenses have been disturbed, including the extravagant, wasteful and unbusinesslike expenditures which would not be under municipal operation. They include what brokers and money-lenders exacted on loans also charges which belong to other and less profitable properties of the companies and not operated as part of Contracts 1, 2, 3 and 4.

I direct attention to the fact that in these schedules no account has been taken and no interest charged on the city's investment of over $240,000,000, under contracts 3 and 4. In other words, whilst the roads have earned a profit for the companies, the result has been a loss to the city of about $10,000,000 a year.

There can be no question but that under municipal operation the income from our subways, will not only provide for all operating and maintenance expenses, depreciation and interest on investment, but furnish substantial sums for the construction of future subways. Annexed hereto, marked Exhibit E, is an analysis which supposes *complete municipal operation* of the Brooklyn Rapid Transit lines, assuming the payment of interest on investment, at the rate which the City is required to pay, *but not in any way questioning any of the expenses of operation* of the railroad company, for the year ending June 30, 1924, except taxes. It will be noted that without disturbing or questioning any of these expenditures, and by merely calculating interest at the rate of 4 per cent. per annum upon the investment of both city and company, and much of this investment does not represent real cost of construction or equipment, and taking the B.-M. T.'s old elevated lines at the Transit Commission's valuation of $28,534,060, there would be sufficient from income to pay all of these charges besides a small sum of about $7,000, and that, on the basis of the net revenue reported by the B.-M. T. for the first three months of the current fiscal year, that there will be earned from its rapid transit lines, after the payment of interest at 4 per cent. per annum on the company's as well as the city's investment, a total of $240,000,000, a net profit of $1,390,000.

Annexed hereto, marked Exhibit F, is an analysis and schedules showing that if the city, instead of the I. R. T. had operated the subway lines under Contract No. 3, and the city only paid 4 per cent. interest, which it does, without in anyway disturbing any of the expense items reported by the company, there would have been earned from the operation of the I. R. T. subway lines during the year ending June 30, 1924, a sum sufficient to pay interest on the combined investment of both the city and the company, and besides a net profit of $4,340,000.

If the computation of interest is made upon the basis of the investment of the city and company, properly depreciated as it should be, namely upon $250,000,000; after the payment of all operating and maintenance expenses and interest, there would have been a profit of $5,950,000 during the same year.

Exhibit G, hereto annexed, shows in connection with Contract No. 4, the Brooklyn system, that for the year ending June 30, 1924, assuming complete municipal operation, and payment of interest at the rate of 4 per cent. per annum, and adjusting the operating expenses and taxes of the New York Rapid Transit Corporation (subsidiary of the B.-M. T.) that after paying interest on both the company's and city's investment and all expenses of operation, there would have remained a net profit of $2,537,375. for additional depreciation, sinking fund requirements and improved service.

Much testimony was given as to the cost of construction of future subways. It was claimed that because of increased costs of labor and material, that the cost of new construction will be 125 per cent. higher than was the cost of construction under the dual contracts. The cost of construction will undoubtedly be higher than it was under the dual contracts, but it is very doubtful whether the advances will be as great as it is claimed.

Exhibit H, hereto annexed, is a copy of a valuation report made by the present Transit Commission of properties of the Brooklyn Rapid Transit system as of June 30, 1921, showing both the original cost and 1921 reproduction cost. It will be noted that the New York Consolidated Railroad Company, the lessee under contract No. 4 of the New York Municipal Railway Corporation, then had invested under Contract No. 4 about $75,000,000. Its total investment to date is $88,000,000 so that in 1921 about 85 per cent. of its investment under Contract No. 4 had been made, and you will note that the 1921 price basis for this investment was only $106,000,000. In other words, the 1921 value was about 42 per cent. in excess of the original cost. I understand the costs in 1921 were fully as high, if not higher, than they are today.

It is to be borne in mind that much of the construction under Contracts 3 and 4 took place after prices of labor and material had advanced above the levels obtaining in 1913, when the dual contracts were made. Undoubtedly, with respect to that portion of the construction, under the dual contracts which occurred after January 1, 1918 the cost was fully as high as it is today. Very probably the cost of future construction will not be in excess of 75 per cent. above the average costs of construction under the dual contracts.

However, it is to be borne in mind that for this increased cost there will not merely be a duplication in construction of the present subways. We will have modern construction and equipment. The stations will be built to accommodate local as well as express ten-car trains. Adequate provision for ventilation, emergency exits and sanitary conditions will be provided, resulting not only in increased capacity, but in invitation to those who, because of present conditions, resort to other means of transit, so that whilst the cost of construction will be higher the modern structure will have a greater earning power.

For the purpose of further study of the problem, I have caused to be prepared and am annexing hereto Exhibit I, in which municipal operation by the I. R. T. is assumed for the fiscal year 1924. The cost of construction and equipment is assumed to be 125 per cent. in excess of what it actually was, namely, $565,000,000 instead of $250,000,000 as depreciated. Adjustments are made upon the basis of estimated increased gross income and corresponding expenses of operation and maintenance, from which it appears that were it even assumed that the cost of construction of our existing lines were 125 per cent. higher than they actually were, there would be a net profit from operation of $6,353,000, after the payment of 4 per cent. interest on the entire city and company investment and all expenses.

Further, it should not be overlooked that the deficits from subway operation on both lines, an aggregate of $110,000,000, are attributable to other causes besides extravagance, mismanagement and receivership.

The Manhattan Elevated Lines operated under lease from the Manhattan Railway Company at a rental equal to interest on $45,000,000 outstanding bonds, and 7 per cent. interest on $60,000,000 outstanding stock of the Manhattan Company, has been operated at a huge loss, and the earnings from the subways have been diverted to make good this loss (p. 2600).

Lastly, there is the astounding fact that the B. R. T. paid out prior to 1918, in dividends $36,000,000 on its common stcok of $74,500,000, which in June of 1923 sold at a dollar a share, an aggregate of about $775,000 and that the I. R. T. paid out prior to 1919, $65,000,000 in dividends on $35,000,000 common stock, which in June of 1923 was sold at $9.50 a share, an aggregate of $3,325,000.

This sapping of the financial vitality of these companies prevented necessary capital improvements and resulted in what Commissioner McAneny euphemistically calls "deferred maintenance"—a technical term for gross disrepair.

CHAPTER III

The City's Plight

TRAFFIC CONGESTION—CURTAILED SERVICE—INSUFFICIENT CARS—DILAPIDATED ELEVATED STRUCTURE—DANGEROUS DEFECTS—WOODEN CARS—ACCIDENTS

When the Legislature in 1921 spoke of an emergency in our traffic situation, it had in mind the intolerable transit conditions which the public in the City of New York were suffering—specifically the herding, jamming and crowding, long waits between trains, bedlam, particularly at congested points at the beginning and end of rush hour periods, strap-hanging during non-rush hours, insufficiency of conductors in trains, and guards on platforms and stations, the filth on the windows and elsewhere in the trains, the unsanitary conditions and "out-of-order" signs in comfort rooms, and the dangers from defects in the roadbed and structure of the elevated lines due to long neglect.

Of course, the Legislature contemplated, that ultimate relief might come by the construction of new subways, but that immediate relief could come only by a correction of these conditions on our existing lines. That, constituted the primary duty of the Transit Commission. The obligation of the transit companies to remove these conditions and to give decent service was clear, fixed both by contract and statute. Section 26 of the Public Service Commission law defines that obligation in the plainest terms, namely:

> "Every corporation, person or common carrier performing a service designated in the preceding

> section, shall furnish, with respect thereto, such service and facilities as *shall be safe and adequate and in all respects just and reasonable.*"

So, too, it is provided in Contract No. 4 with the Brooklyn Company, and a similar provision is contained in Contract No. 3 with the New York Company.

> "The principal object of the city in making this contract is to secure for the public convenience *an adequate, comfortable and rapid system of passenger transportation* in the portions of New York which will be served by the Railroad and the Existing Railroads. By the foregoing provisions of the Lease the Lessee has covenanted, among other things, *to operate the Railroad* and Existing Railroads *carefully and skillfully,* according to the highest standards of railway operation; to supply *adequate equipment, to run trains so as to furnish adequate service; to use the best safety devices; to keep the Railroad and Equipment and Existing Railroads clean, dry, well lighted, heated and ventilated; and to do other things, as hereinbefore set forth, for the convenience and accommodation of the public.*
>
> "These covenants on the part of the Lessee are among the *principal moving considerations to the city* in making this contract, and any breach thereof will entitle the city to the remedies in this contract. If at any time Additions to the Railroad or Equipment or to the Existing Railroads or any change in the mode of operating the Railroad or the Existing Railroads or conducting the business thereof are necessary in order to carry out the purposes of the Lease in securing service and facilities as shall be

safe and adequate and in all respects just and reasonable *the Commission may direct the provision or construction of such Additions and the making of such changes in the mode of operation of the Railroad or the Existing Railroads or in the conduct of the business thereof as may be necessary to accomplish such purpose.*"

Section 49, Sub. 2 of the Public Service Commission Law, provides that

"Whenever the commission shall be of opinion * * * that the regulations, practices, equipment, appliances, or service of any such common carrier, railroad corporation or street railroad corporation in respect to transportation of persons * * * are unjust, unreasonable, unsafe, improper or inadequate, the *commission shall determine* the just, reasonable, safe, adequate and proper regulations, practices, equipment, appliances and service thereafter to be in force * * * in such transportation of persons * * * and *so fix and prescribe the same by order to be served upon every common carrier,* railroad corporation and street railroad corporation to be bound thereby, and thereafter it shall be the duty of the railroad * * * *to observe and obey* each and every requirement of every such order so served upon it, and to do everything necessary or proper in order to secure absolute compliance with and observance of every such order by all of its officers, agents and employees."

and under Section 50, it is provided:

"If in the judgment of the commission * * * additional *equipment, facilities or device* for use by any common carrier * * * or in connection with the transportation of passengers * * * ought reasonably to be provided, or *any repairs for improvements* to or changes in any thereof in use *ought reasonably to be made* * * * in order to secure adequate service or facilities for the transportation of passengers * * * the commission shall * * * make and serve an order directing *such repairs, improvements, changes or additions to be made within a reasonable time* * * * and every railroad corporation * * * is hereby required and directed to make all repairs, improvements, changes and additions required of it by any order of the commission served upon it."

and under Section 51:

"If, in the judgment of the commission * * * any railroad corporation or street railroad corporation does *not run trains enough or cars enough*, or possess or operate motive power enough, reasonably to accommodate the traffic * * * or does not run its trains or cars with sufficient frequency or at a reasonable or proper time, having regard to safety, or does not run any train or trains, car or cars upon a reasonable time schedule for the run, *the commission shall* * * * *have power to make an order directing any such railroad* * * * *to increase the number of its trains or of its cars* * * * *or to change the time for starting its trains or cars or to change the time schedule for the run of any train or car or make any other suitable order that the commission may determine reasonably necessary to accommodate and transport the traffic* * * *."

and under Section 51a:

"The commission shall have exclusive power to make an order fixing the maximum number of passengers that may be carried on any car * * *."

Thus, there was specific provision in our transit laws which empowered the Transit Commission to abate each of the "disgraceful" conditions, which constituted the "emergency" for the relief of which the Transit Commission was created. The question naturally presents itself, how expeditiously and to what extent, the Transit Commission, after it came into office on April 25, 1921, directed its activities to that end.

We have it from the mouths of the Commissioners themselves that they have slept on those powers, and that they did not even commence an inquiry, into the service of the companies, until eleven months after the Transit Commission came into office—March 15, 1922.

Not a single order was made requiring any change of schedules, by increasing the frequency or numbers of the trains, not a single direction that the transit companies purchase additional cars, not a single mandate that the defects and dangers in the roadbed, structures and equipment be removed, not a single request that the railroad companies add to their equipment of conductors and guards both in and out of cars, was made until more than a year after the Transit Commission came into office, and then, the orders which they gave were ignored, and no steps were taken to enforce them to this very day.

The first service hearings which the Transit Commission conducted were into conditions of operation of the I. R. T. These commenced on March 15, 1922, and continued until April 12, 1922 (McAneny, pp. 155-157). During these hearings the I. R. T. urged that it be not compelled to improve its service and to operate more trains because of its financial inability and because of the alleged excuse of lack of repair, inspection and storage facilities (McAneny, p. 179). This hearing resulted in the so-called service order in May, 1922, by which the I. R. T. was directed, from its then *equipment, and without the addition of any new cars to add* 360 *trains daily.* The company was also ordered to make arrangements for the purchase of 350 cars, 100 immediately, 50 during the following summer and 200 when the additions to the Lenox Avenue repair shop would be completed (pp. 195-196). At that time the equipment of the I. R. T. consisted of 1935 cars.

The equipment of the B. R. T. then consisted of 907 wooden cars and 900 steel cars. There are carried 1,314,000,000 passengers per annum, or about four millions a day in this inadequate equipment.

Reverting again to this service order of May, 1922, which required the addition by the I. R. T. of 360 trains daily, a coal strike followed, with the result that the Transit Commission deferred the order until September 18, 1922 (p. 209). The I. R. T. took the position that the order was impossible of performance, and offered in support of its claim a report by engineers Gibbs and Hill. Apparently the order was not recognized by the company and the additional trains did not come. Nine months after it was issued, the company sought a modification and the application was formally denied, but apparently this service order was not honored or obeyed by the company (pp. 183-223), except that in August, 1923, it added 100 new cars to its equipment and within the last few months an additional 100, making the total equipment 2135 cars (p. 229), which carried during the last year, 714,000,000 passengers (p. 227).

Since the presentation of the Board of Estimate's charges against the Transit Commission on November 12, 1924, the Transit Commission acquired new life and began a new service hearing on November 14, 1924, and requested the I. R. T. to submit new schedules for train operation (p. 228).

A similar service hearing was commenced as to the Brooklyn Company on April 17, 1922 and continued until July 13, 1922, and resulted in an order effective August 15, 1922 requiring the addition of 100 cars daily from its then equipment, and the purchase of 50 new cars (pp. 237-239). These 50 cars were likewise not delivered until the fall of 1924, making the total equipment 950 steel cars and 907 wooden cars to carry over 600,000,000 passengers a year.

A new order has been recently made (since the charges were filed) that the B. M. T. purchase 100 additional cars (p. 248).

The reason assigned for this inactivity of the Transit Commission and its failure to even attempt a relief of congestion on our existing lines was very plainly stated by Commissioner McAneny (p. 261) as follows:

> "Now as to the time that elapsed between that date (April 1921 when the Commission came into office) and May, (1922) *our inquiry was turned immediately to the financial condition of all of these companies.* We had many sessions lasting for weeks; we examined their auditors, their books and the whole thing in the minutest fashion. If we had attempted to put out a service order at that time, for which there was no money, we should have found ourselves in the position of attempting to enforce a confiscatory proceeding and that as you know, would not have held water for a minute, *Therefore, our first duty was to find out not only what the financial condition of the companies were, but what might be done to improve them and put them in a position where our orders would really*

count and amount to something and we did that through forcing the reorganization of the Interboro Company in such a fashion that the money could be yielded."

We shall see how the Transit Commission "forced" the reorganization of the Interboro Company and how "that money" was "yielded." There remained only a deficit after the "yielding" (McAneny, p. 261).

But for the fact that these are the words of McAneny himself, it would seem incredible that the public interests were so ignored. It is unnecessary to describe the condition of traffic in our subways. It is claimed that they are operated to capacity during rush hours. It was pointed out by Mayor Hylan that the traction companies, apparently with a view to further harassing the public, to the end that it may be coerced into consenting to increased fares, pursues the "method of turning trains back, putting on trains shortly after rush hour starts, taking them off before the rush hour ends, and then curtailing the service on trains all day long to keep people crowded in cars. I know the method of switching trains back before they reach where they might go on to the terminal, dumping the people out on the way and crowding them in already crowded cars, and going on to their destination" (Hylan, pp. 1138-1139).

The remedy would come, if as the Mayor says, "The Transit Commission would not spend so much time worrying about the finances of the B.-M. T. and the I. R. T., and compel them to give a little better service for the people—they would not be in their mixup today" (Hylan, p. 1181).

Further, "It needs a Transit Commission who are in a little sympathy with the people, to compel any railroad company to perform its duty to the people that they are trying to serve" (Hylan, p. 1140).

"There is no reason in the world why people should be standing up after the rush hour and before the rush hour begins * * * crowding people in like sardines * * *." "It is not an engineering problem," says the Mayor, "It is common sense. All they have got to do is to put on an additional car or two and serve the people" (Hylan, pp. 1147-1148).

"The trouble is with the Transit Commission that they take testimony, and testimony * * * and do not act. Although all they have to do is to give these people an order, and make them live up to the order" (Hylan, p. 1179).

Of course, marked improvement could come in many ways. In the first place, the stations on the old I. R. T. subway, contracted under Contracts No. 1 and No. 2, are not long enough to accommodate ten-car local trains which are necessary. Under Contract No. 3 the Interboro is required to pay one-half of the cost of lengthening the stations. Under Contract No. 4 with the Brooklyn Company the city bears the entire expense (McAneny, p. 182). The matter of lengthening the Interboro stations has been considered. It will cost $12,000,000 of which the Interboro must bear $6,000,000 but to use the language of President Hedley of that company. "The Interboro Railroad have not got $6,000,000 to put in for anything just now."

So, too, the Dekalb and Myrtle Avenue platforms accommodate only six-car trains and the Pacific Street station only seven-car trains (p. 1095). That matter was considered by the Conference Committee in 1923 (p. 1094). On January 14, 1924, it recommended the lengthening of these stations to the Board of Estimate (pp. 1094-1096). On February 15, 1924, the Board of Estimate voted $282,000 for that purpose (p. 1096). The Company pays nothing.

The Mayor besides made suggestions as to how the present service of both the I. R. T. and the B.-M. T. might be decidedly improved (p. 1168). He submitted to Commissioner McAvoy a memorandum dated December 9, 1924, entitled "Lines Where Service Should Be Increased." This is annexed as Exhibit "J."

Naturally, when railroad companies become insolvent and receivers operate their lines and those receivers are only appointed to protect the creditors and stockholders, and the roadbed, structures and equipment are permitted to deteriorate during a long period of receivership (such as that of the B. R. T. which endured for four and one-half years), and there is no governmental agency interested in anything except the financial rehabilitation of the companies, something must happen,—and it did on our rapid transit lines.

The first serious accident during the regime of the Transit Commission happened on June 25, 1923, on the B. R. T. lines. A train was wrecked at the curve of the elevated road running from Fifth Avenue into Flatbush Avenue; two wooden cars, fell from the elevated structure into the street—the result, seven passengers killed and seventy injured. The wreck was due to rotten and defective guard rails and wooden ties, and because the spikes holding the rails to the ties were not in contact with the rails, and many of the bolts holding the ties to the steel structures were loose. As a result of this accident, the Board of Estimate on July 13, 1923, adopted a resolution by which the Committee on Transportation Facilities was appointed to investigate and report, on the condition of the cars and road equipment in use on all the elevated lines in the city, giving first consideration to the older structures in the Borough of Brooklyn, and next to the older ones in the Borough of Manhattan. This Committee consisted of John H. Delaney, Arthur S. Tuttle and George P. Nicholson. Upon the appointment of this Committee there was organized a Joint Commission of Engineers consisting of Robert Ridgway, Chief Engineer of the Transit Commission, Dr. George F. Swain, Professor of Civil Engineering at Harvard University, representing the Board of Estimate and Apportionment, and Eugene Klapp of the firm of Parsons, Brinckerhoff and Klapp, representing the railroad. This Commission investigated and made a report on the condition of cars, road and equipment of the B.-M. T. It commenced its work on July 26, 1923, and finished on January 4, 1924, when it made a written report. The Transit Commission, according to the testimony of McAneny, concurred "in every finding" of this Joint Commission of Engineers (p. 357).

Specifically this report found that on the Brooklyn elevated structures, 2,590 outer guard timbers (p. 329), 19,000 ties (p. 3336), 77,620 inner guard timbers (p. 343) and 14,910 joints (p. 345) *required immediate replacement for the safety of the riding public,* that the elevated structures were corroded and required painting, that the columns carrying the structures and the live weight of long trains filled with passengers, were corroded and that the bases were receptacles for ice, dirt and rubbish (p. 345). It was found that the wooden cars (to the danger from the use of which reference will be made later) lacked the modern "dead man's button," device, by which, if the motorman is rendered unconscious and his hand removed from the master controller, *the power is automatically shut off and the brakes applied.* The finding of the Joint Commission with respect to the necessity for the "dead man's button" on all of these wooden cars is as follows:

> "The Committee calls attention to the fact that the electric control equipment of the cars includes a master controller of the current and a 'dead man's button,' the purpose of which is to cut off the current automatically when the hand of the motorman is removed from the master controller as it would be if the motorman should have a sudden attack which would incapacitate him. The 'dead man's button' performs this function properly but it would not apply the brakes. If a motorman should die suddenly at his post, or faint, when his train was going at full speed, although the electric current would be cut off, the train might be approaching a curve around which it would pass at too high speed and an accident might result; or a collision might take place with a train ahead. *The modern 'dead man's button' is so arranged that when the hand of the motorman is removed from the controller not only is the current cut off but an emergency application of the brake is made.*
>
> *"It seems obvious to the Board that it would be desirable, as suggested by the Committee, that this modern form of the 'dead man's button' should be used.* The steel subway cars are already so equipped and the company is planning to equip similarly about 50 per cent. of the wooden cars."

The Transit Commission concurred that the conditions existed as found in the report. Of course they did not arise suddenly. *They had existed for a long time. They had become aggravated through inattention.*

On April 21, 1924 the report of this Joint Commission of Engineers, together with a supplementary report by the Committee on Transportation Facilities, was presented to the Board of Estimate and Apportionment and resulted in a resolution, which in part reads as follows.

> "The Board of Estimate and Apportionment has no power to take action to enforce compliance with any of these recommendations, such power being vested by law in the Transit Commission. As the report of the Joint Committee of Engineers is unanimous, it is to be inferred that the Transit Commission and the operating company itself will recognize the justice of all the recommendations made and will cooperate to carry them out * * *.
>
> "*It is recommended that the Transit Commission be requested to give its immediate attention to the elimination of the defects reported by the Joint Committee of Engineers* and to the need for a general improvement of the elevated railroad facilities as disclosed by this investigation, giving particular attention to the report of the Equipment Committee of the Joint Committee of Engineers, contained in Appendix VI of the Joint Committee report."

With respect to the recommendation by the Board of Estimate that "it give immediate attention to the elimination of the defects reported by the Joint Committee of Engineers and to the need for a general improvement of the elevated railroad facilities as disclosed by this investigation" *the testimony of Commissioner McAneny is that he regarded that recommendation "as a bit of humor"* (p. 338).

Notwithstanding the concurrence of the Transit Commission in every finding of this report, *it is the startling admission of the Transit Commissioners that they took absolutely no steps, and never made any order to the railroad companies, requiring the elimination of any of the defects or replacements* recommended by the Joint Committee of Engineers (McAneny, p. 358). The explanation for this gross neglect of duty is as follows:

McAneny says (page 346) that they (the transit companies) "haven't the money to spend on paint"—inferentially, much less to make the recommended replacements and remedy the defects. That was (April, 1924) nine months after the B.-M. T. reorganization, when $26,000,000 new money was invested; the very month in which the B.-M. T. paid dividends on preferred stock; and the year for which the B.-M. T. reported a net profit of $4,022,000. Every single joint of the 14,910 found defective, every spread of the 19,000 ties which were rotten, every span of the 77,620 inner guard timbers and 2,590 outer guard rails, every oxidized column upon which the elevated structure rested, presented a source of potential danger to the great mass of humanity that travels on our elevated lines. Much is made by the Commission, of the fact that the Joint Committee of Engineers gave the opinion that the elevated system was generally safe. The Engineers are to be commended for their diplomacy. It would have been grossly indiscreet to have spread a public alarm of the unsafety of these structures, which the public are compelled to use. The psychological effect would have wrought serious consequences, but they gave the facts, from which there can be but one inference.

The Transit Commissioners admitted that these conditions of deterioration were unknown to them until the reports of the engineers was made. This likewise supports one of the charges that the Transit Commissions maintained an inadequate and insufficient inspection body. The fact is, as was admitted, that while the railroad companies have in the aggregate 5,000 inspectors on their roads, the Transit Commission employed only 30 inspectors to check up their work and to investigate defects and compliance with orders and to recommend improvements (pp. 310-333).

This accident and report did not bring any activity among the Commissioners and soon another accident happened.

On July 30, 1924 a wreck occurred at the Sunnyside Yards of the Long Island Railroad, as a result of which one human being was killed and many others were seriously injured. The Grand Jury of Queens County made inquiry into this wreck, and found that the direct cause thereof was the throwing by hand of a switch under a moving train which caused the derailment of the last three cars; that there was no excuse for the operation of this switch by hand; that the operation of the switch should have been included in the interlocking system of the railroad which was in operation within ten feet of the switch. The Grand Jury, among other things, made its presentment as follows:

> "The Transit Commission has a large number of experts and the operation of the Long Island Railroad in the Greater City of New York is under its jurisdiction. *The control and operation of this switch at the time of the wreck is now condemned by the engineers of the Transit Commission.* As the Commission now condemns the switch and its

operation as antiquated and obsolete, it must have been antiquated and obsolete before the wreck and that being so it was the duty of the Commission to have ordered and required the removal of the switch and the installation of the safe method of operation it now recommends. The criminal responsibility for the wreck must be placed on the railroad company and its employees, but that does not relieve the Transit Commission for its failure to properly and adequately function in its control of the railroad."

and concluded as follows:

"We condemn the failure of the Commission to take proper action for the removal of this condition before the disaster and for its very evident policy that 'anything is good enough' until the contrary is proven by a disaster costing human lives, and we also condemn the officials of the railroad company above named for their neglect to take the initiative in the adoption of ways and means for the protection of human life and for their total disregard of their responsibilities.

An independent investigation into the cause of this wreck was made by the United States Inter-State Commerce Commission and resulted in a report by the Director of the Bureau of Safety of that Commission. That report was received in evidence before Commissioner McAvoy and in it the Director says: "It is *probable* that had these switches been interlocked and operated from the tower, this accident would not have occurred. It is believed that the traffic conditions on this road at this point amply justify the recommendation that these switches be made inter-locking and their operation controlled from the 'H' tower." The engineers of the

Transit Commission also recommended this extension of the interlocking system, *but the recommendation has not been adopted by the Transit Commission* (p. 365).

Then came within a few days thereafter, the wreck at Ocean Parkway Station of the Brighton Beach line of the B.-M. T. A train, consisting of six wooden cars, crashed into a train of seven steel cars which were at a standstill with the result that the roof of the first car of the wooden train telescoped over the roof of the last car of the steel train, and the after part of the roof of the same first wooden car telescoped over the forward part of the second wooden car. The forward platform of the second wooden car was crushed, and as a result of this wreck, one human being was killed and thirty passengers were injured, fifteen were removed to hospitals. The wooden cars were as follows: the first and colliding car, No. 1080; and the following Nos. 845, 1051, 47, 1078, 904. None of these cars were equipped with the modern "dead man's button." In fact, it was admitted at the hearings by the Transit Commission, that no orders were given by the Company for the installation of the "dead man's button" until after this accident, notwithstanding that it was recommended for installation by the Commission of Engineers on January 4, 1924, seven months before this accident.

The first car, No. 1080 was built in 1903, and it, together with cars Nos. 1051 and 1078, both built in 1902, were included in Group A required by Contract No. 4 to be retired from service prior to January 1, 1924, as will be indicated. Car No. 845 was built as a steam coach in 1887; Car No. 47 was likewise built as a steam coach in 1884, and Car No. 904 built in 1898; Cars Nos. 1051 and 904 were the subject of the last mentioned investigation of the Joint Commission of Engineers following the disaster of June 25, 1923. The motorman claimed at the time of the accident, that the brake handle, controlling the brakes of the first car, No. 1080, failed to function, and the brakes were not applied. Of course, this accident would not have happened if the car had been equipped with the "dead man's button". Nothing was said by the Transit Commissioners at the hearings about this accident except that it, like the Sunnyside Yards accident, was due to "man failure". There would have been "no man failure" if the switch in the case of the Sunnyside Yards accident had been interlocked, and there would have been no death and no injuries in this instance, if the cars were of steel instead of wood, and no accident if the cars had the "modern dead man's button".

It is claimed by the Board of Estimate in Charge 1 that these accidents were due to the culpable negligence of both the officials of the B.-M. T. and subsidiary company, and of the Transit Commission in permitting the "continuance and operation of, and failing to abate and remove, the aforementioned wooden. dangerous and unsafe cars, and in failing to require the B.-M. T. to keep its roadbed and structures in proper and safe condition".

There remains to be considered the situation with respect to the continued use of wooden cars by the B.-M. T., particularly in the Center Street loop. The condition of danger which that use presents has been often referred to and was emphasized by the Mayor at the hearings (p. 1282). There is no excuse for the use of these wooden cars, particularly in our subways, where any day they may become fire traps for the destruction of human beings. The obligation of the company to remove these wooden cars from service is very clearly fixed in Contract No. 4. It is provided in that contract as follows:

"On the dates given in the following schedule, the Lessee shall pay out of its own resources into the Depreciation Fund for the Existing Railroads provided for in paragraph 55 of Article XLIX the following amounts representing depreciation accrued upon the properties stated in the schedule prior to January 1, 1914."

SCHEDULE OF ROLLING STOCK OF EXISTING RAILROADS INCLUDING DATES OF ESTIMATED RETIREMENT AND ACCRUED DEPRECIATION.

Item No.	Date of Retirement	Accrued Depreciation					
1	Jan. 1, 1924	$240,058.00	Bodies and Trucks of Group A				
2	" 1, 1929	526,249.00	"	"	"	"	B
3	" 1, 1929	622,904.00	"	"	"	"	D
4	" 1, 1934	240,263.00	Equipment			"	A
5	" 1, 1936	388,951.00	"			"	B
6	" 1, 1936	338,711.00	Bodies and Trucks of Group C				
7	" 1, 1936	499,724.00	Equipment			"	C
8	" 1, 1946	35,680.00	"			"	D

Group A comprises 118 converted motor cars bearing the following numbers:

No. 1000—1078 inclusive
No. 1080
No. 1082—119 inclusive

Group B comprises 236 rebuilt motor cars bearing the following numbers:

No. 600—683 inclusive
No. 700—743 "
No. 745—758 "
No. 800—816 "

No. 818—820 inclusive
No. 822—859 "
No. 900—935 "

Group C comprises 306 motor cars bearing the following numbers:

No. 684, 817, 936, 993, 1079, 1081.
No. 1200—1499 inclusive.

Group D comprises 268 trailer cars bearing the following numbers:

No. 1— 6 inclusive
No. 8— 81 "
No. 83—125 "
No. 127—271 "

The dates cited in the above schedule represent the estimated date of retirement of the car bodies, trucks and equipment named in the schedule."

This schedule makes it clear, that, at the dates mentioned, the company agreed to retire from use, certain cars classified in Groups A, B, C and D—*Group A comprising* 118 *converted motor cars bearing the numbers* 1000 *to* 1078 *inclusive, No.* 1080 *and* 1082—1119 *inclusive, the date fixed being January* 1, 1924. Car. No. 1080, the colliding car, and cars Nos. 1051 and 1078 of the Ocean Parkway Wreck, are in this group.

Commissioner Harkness says that *this provision* in Contract No. 4 does not mean what it says, that it does not mean that the cars shall be *actually physically retired on the dates specified,* but that it has reference only to payments to be made into the Depreciation Fund, and he says further that it was so understood by McAneny, who negotiated the contract, and by himself who drew it (1214-15). We do not permit authors and scribes of contracts, which are clear and unambiguous to interpret them for us, to distort their language and to give them a meaning which does violence to their plain words. "Retirement" means "retirement" and not payment into depreciation funds. True, McAneny corroborates Harkness in his interpretation (p. 276). It is singular how these contracts are always interpreted by these Commissioners against the city. McAneny says that the Commission took no steps to direct the retirement of wooden cars and "will direct the retirement of no part of these wooden cars until their usefulness has ceased" (p. 274).

The excuse of the Transit Commissioners for the continuance in service of the wooden cars of the B.-M. T. is, that their replacement will cost about $60,000,000. *Again, human lives are weighed with dollars.* Besides, it is urged that steel cars in accidents topple from elevated structures into the street, *but they were wooden and not steel cars which fell from the elevated structure into the street in the Flatbush Avenue accident.*

Unfortunately for the Transit Commissioners, besides the plain language of the contracts, we have the conduct of Harkness which shows that in the beginning, he interpreted the contract clearly, and according to its plain language. On January 9, 1917, Mr. Harkness was the Chief of Rapid Transit of the then Public Service Commission of the First District. On that day there was addressed to him a communication by Daniel L. Turner, then Acting Chief Engineer of the Public Service Commission, in which, among other things, was discussed the operation of wooden cars in the Centre Street Loop, and in which Mr. Turner says, in part, as follows:

> "In the above, consideration has been paid only to the matter of safety of operation and to the pur-

chase of sufficient steel cars to provide the same passenger capacity as is not obtained with the present wooden equipment." * * *

"I recommend that the New York Municipal Railway Comporation be required *to provide the necessary steel cars for operation in the Centre Street loop and put these cars into operation as soon as the physical charges necessary can be made and the company can obtain the cars."* * * *

"Judging from the standpoint of ability to construct and deliver these cars, they probably could be provided within two years."

It is to be borne in mind that this was on January 9, 1917, and that the two year period ended on January 9, 1919

Acting upon this recommendation the same Mr. Harkness then, January 1917, addressed a communication to the Public Service Commission in which he said as follows:

"I therefore concur in the recommendation of the Acting Chief Engineer that the Railway Corporation 'be required to provide the necessary steel cars for operation in the Center Street Loop and put these cars into operation as soon as the physical changes necessary can be made and the company can obtain the cars.' "

The physical changes necessary for the operation of these steel cars in the Center Street Loop were concededly completed in about one year, because in January, 1918, there appears in the Public Service Record, the official publication of the Public Service Commission, an announcement which reads as follows:

*"Early in January the changes necessary to permit the use of the new **B. R. T.** steel subway cars on the Broadway-Myrtle Avenue elevated lines in Brooklyn were completed.* As a result some 70 of these cars have been placed in operation, affording a very considerable relief to traffic. Seven of these steel cars are approximately the equivalent of 10 of the old type of wooden elevated line cars and in addition to the increased capacity and increased service made possible by them, add a very considerable factor of safety to the operation in the Center Street Loop. The Commission has been for some years steadily pursuing a policy of getting wooden cars out of subway operation, having completed such work in reference to the First Subway operation by the Interborough Company early in 1916. *There are still some wooden cars operated through the Center Street Loop and their removal from that operation will not be possible before the completion of changes now being made by the Brooklyn company to its East New York yards. When those changes are completed, which is looked for during the present year, it will be possible to operate the large steel cars over the Broadway and connecting lines as well as over the Broadway-Myrtle Avenue line, thus making unnecessary the further use of the wooden cars on these lines.* At the same time a large number of wooden cars will be released for use on other elevated lines not connecting with subways."

The situation with respect to these wooden cars is, that after the charges were filed against the Transit Commissioners, they ordered the withdrawal of all wooden cars, except 100 from operation in the Center

Street loop, *and these* 100 *wooden cars* are at this very moment in use in that service (p. 2380).

It is claimed that when in 1922, the Transit Commission ordered the B.-M. T. to buy 50 new cars, it was intended that they would be placed in the Center Street loop service, but say the Commissioners, that, without consulting them, the company placed them into the Brighton Beach line, and that their withdrawal would embarrass that service (p. 2380).

Not only have the Transit Commissioners taken no action looking to the withdrawal of these obsolete wooden cars from service, but they have embarked upon a plan to permanently retain them in the service by subterfuge. They have agreed with the B.-M. T. that about one-half of the present wooden equipment be reconstructed into 150 three car wooden units, each consisting of two motor cars, with trailer car between, permanently connected together and operated as a single three-car "articulated unit."

On June 10, 1924, the Transit Commission approved the construction of 50 of such wooden cars in violation of the plain language of Contract No. 4 that these wooden cars be retired from service. This avoidance and evasion by the Transit Commission of the provisions of Contract No. 4 is the basis of Charge No. 11.

CHAPTER IV

The Legacy

UNCOMPLETED CONSTRUCTION UNDER CONTRACTS 3 AND 4

At least 50 per cent of the record made before Commissioner McAvoy has been devoted to what remained undone under Contracts 3 and 4 when the present City administration went into office, January 1, 1918. It has already been pointed out, that under the terms of the Dual contracts they were required to be fully completed on January 1, 1917. Apparently, therefore, the responsibility for the non-performance of these contracts in the first instance, rests elsewhere than upon the present administration. Had the work been done in 1915 and 1916 there would have been a huge saving to the City.

When the present administration came into office it attempted to ascertain what portions of the subways and facilities embraced under Contracts 3 and 4 remained uncompleted. It sought this information from the then Public Service Commission but it was not until the end of the year 1918, that any list was furnished by the Public Service Commission (Craig, p. 1986).

Immediately thereafter and in January or February, 1919, the Board of Estimate and Apportionment committed itself by resolution to expedite the completion of that work. The subways and facilities then remaining unfinished were as follows:

(a) The Fourteenth Street-Eastern Line, running from Sixth Avenue in New York to East New York for service to Brownsville section;

(b) The Nassau-Broad Street Line, one-half mile, intended in 1913, when the contracts were made, as a connection between the Centre Street Loop and the Montague-Whitehall tunnel; and

(c) The construction of additional repair and inspection shops and storage yards of the Interborough system, as well as additional facilities, if necessary, for the Brooklyn system.

(d) The continuation of the Queensboro Line under 42nd Street from Grand Central Station to 8th Ave.

These items of unfinished work will be separately discussed.

(A) FOURTEENTH STREET-EASTERN LINE

This consists of two parts—Section 1 which runs as a subway from Sixth Avenue in New York under Fourteenth Street and the East River to Montrose Avenue in Williamsburg; and section 2 from Montrose Avenue to East New York, a distance of about two miles, projected as an elevated structure under Contract 4. Neither section was built when the present administration commenced. The present administration proceeded with the construction of the New York section. Difficulties and delays were encountered, owing principally to strikes against the contractors, increased costs of labor and material, the abandonment by the contractor of his contract and the necessity for a reletting at increased expense to the City. Finally that section was completed, requiring only tracks, stations and equipment, when the present Transit Commission came into office; was opened for operation in 1924 and is now in use.

The two mile section from Montrose Avenue to East New York has not been constructed. The delay has been attributed by the Transit Commission to the city. If there had been a delay, it has been solely in deference to public sentiment.

The record with respect to that construction is as follows:

In June, 1920, when Mr. John H. Delaney was Transit Construction Commissioner he laid out the routes for that elevated structure and they were promptly validated by the Board of Estimate and Apportionment and approved by the Mayor in that same month (McAneny, p. 450). Then there developed an agitation, by property owners and civic associations from the locality affected, against the construction of these elevated lines. Since 1913 there has spread a movement for the removal of all elevated structures in congested sections and the position which they took was that the City should not build elevated structures, which eventually would be destroyed, and that its investment should be in the more permanent construction of a subway. Representatives of these organizations appeared before the Transit Commission and registered their protests. The Transit Commission communicated with Mr. Garrison, who then was the Receiver of the B.-M. T. To effect this substitution from elevated to subway it was necessary to secure the railroad company's consent. Mr. Garrison refused such consent. The Transit Commission, heedless of the public's protestations, Commissioner O'Ryan dissenting as I understand, advertised for and proceeded to let contracts for this elevated structure and submitted the same for approval to the Board of Estimate and Apportionment in March, 1922. The Board of Estimate and Apportionment, heeding the public demand and realizing its merit, refused to approve these contracts (McAneny, p. 463). Nothing was done by the Transit Commission, in fact nothing could be done until the Receiver was discharged. That was in June, 1923.

In December, 1923, Mr. Menden the new President of the B.-M. T. indicated his willingness to consent to a modification of Contract 4, to permit the construction of the subway (McAneny, pp. 464-467).

Then in February and in April, 1924, the Transit Commissioners again submitted routes for this construction but they were again objectionable because they provided for part subway and part elevated, and the Board of Estimate and Apportionment rejected their last route on June 20, 1924 (McAneny, p. 470).

The Board of Transportation came into office on July 1, 1924. It proceeded most expeditiously in connection with this construction. On July 5, 1924 it sent a route for one section, to the Board of Estimate and it was validated and approved on August 21, 1924. The remaining route was sent to the Board of Estimate on September 30, 1924 and approved October 10, 1924. Construction work, for the *actual* building of this line has, according to Commissioner McAneny's own admission, been let (p. 472). Some difficulty in connection with the phraseology of the contract has developed, due to objection from the B.-M. T., but I understand they have been for all practical purposes adjusted, and the Fourteenth Street-Eastern Line is a closed chapter in the history of rapid transit construction in this City.

(B) NASSAU-BROAD STREET LINE

Nobody seriously urged the building of this line, realizing its uselessness, until recently when the B.-

M. T. discovered that its insistence thereon might be helpful in connection with a suit which the B.-M. T. has brought against The City of New York for the recovery of $30,000,000 damages, for alleged breaches by the City of Contract No. 4.

The Nassau-Broad Street Line was projected in Contract No. 4 as a tunnel, about one-half a mile long, running from the terminus of the subway under the Municipal Building, underneath the narrow streets of Broad and Nassau to connect at about Whitehall Street with the B.-M. T.'s line running through the Montague-Whitehall tunnel.

When the City administration first received its list of unfinished work under the dual contracts at the end of 1918, the Nassau-Broad Street tunnel, to use the language of Comptroller Craig, was "last in order to be done—if ever". Putting this Nassau Street Line "in this position meant indefinite postponement" (Craig, p. 1987).

Apparently the Transit Commission shared in this view until March of 1923, when for the first time it advertised for bids for the first section of this half mile tunnel. The lowest bidder was one Patrick McGovern, whose bid was $5,376,035 (p. 542). The original estimate in 1913 of the cost of the entire tunnel was $5,000,000. On the basis of McGovern's bid it would cost over $11,000,000. The contract was sent to the Board of Estimate for approval on March 23, 1923 (McAneny, p. 542). The Board of Estimate and Apportionment referred this contract to a Committee of One, consisting of Mr. John H. Delaney.

Prior thereto and on November 13, 1919 Mr. Daniel Turner who, together with Mr. Robert Ridgway are admitted by everybody to be perhaps the best informed persons on subway construction, and who, was the Chief Engineer of the Transit Construction Commission and *is at this moment the consulting engineer of the Transit Commission,* wrote a letter to then Transit Construction Commissioner John H. Delaney in which he said with reference to this Nassau-Broad Street tunnel in part as follows:

> "The real question is whether or not the money to be spent on the Nassau Street Line would not result in Brooklyn being better served if spent somewhere else.
>
> * * * * * * * * * *
>
> "There can be no excuse for running new trains to the Montague Street tunnel which are to be deflected through the Nassau Street line and returned immediately to Brooklyn via the Manhattan Bridge without traversing upper Manhattan (p. 774).
>
> "In other words, the Nassau Street branch will be used to save the car mileage, to the detriment of the character of the service furnished to Brooklyn passengers" and in which he concluded with the statement:
>
> "I believe that the *money* necessary to build it, although it will be of convenience to some people travelling through the Centre Street loop *could be spent to better advantage in providing additional facilities from Brooklyn to Manhattan for Brooklyn people."*

In the light of this letter and his own judgment, Commissioner Delaney recommended to the Board of Estimate and Apportionment the rejection of these contracts, and such rejection was made by the Board of Estimate on July 25, 1923 (McAneny, p. 546) upon grounds which the Mayor very tersely gave in his statement, in advance of his testimony before Commissioner McAvoy as follows:

> "1. That the plan for construction was not in accord with the general plan of construction adopted by the Board of Estimate in 1912 or 1913, when the route was originally approved, because it provided for a two-track reservoir or spur, extending under Broad Street, below Wall Street, which was not described in the general plan at the time it was originally adopted.
>
> "2. That there was doubt as to the obligation of the city to appropriate any more money under the terms of Contract No. 4, for the reason that the amount which the Board could legally appropriate in 1913 had already been exceeded (see also Craig, p. 2018).
>
> "3. That the Nassau Street line would not provide for additional service for the travellers on the rapid transit line, but merely furnished an operating convenience and that the amount which it would cost to construct should be applied to serve localities not included in the existing system."

And the position of the City with respect to this line is, that it will not waste this money and will not construct this spur, except upon judicial decree.

(c) SHOPS AND YARDS

In order that there may be efficient transit service there must be adequate facilities in which to inspect and repair rolling stock. About half of the record before

Commissioner McAvoy consists in discussion of the lack of these facilities to the Interborough, as the excuse both for the intolerable service on our existing lines, and for the failure of the Transit Commission to direct the purchase of new cars. Briefly stated, the excuse is couched as follows: During rush hours, says the Transit Commission, the lines are operated to capacity and no additional cars can be added. With respect to the practice of placing cars in operation after the commencement of the rush hour peak and the withdrawal of cars from operation before the termination of the rush hour, resulting in the chaos, confusion and jamming from which the public has been suffering, and about which so much public complaint has been made by our Mayor, and with respect to the failure to furnish additional *cars during non-rush hours,* when passengers are crowded and compelled to stand without reason, the excuse is, that if more cars are run they will wear more, and if they wear more, they will require more repairs and more facilities for repairs, and that the failure of the Transit Commission to require the companies to give improved service, and of the companies to operate more cars was due to insufficient shops and yards, which under Contract 3 the City was required to build.

This chant of the lack of shops and yards continues through the record, sung in varying tones, scales and harmonies. That subject would be deserving of extended consideration but for two incidents, unfortunate for the Transit Commissioners. One, was the fact that the Mayor himself, before giving his testimony, personally visited the shops and yards where it is claimed facilities are lacking, and saw and told that they are not in use—that inspection pits are boarded up so that they may not serve for repairs, and that endless tracks are empty. Photographs were received in evidence, descriptive of these conditions.

These physical facts are not, cannot be and were not denied by the Transit Commissioners. Against that, we have a mass of tabulations, data and statistics that sink into insignificance in the light of the results of the Mayor's personal inspection. But most unfortunate for the Transit Commissioners was the testimony of Commissioner O'Ryan. It must be admitted that he was not properly prepared. He, to use the vernacular, "Let the cat out of the bag" and destroyed the Commission's entire alibi for failing to give the people proper service on our transit lines. He too was questioned with respect to the shops and yards and he directed attention to the fact that there was a difference of situation between the shops and yards of the B.-M. T. and those of the Interborough. He said quite truthfully:

> *"I had a lot of experience with people in passing the buck and I believed that the company frankly was trying to pass the buck in relation to service, by pleading lack of adequate shop facilities"* (p. 2436).

How eloquently this tells the whole tale.

He says that he personally had charge of the B.-M. T. situation; that Menden "strongly urged that the then existing shops at 39th Street in Brooklyn be extended by the construction of additional buildings"; that the property on which these shops were, was owned by the South Brooklyn Railroad Company, "which leased it to the B.-M. T. in several parcels" upon different rentals and for different terms. Commissioner O'Ryan says:

> "It seemed to me very unwise for the City to make an investment of any considerable amount in the construction of shops to be built upon property that they did not own" (p. 2433).

He recommended that the City build its own repair shops. General Andrews, chief executive officer of the Transit Commission, was directed to find the site, which he did near Coney Island Creek. The City approved it and appropriated $10,000,000 for its construction (O'Ryan, p. 2434). The electrical repair shop is in process of construction and the contracts for the remainder are ready for letting (Harkness, p. 2373).

Surely nothing need be added to this recital. The B.-M. T. was not lacking in shop facilities. The Transit Commissioners so admitted. No contracts for the construction by the City of any additional shops for the Brooklyn system were sent by the Transit Commission to the Board of Estimate from April 1921 to May 7, 1924 (p. 67).

The B.-M. T. never claimed that shops were lacking until it appeared to it to be a plausible basis for damages in the suit which it recently brought against the City.

There remains to be considered the shop and yard facilities of the I. R. T. It has six yards. The principal repair shop of that Company is at 148th Street and Lenox Avenue. Its other principal yards are at 239th Street, Livonia Avenue, Westchester Avenue and Jerome Avenue (Delaney, p. 567).

Contract 3 obligates the City to build additions to shops and yards. It was arranged that there should be three additions to the repair shop at 148th Street and Lenox Avenue. The first addition was intended to increase the capacity of that shop from 500 to 900 cars, and the second and third to further enlarge the capacity. Pending the construction of these permanent additions, the Transit Commission recommended the construction of temporary shops, which recommendation the Board of Estimate rejected as a waste of City's money, and the companies provided such temporary structures themselves (McAneny, p. 2021).

The city has been engaged in constructing these additions. The condition with respect to inspection and storage yards has been "satisfactory," according to the testimony of Harkness himself since 1923 (p. 2373).

With respect to the repair shop (the only further facility required by the Interborough), the alleged lack "is overcome," as Harkness admits; the second and third additions to this repair shop have been fully equipped and the railroad companies have taken possession (pp. 2372-2406-2407).

Harkness says that the storage barn capacity is 150 percent more than it was in 1912, a very "satisfactory condition." One-half of this addition was made in 1919, and the other in 1924. There will be in the immediate future storage capacity for the I. R. T. of 2805 cars. The present equipment consists of 2135 cars (Delaney, p. 887).

Chief Engineer Ridgway of the Board of Transportation testified that all yards of the I. R. T. are ready, including the repair shop at 148th Street and Lenox Avenue with the exception of the Westchester yard, which is being graded; the foundations are being placed for sheds which will cover the inspection pits; steel for the structure is being fabricated (pp. 1969-1970).

Commissioner Delaney testified "they have ample storage facilities" (p. 570). * * * "there are proper means of inspection" (p. 571) and at p. 586 he said:

> "The record of the first two or three days, as I have read the testimony of the preceding witness, would create the opposite impression—that storage yard provision should be made for all of the cars on the system; which means that they would be a *bedroom for the cars* when they ought to be in operation."

The City has expended about $7,000,000 for shops and yards (p. 869).

Notwithstanding the claim of the I. R. T. and the Transit Commission of lack of facilities, as the cause of the intolerable present service on our transit lines, it is a conceded fact, that although it has ample space in yards for storage, the I. R. T. finds that storing cars on tracks is more to its convenience. The I. R. T. as far back as February 1918, requested that the City defer building additions to yards, because of the financial inability of the company to bear the expense of equipment (pp. 902-904).

Much has been said in the record by the Transit Commissioners, before Commissioner McAvoy as to the refusal of the Board of Estimate and Apportionment to validate appropriations for construction of shops and yards, resulting in unnecessary delays. The fact is, as was established before Commissioner McAvoy, that there were before the Board of Estimate and Apportionment from the Transit Commission between May 2, 1921, and December 2, 1924, in all about 372 contracts; that 249 of these contracts were approved in the first instance, and the requested funds furnished; that 8 contracts were withdrawn by the Transit Commission; that 39 were referred back, and only 27 disapproved; 11 failed of adoption because of necessary votes; 28 because of intervening circumstances which rendered the proposals ineffective, and of the 27 which were disapproved and of the 11 which failed of adoption, in many instances they represent contracts which were subsequently approved, after readvertising, resulting in savings to the City of hundreds of thousands of dollars.

I call particular attention to the fact that the Transit Commission proposed certain contracts for the construction of additions to the shop at 148th Street and Lenox Avenue for $456,191.50; that the Board of Estimate rejected these contracts; that upon readvertisement a contract for a lower amount was again submitted to the Board of Estimate and again rejected, and that finally upon the third advertisement a contract for $313,154.50 was let, and approved by the Board of Estimate and Apportionment at a saving to the City of $143,000.

With respect generally to the disapproval by the Board of Estimate and Apportionment of contracts proposed by the Transit Commission, it was to be expected, that there would be a difference of judgment between the members of the Board of Estimate and Apportionment and the Transit Commissioners. If the law contemplated that the Board of Estimate's approval should be merely formal, and not based on independent judgment, it would not have required any approval.

Surely, the Board of Estimate and Apportionment is not subject to criticism because it discharged the duties imposed upon it by law and when the interest of the city so required, it exercised its veto power, with a resultant large saving of the City's money.

Besides, and in connection with the same subject matter, account should be taken of the status of the Transit Commission at the time when most of these disapprovals occurred July 1921.

The Transit Commission came into office on April 25, 1921. It brought with it a threat, embodied in the law of its creation, to nullify the dual contracts, to destroy whatever rights were saved to the city under those contracts, including the five cent fare, and to impose upon the city by purchase, our entire transit system including the old elevated and obsolete surface lines, at prices to be fixed by agreement with the traction companies.

The City then had an investment of $300,000,000 in subways. It had received no return on $240,000,000. It was loath, as the Mayor well stated it, to invest any more money in so unbusiness-like a venture. Besides, the City was then challenging on constitutional grounds, the legality of the Transit Commission and its powers, particularly with respect to the plan of readjustment, which made its appearance from the Transit Commission shortly after its appointment. It was not until January, 1922, that the Court of Appeals decided that the Transit Commission was a legally constituted body.

It would have been inconsistent for the City, in the one breath to challenge the legality of the Transit Commission's creation and at the same time to recognize that legality by approving its proposals. But the City's interest was in no case prejudiced by any of the disapprovals, because as was proved by the record of proceedings before the Board of Estimate which was received in evidence before Commissioner McAvoy, in every instance, pending the litigation, where delay would have injured the City, the contracts were approved with a stipulation reserving the City's rights.

Criticism is made of the fact that after the decision by the Court of Appeals in January 1922, it was necessary for the Transit Commission to make three applications to the Appellate Division for orders requiring the Board of Estimate and Apportionment to honor their requisitions for expenses. That all occurred before May, 1922. During that time the appealability of the Court of Appeals determination to the United States Supreme Court was under consideration. Concededly the opposition to these applications, in the Appellate Division, made by the Corporation Counsel, was merely perfunctory and to preserve the City's rights (Harkness, p. 2363). And it is important to remember, that the only question which was decided by the Court of Appeals in January, 1922, was that the Board of Estimate and Apportionment was required by law to approve the requisitions of the Transit Commission for its alleged expenses. The question of the power of the Transit Commission to put into effect its plan to buy all of the existing lines, to nullify the dual contracts and the five-cent fare, was not decided by the Court of Appeals but was specifically saved for future determination, and cannot be raised until the Transit Commission takes its first step to put that plan of readjustment into effect. That has not yet been attempted.

The extension of the Queensboro line by continuation of the subway from Grand Central Station to 8th Avenue is entitled to but passing comment. No criticism is made by the Transit Commission of the City administration about that construction. The contracts were let by the Transit Commission to Bowers and Kennedy, approved by the Board of Estimate and Apportionment in

March, 1922, and the construction has proceeded since, and will be completed in about a year and a half (McAneny, 2527).

CONSTRUCTION NOT EMBRACED IN DUAL CONTRACTS

Besides the work which was done in completing the construction of subways under the Dual Contracts, certain additions were made to subways not provided for under these contracts. The Board of Estimate and Apportionment in May, 1923, approved the contract for the construction of an additional one mile of subway connecting Corona with Flushing (p. 2501) at a cost of $3,600,000 and extending the Fourth Avenue line to Fort Hamilton at a cost of $1,700,000.

The City has recognized the necessity for the construction of a passenger and freight tunnel connecting Staten Island with Brooklyn. Such necessity is very clearly set forth in Mayor Hylan's recent statement in which he says:

> "Practically all commerce and trade between Brooklyn and Queens and the major portion of the United States is floated over the water barrier which separates these boroughs from the rail terminals of the trunk line railroads on the westerly side of the Port. For this reason the population of these boroughs has been said to live a 'hand to mouth' existence and in time of stress caused by bad weather, ice, harbor congestion, marine strikes and the like, the supply of actual necessities in these boroughs is not only seriously curtailed, but has actually been in danger of being entirely cut off. Despite the fact that this portion of the greater city is but about one hundred and fifty miles from the anthracite coal fields there occurs as regularly as cold weather appears the usual danger of a scarcity of coal.

"The construction of the Narrows Tunnel will provide a direct rail route connecting with most of the trunk lines that serve the Port of New York and will afford the means of supplying Long Island with the necessities of life and trade at all times regardless of weather conditions and other hazards to which the existing system of transportation is exposed. By means of the tunnel it will be possible also to avoid centers of congestion and to deliver freight via a 'back door' route to Brooklyn and Queens, and by affording new points of receipt and shipment for freight it will be an important factor in the development and expansion of freight facilities.

"Brooklyn and Queens consume upwards of 7,500,000 tons of coal annually which in general must be supplied as required. It requires no imagination to picture what it would mean in a time of serious coal shortage to be able to haul coal in quantity by fast freight over one of the trunk line railroads and then over the Narrows Tunnel line into Brooklyn and Queens for distribution to consumers. Under these conditions relief would be but a matter of hours rather than days or perhaps weeks and the resulting benefits would be incalculable. The illustration need not be applied only to coal; it will serve as well for milk, and for food, once the bulk of the city's food supply comes to New York over the railroads which terminate on the New Jersey side of the Port.

"The railroads terminating in New Jersey handle upwards of 21,000,000 tons of Brooklyn and Queens freight annually, exclusive of the many tons of freight transferred directly between lighter and ship along the Brooklyn waterfront in connection with foreign and coastwise commerce. Upwards of 6,000,000 tons of railroad freight are handled each year at Bay Ridge in the vicinity of the tunnel line, the major portion of it being destined for movement through Brooklyn, Queens, the Bronx and on into New England. All of this freight is subject to the delays and expense incident to its movement through congested waterfront terminals on the New Jersey side of the port and its transfer in various forms of marine craft across the intervening waterway to again pass through congested waterfront areas on the Long Island side. The Narrows Tunnel when in operation will make it possible to move a larger volume of railroad freight expeditiously and economically from one side of the port to the other by avoiding congested terminals and cross currents of traffic. It will permit the delivery of freight to inland points in Brooklyn and Queens and thereby reduce many of the long trucking hauls that are now necessary. It will also relieve waterfront congestion by making it unnecessary to pass through waterfront freight stations much of the freight that is not destined for waterfront delivery.

"The city in cooperation with the Federal Government has undertaken the development of a modern seaport at Jamaica Bay. This territory, surrounded as it is by a large and densely populated area, where there is plenty of land available at reasonable prices for the erection of factories and homes, where the cheapest and most efficient water connections may be had, is sure to develop rapidly and become a great commercial and industrial centre if rail connection is provided. With direct rail and water transportation facilities available, Jamaica Bay will also afford a much needed opportunity for the location of heavy industries which require extensive space at reasonable cost. There is no question but Jamaica Bay can be made an asset of tremendous value to the City of New York.

"Under existing transportation methods the commercial and industrial development of Jamaica Bay will be slow and uncertain. Its full degree of usefulness and efficiency will not be attained until it is connected directly by rail with every trunk line railroad serving the Port of New York, so that direct shipment in standard cars, without breaking bulk, will be possible between Jamaica Bay and all ports in the country. The Narrows Tunnel will provide the means of a physical connection between the trunk lines on the easterly and westerly sides of the Port District and the plans for the project have been formulated in such a manner as to permit of a direct extension from Bay Ridge to Jamaica Bay either by way of the Long Island Railroad or by an independent line, in order to provide adequate rail connections for the extensive harbor and terminal facilities contemplated for Jamaica Bay.

"The construction of the Narrows Tunnel should result in the development of a railroad line connecting four of the Boroughs of New York City with the New England States to the east and with the mainland to the west, with numerous attending advantages in the way of favorable freight rate adjustments, the establishment of additional, convenient and efficient freight and passenger terminals, the curtailment of trucking and resulting relief from vehicular congestion, the elimination of delays caused by weather and congestion on the waterways, and in conjunction with the Stapleton piers and the development of Jamaica Bay, by increasing the number, capacity and efficiency of terminals secure for the Port of New York facilities comparable with any in the world."

Two shafts have already been built for this subway. Two million dollars have been spent. Two million five hundred thousand dollars more have been appropriated (pp. 73-76). That tunnel will run from the neighborhood of about 65th Street, Bay Ridge, Brooklyn, under the Narrows to St. George, Staten Island (p. 2548).

There was introduced in evidence before Commissioner McAvoy, as a basis for comparison, the record of the moneys appropriated for municipal purposes during the seven years of the present administration, and the appropriations during the seven years preceding, a resume of which is as follows:

Purposes	Appropriated from January 1, 1918, to December 31, 1924	Appropriated during seven years preceding January 1, 1918
Schools	$173,865,000	$36,395,000
Facilities for Commerce and Traffic Docks and Ferries	70,378,000	32,000,000
Rapid Transit	54,750,000	170,000,000
Street Cleaning	11,754,000	1,051,000
Hospitals	12,788,000	15,707,000
Parks	11,490,000	7,235,000
Public Markets	22,500,000	....
Police and Fire	5,954,000	6,113,000
Roads, Streets and Public Buildings	52,240,000	35,668,000

In the Transit Commission rested the sole duty and power to provide for new rapid transit construction for over three years. The rapid transit appropriations in the foregoing table in a measure reflect the extent of that Commission's activities in this direction.

CHAPTER V

The Fruits of Greed

BROOKLYN RAPID TRANSIT CORPORATION REORGANIZATION

The Board of Estimate, in its presentment to the Governor, charged that in connection with the reorganization of the B. R. T. into the B.-M. T., the Transit Commission was guilty of dereliction of duty in permitting the reorganization, upon the basis of an inflated capitalization, dividends on which will bring the imposition of unwarranted and illegal burdens upon the public; that the reorganization concealed and continued, by the issuance of both common and preferred stock *without par value*, the watered capitalization of the B. R. T. and in permitting the B.-M. T. to be organized as a ***business*** corporation instead of a *railroad* corporation; and in permitting the B.-M. T. on its books immediately after reorganization to value its no par common stock at $54 per share, thereby laying the foundation for prospective dividend distributions upon the basis of this fictitious value, and in permitting the diversion of its assets to the payment of dividends instead of applying them to make safe, adequate and convenient the operation of its transit lines; in permitting the B.-M. T. to be governed by a directorate and officers, some of whom are serving in dual and antagonistic capacities, some of whom are primarily interested in the manipulation of prices and sales of stock and bonds of the B.-M. T.; and in permitting the B.-M. T. to be managed and controlled largely with a view to favorable action of its securities on the stock market, and not in the interest and for the comfort of the traveling public; and in permitting the B.-M. T. to divert its moneys for the advertisement and acceleration of a movement for increased fares and to misrepresent and deceive the public as to the responsibility for the present intolerable transit conditions and to wrongfully arouse an unwarranted public indignation against the City authorities, and to wrongfully shift the responsibility for the same from the B.-M. T. and operating companies, to the city.

This charge was before Commissioner McAvoy.

I specifically direct your attention to the fact that no inquiry was made as to the affiliations of the directors of the B.-M. T. with enterprises engaged solely in Wall Street operations, and for the purpose of ascertaining whether or not these directors were really serving the company or serving other hostile private interests; that in fact no serious effort was made to ascertain the capitalization of the reorganized company, in relation to the value of its assets or the capitalization of its predecessor; that whenever reference was made to this charge it was simply the occasion for an opportunity to the Transit Commissioners to give such explanation as they saw fit, which were accepted at par, and with no attempt on the part of the interrogator, Mr. Sherman, to pursue the inquiry or ascertain the real facts. There is not even a reference to the charge that the B.-M. T. diverted its funds, for which it is accountable to the city under its contract, in accelerating a movement to discredit the city administration by propaganda, and to secure an increased fare.

An analysis of the B. R. T. reorganization will bring to light in a large measure the causes which from time to time have brought about the collapse of our transit companies and the public's painful experiences with receiverships.

The B. R. T. was organized in 1896 as a successor to the Long Island Traction Company. At the time of its receivership it owned the power plants, operated certain railroad facilities and controlled through the ownership of stocks, bonds and instruments of indebtedness, the companies operating the subway and elevated rapid transit lines and street surface railways of this system. Its subsidiary, the New York Municipal Railway Company was the lessee under Contract No. 4. It in turn subleased to the New York Consolidated Railroad Corporation, which owned the old Brooklyn elevated lines, and operated those lines, together with the subways under Contract 4.

The B. R. T. also owned the entire stock of the Brooklyn Heights Railroad Company, the Nassau Electric Railroad Company and the Coney Island and Brooklyn Railroad Company, including the DeKalb Avenue and North Beach Railroad Company, the Brooklyn, Queens County and Suburban Railroad Company, South Brooklyn Railway Company and subsidiaries, the Coney Island and Gravesend Railway Company, Brooklyn and North River Railroad Company, which operated tracks over the Manhattan Bridge. The Brooklyn Heights Railroad Company also operated the tracks over the Williamsburg Bridge leased to the Bridge Operating Company by the City.

The B. R. T. controlled the operation of 138 miles of surface lines besides 107 miles owned by the Brooklyn City Railroad Company, under lease to which reference is later made.

It and its subsidiary companies claim to have invested $46,177,000 in equipment and contribution to construction of subways under Contract 4, and $41,823,000 in extending and tracking its old elevated lines, a total of

$88,000,000 under Contract 4; its old elevated lines and equipment which were valued by the Transit Commission as of 1921 at $22,240,000, but for purpose of reorganization and in order to justify the new capitalization this figure was forced up by the Transit Commission to $28,000,000. As elsewhere indicated $20,000,000 is a charitable estimate of its value. Besides its surface lines which the Commission valued at $52,000,000, represent in part obsolete and about-to-be discarded lines and constantly diminishing values because their usefulness is gradually disappearing. Thus the total value of its principal assets at the time of reorganization was $168,000,000, but if the elevated lines are valued at $20,000,000 and the surface lines at one-half of their Transit Commission valuations, the value of the assets is reduced to $134,000,000.

On December 31, 1918, because of insolvency it went into receivership and the receivership continued for four and one-half years until June 14, 1923. The subsidiary companies were likewise in receivership from July 14, 1919, and were so continued until reorganization. Mr. Lindley M. Garrison was the receiver. Two of the smaller surface lines survived without receivership. No explanation is given for the continuance of the receivership for these four and one-half years.

It is needless to recite the conditions of the service on the B. R. T. rapid transit and surface lines during the period of receivership, including the additional burdens imposed by the discontinuance of free transfers upon abrogation by the receiver of the lease of the Brooklyn City Railroad Company and the return to it of its properties in October, 1919.

Commissioner Harkness in his opinion of June 4, 1923, in approving the reorganization says:

"The receivership has now continued for about four and one-half years, and as is common to receiverships has been marked by disintegration, by restricted capital expenditures and improvements and for its earlier period by greatly restricted service."

Notwithstanding, later in the opinion he says:

"The claim that the company has not been living up to its obligations is a contention unsupported by the evidence. On the other hand, the reports to the Commission by its inspectors show that the company is and has been in good faith living up to the service orders of the Commission."

In other words, Commissioner Harkness says that the public got during the receivership just such service as it deserved because presumably, if the company had not given what the Commission regarded as proper service, orders would have been issued by the Commission for its improvement.

It may be in place at this stage to consider a matter which was not presented in the investigation, but which will be all important in the event of future receiverships of our transit companies. It was assumed throughout the investigation, and has apparently always been the position of the Transit Commission, that upon the incoming of the receiver the control of our transit lines passed into the court of his appointment and that in effect the Transit Commission became *functus officio.*

Our Public Service Commission Law and Rapid Transit Act, Chapter 4, Laws 1891 as amended, fixes the obligations of carriers of passengers and the powers of our transit regulating commissions. Franchises to railroad companies are held subject to the compliance by them with the provisions of these laws and the orders of these commissions.

When a receiver is appointed of the properties of a railroad company, he merely becomes the custodian and entitled to their possession, solely, however, *for the benefit of the company, its stockholders and creditors, and not for the public.* He takes only what the traction company has, charged with all of its obligations, both under law and under contract. It is clear that by the appointment of the receiver of the B. R. T. and its subsidiaries, the obligation resting upon those companies was not in the slightest degree impaired, suspended or changed.

Much is said in the record about the financial inability of the traction companies to give the service which was required by law and contract. With respect to that, too, there appears to be misapprehension. The obligation of a carrier under its franchise and particularly under specific contract is not lessened or discharged because of financial inability to perform. *The duty of the Transit Commission to secure adequate and safe service for the traveling public is not affected, suspended or changed in the slightest way by the appointment of a receiver or the insolvency of the carrier.* It is by law charged with the duty of securing service regardless of these contingencies. *It was for it, having ascertained the deplorable conditions which it reported in* 1921, *to have issued adequate orders for the removal of those conditions and for proper service.* The receivership and financial inability of the traction companies were not its concern. The companies were bound to comply with these orders. They had their choice of either complying or abandoning their contracts and franchises. Their physical assets were in the possession of the United States Court; foreclosure proceedings of mortgage thereon were pending. Orders from the Transit Commission, non-compliance, resultant proceedings for cancellation of contracts and franchises would have brought a prompt sale of the railroads, presumably into strong financial hands, with adequate capital to rehabilitate them and to provide for necessary improvements and better service. Such should have been the course of the Transit Commission. Had it been the public would not have suffered the results of the four and one-half years of receivership. With respect to the reorganization, the position of the Transit Commission seems to have been that it was helpless, and that approval by it was compulsory. Here again is a mistaken fundamental conception. The Transit Commission might have disapproved any but a proper reorganization; might have insisted that it take place expeditiously after it went into office; that otherwise the foreclosure suits proceed to judgment and sale. It might have ordered additional equipment and improvement of service, failing which the door would have been opened for remedies which the law gives.

However, those were not the thoughts and actions of the Transit Commissioners. After four and one-half years of receivership the reorganization was approved. Huge sums were spent in maintaining the receiver, his counsel, engineers and accountants, clerical staff, all of whom were concerned only with stock and bond holdings. Some of that expense curiously enough has been charged to the "cost of construction" of our subways. The remainder, to use the language of one of the Transit Commissioners, was "absorbed" by the company and a substantial "part charged to the operating expense" in its account with the city.

Before the reorganization of the B. R. T. it had outstanding 755,000 shares of $100 par stock. That stock was selling at one dollar per share at the time of reorganization. Its market value was $755,000. The bonds, bank loans and notes aggregated $120,000,000; interest and other charges had accrued. There were $12,500,000 of receiver's certificates outstanding. It had $8,000,000 in the bank. All this at the time when McAneny says it did not have enough "money with which to buy paint" for its corroded structures; this, at the time when the Joint Committee of Engineers found that 2,590 outer guard timbers, 14,910 joints, 1,900 ties and 77,000 inner guard timbers were rotten and required immediate replacement and the installation of the "dead man's button" was imperative.

Thus the total of its outstanding bonds, notes and receiver's certificates (not including accrued interest) and the market value of its outstanding capital stock was under $134,000,000. Of course, the market value of its bonds and notes was much below par and on that basis the amount would be much less.

The company was reorganized and the smooth-tongued Harkness naively says that the reorganization meant the squeezing out of $107,000,000 of water (Harkness, pp. 612-614). The fact is that at least $75,000,000 of new water was added on the basis of prevailing market valuations. The B. R. T. was reorganized into the B.-M. T. The B.-M. T. has an authorized capitalization of 350,000 shares preferred stock, no par value, but for all purposes treated as of the value of $100 per share, and 850,000 shares common stock, no par value. There were issued, as of October 8, 1924, 249,468 shares of preferred stock and 769,911 shares of common stock, 6 per cent. B.-M. T. bonds aggregating $92,000,000; underlying bonds aggregating $47,000,000, an aggregate of $139,000,000 in bonds, besides $25,000,000 preferred stock, a total of $164,-000,000 bonds and preferred stock. That is the capitalization to which Mr. Harkness refers when he speaks of the squeezing out of water. How convenient it is to forget 769,911 shares of common stock. How easy it is to wipe out $75,000,000 (par value of B. R. T. common stock) for the consumption of the riding public by merely changing the "R" into an "M" in the name of the company, and the name of the stock and calling it "no par value." A little thing like fourteen thousand shares of additional common stock has escaped Mr. Harkness' notice. But it was another story in relation to Wall Street. Before the ink of Mr. Harkness' signature of approval of this plan of reorganization was completely dry a balance sheet was prepared by the B. M. T., the common stock acquired a real value and on the first balance sheet which came to light after the reorganization the common stock was valued at $41,596,190, or at the rate of $54 per share—this supposed equivalent of common stock of the B. R. T. which sold the day before at $1 per share. Adding that $41,596,190 for common stock to the $164,000,000 aggregate of bonds of preferred stock, the total is $205,-000,000. It is indeed singular that this figure so nearly corresponds with Commissioner Harkness' value of $201,105,711 on page 11 of his opinion approving the reorganization. Of course that may be a mere accident.

Before the reorganization took place the Corporation Counsel seriously objected to the incorporation of the B.-M. T. as a *holding* company. The Transit Commission's alibi is, that the B. R. T. was and the B.-M. T. is a holding company organized under the business corporation law; that only railroad companies are subject to the direction and control of the Transit Commission (Harkness, pp. 622, 623). Of course, if the Transit Commission had compelled the B.-M. T. to organize as a *railroad* corporation, it would have had the power to inquire into the details of the reorganization, to fix the proper capitalization and to ascertain where the huge sums went which were spent on the reorganization; who received these sums and for what purpose. But the Corporation Counsel's objections were overruled. There can be no question as to the merit of this objection.

I quote from the plan of reorganization of March 15, 1923, page 5. "The Brooklyn Rapid Transit Company is a corporation * * * *owning directly* the power plants of the system," and at the bottom of page 6 and top of page 7 as follows: "The power plants, repair shops, car barns, etc., common to the use both of the surface lines and the subway and elevated lines *were operated* by the B. R. T. itself and the *principal power plants are also owned by the **B. R. T.*** * * * many of the *common facilities* are *owned* by the rapid transit companies and many by the surface companies."

Section 5 of the Public Service Commission Law provides:

> 1. Jurisdiction, supervision, powers and duties * * * shall extend under this chapter to common carriers, railroads, street railroads, etc.
>
> 2. * * * to the manufacture, sale or distribution of gas, electricity for light, heat or power.

Section 2, subdivision 8, provides:

> "The term railroad corporation when used in this chapter includes every corporation, company,

association, joint stock association, partnership and person, their lessees, trustees or receivers appointed by any court whatsoever owning, *operating* or managing any railroad or any cars *or any equipment* used thereon or in connection therewith."

The title to the power plants and the right to operate the repair shops, car barns and other facilities was vested in the B. R. T. before reorganization and passed directly to the B.-M. T. upon reorganization. Surely, *power plants, car barns and repair shops are equipment,* and yet the Transit Commission permitted the organization of the B.-M. T. as a *business corporation, thus placing it beyond the control of the Transit Commission.*

Under Section 55, Public Service Commission Law, it is provided that the capital of a consolidated or merged corporation shall not exceed the capital of the corporations consolidated, *at par value* thereof and any additional sum actually paid in in cash. This section naturally contemplated that a reorganized company could be incorporated *only with par value stock,* because otherwise it would be impossible to apply this section. The Transit Commission approved the reorganization of the B. R. T. with no par value stock, both common and preferred, so that Section 55 was not complied with.

How well the B.-M. T. succeeded in creating a situation where for the purposes of the Transit Commission the capitalization would be one amount, and for the purpose of stock manipulation it would be another, may be inferred from the foregoing comparison of the testimony of Mr. Harkness in which he fixed the capitalization at $164,000,000, and the records in Wall Street showing a capitalization of $204,000,000, not taking into account the earnings and surplus since reorganization. Annexed hereto is Exhibit "K" which I have caused to be prepared, which discloses that the aggregate market value of the outstanding B. R. T. stock and bonds at the time of reorganization, June 7, 1923, together with a sum sufficient to discharge all of its obligations as they were in fact discharged, *is $123,042,936.*

With that sum all of the stock and properties owned by the B. R. T. could have been acquired by purchase in the open market and sufficient would have remained to clear it of its debts. Compare this sum with the $204,000,000 capitalization claimed by the B.-M. T. Simple arithmetic proves at least $80,000,000 of water. That that stock was intentionally watered is proved by its subsequent performances in Wall Street. It first appeared for trading on the stock exchange in October, 1923; shortly thereafter the common stock sold at $9.25 per share. Then appeared the financial statement that it was worth $54 per share, and so it jumped from $9.25 to $40 per share, an appreciation of 31 points or over $23,000,000. That is not taking into account the appreciation of the preferred stock and bonds of the B.-M. T. and all this notwithstanding that it is claimed that subways cannot be operated successfully on a 5c fare. Of course, that is only for the riding public. In the financial district, it was told that for the first year after receivership the B.-M. T. earned over $4,000,000; 10 per cent. of the highest price at which the common stock sold and about 45 per cent. of its lowest price. The effects which will inevitably come from this overcapitalization are clear to anyone who has in mind the history of the finances of the traction corporations in this city. The same B. R. T. paid out $35,000,000 in swollen dividends on its prior watered capitalization. We have the admission that such capitalization was watered in Mr. Harkness' own opinion. The inevitable result will be, as it always has been, that every effort will be strained, under pressure from those who have paid $40 and more for their stock and who are now called investors, to pile up alleged surpluses, dividends will be paid, capital expenditures and replacements will be forgotten, the capital will be impaired, another period of depression will come, and the same tale will be told again.

It will be interesting to observe what the financial status of the B.-M. T. will be when the city recaptures its subway under Contract 4. It will then have left the surface lines, power plants, etc., valued by the Transit Commission in 1921 at $52,000,000, with subsequent additions, but surely not saleable at even $26,000,000; its old elevated lines valued by the Commission in 1921 at $22,400,000, together with about $36,000,000 invested in improvements, extensions and third-tracking under Contract No. 4, a total of $58,400,000 (surely no one will claim its real value to be that sum), and other and current assets over current liabilities, $10,000,000.

An approximate balance sheet of the B.-M. T. upon such recapture will be as follows:

Assets

Cash from City for subways...........	$52,995,000
Surface lines, power plants, etc........	26,000,000
"L" line and improvements	58,400,000
Other and current assets over liabilities..	10,000,000
Total Assets	$147,395,000

Liabilities

Outstanding bonds	$139,000,000
Preferred stock at $100 a share.........	25,000,000
Common stock at $40 a share..........	30,000,000
Total Liabilities	$194,000,000

*There is a good reason why friends of the **B.-M. T.** should be opposed to a "recapture" of the subways.*

It is claimed that $26,048,015 new money went into the reorganization of the B.-M. T. It did, but it did not all stay there. About $5,000,000 was immediately taken out as expenses of reorganization. More will be said on this subject later. That $26,000,000 was raised by assessing each holder of 100 shares of stock of B.-M. T. $3,500, for which he received $2,187.50 bonds and $1,312.50 preferred stock. The aggregate amount of bonds so issued was $16,280,000, and of preferred stock $9,768,000, an aggregate of $26,048,000. These figures are important because deliberate falsehoods have been told with reference thereto, even before Commissioner McAvoy.

Before the preferred stock was issued, it was provided in the plan of reorganization and also in the certificate of incorporation that dividends on the preferred stock should be cumulative from and after July 1, 1926; that means that until July 1, 1926 the holders of the preferred stock could not as of right expect any dividends. There was a reason why that provision was inserted in the plan and certificate of incorporation.

Mr. Harkness in his opinion discusses gross income and estimated expenditures of the company as reorganized. On page 9 he takes into account interest on bonds and operating expenses. He says there are no sinking fund requirements on bonds, by agreement until 1927 (p. 624) and then he says that in view of the desirability of in every way assisting the reorganized company, and "although there may theoretically be a distinction between the sinking funds and depreciation funds in respect of deferred payments, it seems to me that under all the circumstances the new management is entitled to a year's grace in order to get the new company well started. *I, therefore, do not make any deduction from the figures of present earnings to cover depreciation but leave that to future action." That means that the B.-M. T. was told that it need not set anything aside for depreciation except to the small extent to which it had been accustomed.* Of course, to make the situation presentable and consistent it was necessary for the gentlemen engineering the reorganization to display a spirit of intended economy and conservation *and that is why in the certificate of incorporation it is provided that the preferred stock shall not be cumulative as to dividends until July* 1, 1926. That provision served its usefulness the moment the reorganization was approved; the plan of reorganization and the certificate of incorporation were forgotten by both the Transit Commission and the B.-M. T. by April, 1924. Nine months is a long time to wait for dividends, when there is feverish anxiety that the price of stocks advance in Wall Street.

Accordingly, in April, 1924, the very month in which the Joint Committee of Engineers made its report on the causes of the Flatbush Avenue accident and found defects in the B.-M. T. structure requiring immediate remedying for the safety of the public, a quarterly dividend of $1½ or at the rate of $6 per annum was declared on the preferred stock, and it has been paid since. That stock sold only a few months before at $34.50 per share. This dividend meant a return of 18 per cent. on that basis. Commissioner Harkness says the Transit Commission could not forbid the declaration of dividends, but it could have made orders for additional cars and improved service to be paid for out of the million and a half dollars annually which this dividend requires.

The Transit Commission feels and the B.-M T. felt, that the declaration of this dividend required some explanation and we find that explanation in almost in the same words from the company and the Transit Commission. At the time when a dividend was declared in April, 1924, the Chairman of the Board of Directors of the B.-M. T. stated: (I am quoting from the Standard Corporation Records issued August 15, 1924):

> "That the dividend was to be considered as in the nature of interest on the money contributed by stockholders at the time of reorganization nine months ago and was not to be taken as an indication that the company was earning a fair return on its actual investment or on a fair valuation of its property."

and quoting from Commissioner O'Ryan's speech over the radio broadcasting station WAHG on October 30, 1924, as reported in the New York Times of October 31, 1924, he said on the same subject as follows:

> "The Brooklyn-Manhattan Company last year paid dividends on its preferred stock only, nothing more, and the fact is that this preferred stock represented $26,000,000 of *new money* recently paid into the company by the public."

—and at the hearing before Mr. Justice McAvoy, Commissioner McAneny says:

> "The B.-M. T. declared a dividend on the *new money* paid into the treasury at the time of reorganization of the former stockholders" (McAneny, p. 2580).

In other words, these three gentlemen claim in unison *that the dividend was paid on* $26,000,000 *of new money paid in at the time of reorganization. Nothing could be further from the truth.* The fact is that only $9,768,000 preferred stock was issued for new money. The remaining $16,280,000 of new money was represented by new bonds issued to the stockholders and *the B.-M. T. has paid interest on these bonds at* 6 *per cent. since* reorganization. In other words, this 6 per cent. dividend is 6 per cent. on $16,280,000 not represented by any new money.

Interest at the rate of 6 per cent. per annum on $26,148,000 is $1,568,880. The company pays $2,-473,608 for dividends on preferred stock and interest on the $16,280,000 of bonds—*nearly one million dollars more per annum* than the 6 per cent. on $26,000,000 new money. Why this deceit?

There remains but one other outstanding feature of the reorganization which deserves comment. It appears from page 10 of the plan of reorganization which the Transit Commission has approved that $6,484,119 was disbursed, for court costs, commissions, taxes, claims, underwriting and syndicate and other expenses of reorganization. This is a huge sum, and surely required investigation, yet we have the admission of Commissioner Harkness that he did not even inquire into that expenditure (pp. 2319-21).

The Mayor of this city has for months been demanding that a statement be furnished showing how that money was spent and for what purposes. I direct your attention to the fact that it is provided in the reorganization agreement, paragraph 17, page 61 of the plan, that the accounts of the committee shall be filed within one year with the Board of Directors of the new company. That account has apparently not been filed. At the close of Mayor Hylan's testimony before Justice McAvoy, I suggested this inquiry. Nothing having been done, by a letter, a copy of which I am annexing, Exhibit "B," I again directed Mr. Sherman's attention to it. No inquiry was made. Instead there was introduced in evidence a letter and schedule dated January 2, 1925, addressed to Mr. Sherman by Rushmore, Bisbee and Stern, which contains a statement of disbursements of the reorganization. I am annexing a copy, Exhibit "L."

It will be noted that no names are given and that the expenditures are bulked and the purposes not set forth with particularity. It appears therefrom that $1,432,-640.82 was expended as syndicate fees, that the compensation and expenses of counsel, trustees, etc., in connection with defaulted bonds was $1,129,213.04, that representatives of the stockholders and committees and counsel received $440,508.33; that it cost to deposit old and new securities $110,005.86; that engineers and accountants got $51,500; the expenses of receiver, compensation of receiver, counsel, special master, etc., were $254,500, the reorganization committee and counsel took $400,000 and expenses incident to securing deposits of securities were $92,885.21. What did these people do? Who received these enormous sums of money, which should have gone into improvements and for better service of the transit company? Nobody before Commissioner McAvoy was asked and nobody answered. What did representatives of stockholders and contract creditors do that entitled them to nearly half of a million dollars? $2,200,000 was paid to tort creditors and $1,600,000 to contract creditors. I understand that the receiver and counsel collected $470,000 for only a portion of their services during the receivership and before reorganization. That item was the subject of adjustment upon the redetermination of costs. For what did they receive $254,500 more? The reorganization committee charged $400,000 for what? The reorganization committee included Gerard M. Dahl. He was a member of the firm of Hayden Stone & Company. Albert H. Wiggin of the Chase Securities Co. was the chairman of the committee. Hayden Stone & Co., J. & W. Seligman and Chase Securities Company received $1,432,640.82 syndicate fees. What were those syndicate fees? Mr. Harkness says in his order of approval that the organization has been approved by the holders of the majority of the stock of the B. R. T. Apparently they agreed to pay the assessment. Mr. Dahl in his book, "Transit Truths," says repeatedly that the new money was furnished by the stockholders. If that be so, why did the syndicate receive $1,430,000 from the treasury of the B.-M. T? The plan of reorganization provides that the syndicate shall charge 5½ per cent. on the entire $26,000,000 of new money and not merely on any deficiency that they might be required to pay upon failure of stockholders to respond to the assessment. How much did the stockholders contribute —how much the syndicate? Was the arrangement for compensation to the syndicate fair? It was money which otherwise would have gone to make good "deferred maintenance." The reorganization on this basis was approved by the Transit Commission. Should it have been? Should these matters not have been the subject of inquiry by the Transit Commission? Harkness evades the subject and says there were 170 banks in an association which underwrote this $26,000,000. That explanation is not sufficient. J. & W. Seligman, Chase Securities Company and Hayden, Stone & Company did not need 170 banks to help them to finance the comparatively small amount needed because of the failure of some stockholders to pay their assessment.

It is to be borne in mind that this $1,432,000 represents about $2 per share on 750,000 shares of stock of the B. R. T., which was then selling at $1. In other words, the syndicate charged $2 per share for securing the privilege to stockholders to pay $35 per share assessment on stock which was selling at $1 per share. About $4,000,000 went to lawyers, committees and representatives, or at the rate of about $6 per share on the outstanding capital stock of both the new and old companies, and not one cent of this money inured to the benefit of the riding public.

CHAPTER VI

"The Harvest"

DISRUPTION OF UNIFIED BROOKLYN SURFACE LINE SYSTEM —FAILURE TO RESTORE UNIVERSAL FIVE CENT FARE

There are approximately 245 route miles of surface car lines in Brooklyn; 138 are operated by subsidiaries of the B.-M. T., the remaining 107 miles are owned by the Brooklyn City Railroad Company.

The Brooklyn City Railroad Company is the successor of a number of old horse car lines in Brooklyn, some originating before 1850. It owns what has been termed by Commissioner Harkness as "the heart of the surface line system in Brooklyn".

In 1893, the predecessor of the B. R. T., the Long Island Traction Co., acquired control of this system under a 999 year lease from the Brooklyn City Railroad Company to the Brooklyn Heights Railroad Company, now a subsidiary of the B. R. T., at a rental which included taxes, interest on nearly $7,000,000 outstanding bonds of the Brooklyn City Railroad Company, and a guaranteed dividend of 10 per cent. per annum on $12,000,000 stock of the Brooklyn City Railroad Company (Harkness, p. 2389).

The B. R. T. operated these lines as part of its surface system, at the time of the surface line receivership, July 14, 1919. There were at that time over 500 points of free transfer from the lines of the Brooklyn City Railroad Company to other surface lines of the B. R. T.

Prior to its receivership, the B. R. T. had invested

about $10,000,000 in improvements and maintenance, and various other purposes of the Brooklyn City Company (Harkness, p. 2390).

In October 1919 the receiver of the B. R. T. elected to terminate the lease with the Brooklyn City Company, and the lines were restored to that Company and have since, at least ostensibly, been operated by the Brooklyn City Company, separate and apart from the surface system of the B.-M. T. as reorganized.

The result of this severance has been a disruption of the unified surface line system and universal five cent fare as it existed prior to the receivership. At about 500 points of intersection between lines of the Brooklyn City and those of the B.-M. T. where previously free transfers were given, the public is now required to pay additional fares estimated in the aggregate, at least $5,000,000 per annum.

The Legislature in 1921, in creating the Transit Commission, declared, as a measure of relief sought to be accomplished by the Transit Commission, the unification and consolidation of street railway lines with a view to the restoration of the transfer rights which terminated during the receivership.

It is beyond question that it was within the power of the Transit Commission to direct the restoration of transfers between the lines of the Brooklyn City Company and B. R. T. as before the receiverships.

Section 49 of the Public Service Commission Law distinctly provides:

> "That the commission shall have power * * * to require any two * * * street railroad corporations, whose lines * * * form * * * connecting lines of transportation * * * to establish through routes

and joint fares * * * for the transportation of passengers, *and that if upon the expiration or earlier termination of a lease the free transfers * * * of passengers theretofore in effect and permitted by the lessee of a rapid transit railroad * * * is discontinued * * * the commission shall have the power by order to require the companies * * * to continue or to reestablish such through routes formerly existing, and to establish joint rates, fares and charges for the transportation of passengers."*

And further enabling legislation on the same subject is contained in Section 13, Chapter 252, Laws 1884 and Section 101, Chapter 565, Laws of 1890.

When application was made in June, 1923, for the approval by the Transit Commission, of the proposed reorganization of the B. R. T., the City of New York through its Corporation Counsel, objected to the reorganization save upon the condition, that the B.-M. T. secure an arrangement with the Brooklyn City Company, by which free transfers and the unified surface line system of Brooklyn be restored, as before the receivership.

Commissioner Harkness in overruling the objections of the Corporation Counsel and giving approval for the reorganization of the B. R. T. without the inclusion of the lines of the Brooklyn City Company and in giving sanction to the continuance of the disruption of this surface car system, said in part, as follows:

"Of even greater moment is the absence from this reorganization of the Brooklyn City Railroad Company * * * * During the receivership the lease went back to separate company operation. *This was unfortunate for the riding public because* *of the cutting off of transfers and the flexibility of service that had become in a course of over twenty years almost a necessity.* * * * The surface lines are not reorganized, but their bonds were to be reinstated. ***The Brooklyn City Railroad Company** formerly leased and operated as part of the* ***B. R. T.*** *system is not included, but the plan of readjustment contemplates its eventual acquisition."*

The reason assigned by the Transit Commission for its course then was and still is, that it was powerless to compel a lease between the B.-M. T. and the Brooklyn City. That is entirely aside the point. In fact these two companies are inter-related, both in respect to control, and in the operation of their lines. An offer was made, through the testimony of Deputy Commissioner Cornelius H. Sheehan, of the Department of Water Supply, Gas and Electricity, to show, that in fact, the lines and equipment of the B.-M. T. and the Brooklyn City Company, are used inter-changeably. The offer was ignored.

The question is not, and was not, whether the Transit Commission could have compelled leases to unify the surface lines in Brooklyn. The Transit Commission was created to relieve the emergency in the transit situation, including the burdens added by the discontinuance of these free transfers. Much discretion was vested in the Transit Commission, with respect to approval or disapproval of the plan of reorganization, and whilst the Transit Commission might not have had power to compel the two companies to enter into a lease, it could have refused to approve the reorganization except upon the condition that the B. R. T., make an appropriate agreement with the Brooklyn City Company, whereby free transfers would be restored. Nobody should doubt that the B.-M. T. would have been able in the briefest period, to effect such an arrangement.

Commissioner Harkness says: that the Brooklyn City is not included in the reorganization "but the plan of readjustment contemplates its eventual acquisition." Everybody is waiting for the realization of that contemplation. Over a year and a half has passed and nothing has happened.

Commissioner Harkness very frankly admitted, upon the hearing, the power of the Transit Commission under the provisions of the Public Service Commission and other laws, to institute through route and joint rate proceedings which would result in transfer privileges to the public. *But he says, no such proceeding has ever been contemplated, much less commenced.* His explanation is the one oft given. He says that the Brooklyn City is "in good shape" financially. That is beyond doubt. It earned a net profit, after payment of all operating expenses and interest on bonds, of 15 per cent. on its common stock in 1922; 19 per cent. in 1923; and 17 per cent. in 1924.

But says the Commissioner (pp. 2392-2394), the subsidiaries of the B.-M. T. which operate the rest of the surface lines in Brooklyn "are in bad shape," almost insolvent, and are in no position to stand the burden of the restoration of free transfers.

Of course if the primary consideration is the welfare of the railroad company, that is a good excuse, but if the obligation of a railroad company is, as I assume it, to serve the public, under the provisions of our laws, financial debility, may be a reason for the abandonment of its franchise, but it surely is no reason why the Transit Commission should exercise paternalism towards it, at the public's expense.

CHAPTER VII

Financial Rehabilitation

INTERBOROUGH RAPID TRANSIT COMPANY REORGANIZATION

The Interborough Rapid Transit Company, the lessee under Contract 3, underwent what the Transit Commissioners termed a "reorganization," rather "re-adjustment." That so-called "reorganization" occurred in October, 1922, effective November 25, 1922, under the guidance and upon the approval of Commissioner O'Ryan. It was that company which, according to Commissioner Harkness, required nursing and tender treatment, in order that it might be saved the pains of receivership.

It has a capital stock of $35,000,000. Its financial strength endured, at least for the purpose of paying dividends, until suddenly in 1919, it lapsed into financial chaos. Its record of dividend payments is as follows:

Year	Rate	Amount
1904	2. %	$700,000
1905	6.75	2,362,000
1906	8.25	2,887,000
1907	9.	3,150,000
1908	9.	3,150,000
1909	9.	3,150,000
1910	9.	3,150,000
1911	10.	3,500,000

Year	Rate	Amount
1912	15. %	$5,250,000
1913	12.	4,200,000
1914	15.	5,250,000
1915	20.	7,000,000
1916	20.	7,000,000
1917	20.	7,000,000
1918	17.50	6,125,000
1919	5.	1,750,000
	187.50%	$65,625,000

It should be noted that it even paid dividends in 1919.

Harkness' anxiety to prevent receivership was due to the fear that, through it, the lease of the Manhattan Company would end, and, of course, then the earnings from the subways could not be applied to make good the losses of the elevated lines. His fret was, that then there might have been an abolition of free transfers, and an attempt by the "L" company to charge ten cent fare under an ancient charter, and that the I. R. T. might have lost its $43,000,000 investment in third-tracking and extending the "L" lines, under the related certificates of March 19, 1913. It did not occur to Commissioner Harkness that that was not a matter of public concern, and that the tracks and extensions were there, to be used so long as elevated structures are desirable. Nor did it occur to Commissioner Harkness that possibly by a receivership, and the wiping out of stock which represented no value, and of bonds which were inflated, and the coming of the Interborough's properties into strong financial hands, with money for improvements, the public would be best served.

Throughout the record will be found the same solicitude for the financial rehabilitation of these traction companies.

As a measure of justice and relief, and to end the constant and unwarranted diversions of the earnings of the city-owned subways to the stock and bond-holders of the Manhattan Elevated Company, Mayor Hylan had publicly and repeatedly, and long before there was any proposal for the I. R. T. reorganization, urged an equitable reduction of the exorbitant rentals payable out of these subway earnings for these elevated lines.

It will be seen in a moment that the alleged "readjustment" has merely postponed the day of reckoning. The "readjustment" was made, by a modification of the lease with the Manhattan Elevated Company, by which, besides paying taxes and interest on $45,000,000 of outstanding bonds, the Interborough instead of paying 7 per cent. dividends on the $60,000,000 stock of the Manhattan Company, is now required to pay, only out of earnings, for the year ending July 1, 1923, 3 per cent.; for the year ending July 1, 1924, 4 per cent.; for the year ending July 1, 1925, and thereafter, 5 per cent. (Harkness, p. 2313); by a postponement of payments into sinking fund, on the I. R. T. 5 per cent bonds for five years from January 1, 1921; by a provision that the dividend rate on the common stock of the I. R. T. shall be restricted to 7 per cent. per annum, with no disbursements, until July 1, 1926 (Harkness, p. 2315), and by an arrangement for a new security issue of $15,000,000, ten year 6 per cent. notes, of which $10,500,000 was presently issued and absorbed by the holders of the Interborough-Metropolitan 4½ per cent bonds and Interboro stockholders. Thus, so far as finances are concerned, only $10,500,000 additional money was raised, from which must be deducted not only the expenses but nearly $4,000,000 which was immediately paid as an installment of principal on its outstanding 7 per cent. notes, besides about $9,000,000 to and on account of the Manhattan Elevated Company for back taxes, unpaid rental and deferred maintenance, leaving a deficit of at least $2,500,000. That is called "rehabilitation." The net result of this alleged reorganization was, that all new money was paid out on old claims, and nothing left for capital improvements or to make good "deferred maintenance"; besides $2,500,000 had to be taken out of current assets.

The capitalization of the I. R. T. as of June 30, 1924, is as follows:

Capital Stock	$35,000,000
First refunding 5% bonds	162,106,000
Notes	44,833,700
Equipment certificates	3,370,000
Total	$245,309,700
Less sinking fund	8,000,000
Balance	$237,309,700

As against this capitalization it has the following apparent assets:

Its investments under Contracts 1 and 2	$46,000,000
Its investment under Contract 3	110,000,000
Its investment in tracking and extensions of "L"	43,000,000
	$199,000,000

It has, of course, current assets from which must be deducted current liabilities. These assets, in the foregoing schedule, must be properly depreciated. At least one-seventh of the term of the leases has expired. The depreciation is at least $30,000,000. The value of the assets of the Interborough, not taking into account that its Manhattan lease is a real liability, does not exceed $169,000,000 as against $237,000,000 of capitalization, and included in the assets are $43,000,000 invested in "L" improvement. This last mentioned investment has little if any real value. And this has been termed a reorganization of the I. R. T.!

It will be interesting to note what the financial position of the I. R. T. will be when the city recaptures its subway lines under Contract 3. The I. R. T. will then have left $123,000,000 in cash, which it will receive from the city for the subways under Contract 3; its investment in subways under Contracts 1 and 2 of $46,000,000, besides its investment under the lease of the Manhattan Elevated properties, which is only a burden.

An approximate balance sheet of the I. R. T. upon such recapture will be as follows:

Assets	
Received from City under Contract 3—	
Cash	$123,000,000
Investment under Contracts 1 and 2	46,000,000
Other and current assets over liabilities	9,000,000
Total Assets	$178,000,000
Liabilities	
Capital stock	$35,000,000
Bonds, notes, certificates of indebtedness less sinking fund	202,309,700
Total Liabilities	$237,309,700

MORE REHABILITATION—NEW YORK RAILWAYS REORGANIZATION

This company owns or controls all of the surface lines in the Borough of Manhattan with the exception of those of the Second Avenue R. R. Co., Third Avenue R. R. Co., Eighth Avenue R. R. Co., Ninth Avenue R. R. Co. and the New York and Harlem R. R. Co., which operates the 4th and Madison Avenue Line.

The New York Railways Company was petitioned into receivership in March 1919. Mr. Job E. Hedges was its Receiver. That receivership lasted for five years until July 8, 1924, when a so-called "reorganization" was approved, likewise under the guidance of Commissioner O'Ryan. The Receiver is not yet physically out of possession.

These lines, so far as they are useful for operation, have been valued by the Transit Commission as of 1921, at $48,000,000 as depreciated, and at $22,670,000 original cost less cost of conditioning (see Transit Commission Valuations, 1921). Upon reorganization there were recapitalized most of the outstanding and underlying bonds, besides 275,000 shares no par value stock. The old capitalization of the New York Railway system was as follows:

Fixed charge bonds—all Companies....	$39,425,198
Income bonds—N. Y. Railways Co.....	30,609,487
Guaranteed stock—of Subsidiaries......	3,836,700
Non-guaranteed stock—N. Y. Railways Co.	17,495,060
Total	$91,366,445

In accordance with the plan of reorganization, the new capitalization will be as follows:

Underlying New York Railway and subsidiary bonds	$14,653,000
Extended underlying bonds....	600,000
New 6th Avenue purchase bonds	300,000
New prior lien bonds..........	3,800,000

Total fixed charge obligations..........	$19,353,000
New income bonds	19,435,472
New preferred stock, 184,830 shares no par value, rated at $5 a share........	924,150
New common stock, 90,200 shares no par value, rated at $5 a share............	451,000
Total new securities..............	$40,163,622

There would appear to be a squeezing out of water to the extent of $51,000,000. Commissioner O'Ryan so claimed at the hearings (pp. 2428-29). But such is not the fact.

The new shares, no par value stock, common and preferred, for purposes of comparison, must be rated at $100 a share, as was the old stock. The rights of the new stockholders are no different from those of the old, and on that basis the capitalization is as follows:

Total new bonds.....................	$38,778,472
New preferred stock, 184,830 shares....	18,483,000
New common stock, 90,200 shares......	9,020,000
Total	$66,291,472

represented by assets valued by the Transit Commission, original cost, less cost of reconditioning at only $22,-670,000.

These are the surface lines which are gradually ending their usefulness. You may well judge their financial outlook under this "reorganization".

CHAPTER VIII

Other Peoples' Money

DEPRECIATION—DETERMINATION OF COST OF CONSTRUCTION AND EQUIPMENT—COST OF MAINTENANCE AND OPERATION—POOLING REVENUES

A. DEPRECIATION

The subways and equipment are owned by the City of New York. They are leased to and operated by the railroad companies under the dual contracts. One would not believe it from the posters of vilification of our Mayor, to be seen in the B.-M. T. subway cars—all tending to create a disrespect for government, particularly among the uninformed. This matter was brought to the attention of the Transit Commission and is the subject of one of the charges.

The leases will expire in 1962-1964. By the dual contracts the companies are bound to keep both the structure and equipment in proper repair. These provisions in Contracts 3 and 4 are substantially similar (Harkness, 634). The provisions for maintenance are intended to provide for the ordinary wear and tear from use. The depreciation reserve is to cover the wastage and obsolescence to which all property is subject, notwithstanding proper maintenance. It is recognized that all railroad property gradually deteriorates in value, due to progress in science, inventions and modernized construction and equipment.

It was not the intention of the dual contracts that upon their expiration there should be turned over to the city ramshackled and dilapidated structures and equipment, but on the contrary, that during the leases the subways and equipment would be not only kept in proper repair, but that a reserve would be set up for replacements and renewals, the balance to be retained to make good the obsolescence and wastage not saved by repairs. This depreciation fund both upon the expiration of the lease, or upon the recapture, would pass to the city, the theory being that whatever depreciation in value the subways might suffer, would be represented in the depreciation fund, so that in a general way the value of the system would remain constant, and the original investment would be unimpaired. It is provided in Article 49 of Chapter 2, Part III, subdivisions 4 and 5 of Contract 3, and a similar provision is contained in Contract 4, that from the revenues—there shall be deducted "an amount equal to 12 per cent. of the revenues *for maintenance, exclusive of depreciation*, and for the first year of operation—an amount equal to 5 per cent of the revenue for depreciation * * * within thirty days after the 30th day of June following the beginning of the lease and annually thereafter the Commission and the lessee shall determine the classification and amount of depreciation and excess maintenance not covered by the amount set aside in paragraph 4 of this article during the preceding fiscal year and the deduction for such year shall thereupon be adjusted to conform with such determination."

Mr. Delaney became Transit Construction Commissioner on July 1, 1919. Notwithstanding these provisions of the dual contracts for "depreciation funds," no such fund *has been set up to date under Contract No. 3.*

With respect to Contract No. 4 there was no fund created until January 22, 1921, when through the efforts of Commissioner Delaney the depreciation for the entire Brooklyn subway system was *tentatively* fixed at $300,-000 per annum, for the period beginning January 1, 1920. (See T. C. C. record—R. T. 6505.)

That $300,000 is undoubtedly an inadequate reserve for that rapid transit system, involving an investment of roughly, $275,000,000. This inadequacy has been recognized by the Transit Commission. Although tentatively fixed it has continued to date. Mr. Harkness testified that there is some understanding that for the next year it will be increased to $420,000 (p. 648), likewise an entirely insufficient sum. At least one per cent. per annum, namely, two and one-half million dollars, should be set aside as compensation for this "irreparable wear and tear."

With respect to the I. R. T.'s failure to make any provision for depreciation, a conflict developed between Commissioner Delaney and the I. R. T. In May of 1920 Commissioner Delaney addressed a communication to President Hedley in which was included a memorandum in support of Mr. Delaney's view that the failure of the I. R. T. to make provision for depreciation was in violation of the provisions of the contract.

On December 15, 1920, Mr. James L. Quackenbush, the general counsel of the I. R. T. had prepared a memorandum supporting the company's position. In substance it was Mr. Quackenbush's claim that Contract No. 3 provided for an expenditure by the company of 12 per cent. annually for maintenance; that in view of increased costs, that cost of maintenance was in excess of 12 per cent. and that *to the extent of the excess the Company was relieved from making any contribution to the depreciation fund*—in other words, that the contribution to the depreciation fund of 5 per cent. per annum tentatively fixed for the first year would be reduced to nothing when the cost of maintenance reached 17 per cent. He says in summarizing the company's contention:

"* * * * irrespective of the amount which may have been expended for maintenance, and irrespective of the measure of the depreciation fund which may be applied in any particular year, the deduction which will be made from revenue for that year for maintenance and for depreciation will be the sum of 12 per cent. of the revenue and the amount of the year's depreciaton determined in the manner provided in the contract. *Stated in another way, the Company's contention is that in any year when the amount spent for maintenance exceeds* 12 *per cent. of the revenue, the amount of cash to be turned over to the Depreciation Fund Board will be the depreciation for that year, less replacements, diminished by the "excess maintenance";* and conversely, that in any year when the amount spent for maintenance is less than 12 per cent. of the revenue, the amount of cash to be turned over to the Depreciation Fund Board will be the depreciation for that year, less replacements, *increased* by the difference between 12 per cent. of the revenue and the maintenance expenditures. There is nothing in the contract to indicate that whatever is spent for maintenance in excess of 12 per cent. and in the first instance therefor chargeable to 5 per cent. for depreciation *shall be "paid back into the Depreciation Fund at any time."*

Mr. Delaney in his memorandum of May 20, 1920, pointed out the fallacy of this contention. He says, "Experience has shown that the day comes when a unit of equipment, for example, must be retired in spite of all that may have been done to maintain it at the highest possible state of efficiency." "It is proper accounting practice to charge the cost of such a unit against the revenue over the entire period through which it is consumed. The contract and the certificate are interpreted to require that provision be made for that ultimate replacement."

His contention is supported by argument at great length, which is not referred to now, in view of its subsequent restatement in 1921, to which reference will be made. This conflict of views between Commissioner Delaney and the I. R. T. continued without result until March 12, 1921, when Mr. Delaney determined that the interests of the City required a determination of this controversy.

Accordingly, on March 12, 1921, Mr. Delaney addressed to the I. R. T. a communication again restating his position at length and demanding arbitration under subdivision 5 of Article 49, which reads: "If within such period the Commission and the lessee are unable to agree upon the classification and amount of depreciation * * * the amount thereof shall thereupon be determined by arbitration or by the court."

Mr. Delaney pointed out that the word "depreciation" generally means "wastage from use" and is divisible into two parts: "First, the expired life which is currently replaced by expenditures charged against revenue in the maintenance account, and second, *the expired life, the replacement of which is necessarily deferred on physical grounds beyond the current accounting period,*" and that the contract makes separate provision for both of these two elements of depreciation, the former characterized as "maintenance" and the latter as "depreciation"; that "depreciation and maintenance are in a sense dependent variables, because maintenance postponed results in deterioration of the principal parts, thus adding to the amount of depreciation. Therefore, inadequate provision for maintenance necessitates increased provision for depreciation," and he said, "I contend that depreciation begins where maintenance stops. You contend that thorough maintenance obviates depreciation." He called attention to the obligation assumed by the company to make adequate repairs, replacements, substitutions and renewals "at least equal to that of the equipment originally provided" and also that at no time during the term of the lease should the equipment be "less in quantity," and at the end of the lease the railroad should be "fully and perfectly equipped" ready for operation "to the full limit of their capacity; to make certain that these requirements would be observed, the negotiators provided a guaranty fund, deducted from revenue currently in cash * * * not a mere book reserve—and then provided for the adjustment of the maintenance and depreciation accounts annually to conform to the determination of the amount required during the year for these purposes in accordance with the record of the depreciation of each class of construction and equipment * * * twelve per centum of revenue is simply a tentative deduction toward the full amount necessary for maintenance and depreciation and when the annual accounting is made after the close of the fiscal year the actual amount of each is known and then provided."

Accordingly, on March 12, 1921, the Transit Construction Commissioner named as his arbitrator Mr. Milo R. Maltbie, former Public Service Commissioner; on April 19, 1921, Mr. Charles F. Uebelacker was named by the Interborough Rapid Transit Company as its arbitrator, and the Hon. Luke D. Stapleton was chosen as the third arbitrator on June 13, 1922. Judge

Stapleton having died, the Hon. Abel E. Blackmar was named in his stead on October 15, 1923, and he accepted that appointment on November 12, 1923.

I have referred to this matter at length because of its large importance to the city, and because of the attitude towards, and the disposition of it subsequently, by the Transit Commission.

Mr. Harkness testified that the amount involved as of June 30, 1924, according to Mr. Delaney's formula for depreciation, was $12,000,000 (p. 642-3). There can be no question that the amount is at least $30,000,000. The aggregate investment of the city and the company under Contracts 1, 2 and 3 is about $300,000,000. Assuming the probable life of the structure and equipment as a whole, at one hundred years, the depreciation would be 1 per cent. per annum. This is a conservative figure. The probable life of the equipment is not over thirty years. While the subway, so far as it is a tunnel, will endure forever, it is already demonstrated that modern construction and improvements will render it more or less valueless as time progresses. The inadequacy of the tunnel under Contracts 1 and 2 is the subject of daily comment. It is too narrow, not properly ventilated and has not sufficient exits. In fact, because of narrower bore, the cars from the B.-M. T. system cannot be operated on the tracks of the I. R. T. Taking the system as a whole its usefulness will end in much less than 100 years. Be that as it may, even the Transit Commissioners have recognized that both under the dual contracts and as a matter of justice there should be annual contributions to this fund. Yet not only have no steps been taken by the Transit Commission to press this arbitration, but the Transit Commission has abandoned the city's claim and apparently intends to overlook the plain obligations of the I. R. T. to maintain this fund.

Mr. Harkness says: "The attitude of the companies on that, brought into play another theory on depreciation that has been very vigorously contended for by utilities throughout the country. That is what may be called the 100 per cent. rule. That is based on this: Where you have a railroad property, such as the Interborough, with various classes of equipment, with rolling stock of different ages, with that property going through the repair shops all the time, and being maintained up to 100 per cent. efficiency, that there is no depreciation" (Harkness, p. 638). The answer to that contention is apparent.

First, that it is contrary to the fact. The I. R. T. does not maintain its lines in a condition of 100 per cent. efficiency, and second, the contract distinctly provides that there shall be a depreciation fund. The explanation of Commissioner Harkness of the failure of the Transit Commission to safeguard the city's rights and for the abandonment of the city's claim is as follows: He says that when the Transit Commission came into office on April 25, 1921, the Interborough was in financial difficulties and was threatened with receivership; that all interested parties were prompted by a spirit of cooperation to financially resurrect the Interborough. That accordingly, as already indicated, the stockholders of the I. R. T. agreed to raise ten and a half million dollars in cash; the bondholders agreed to postpone their sinking fund requirements for five years; the Manhattan Railway Company agreed to modify its lease as to rentals, and to use the language of Mr. Harkness, "it would be atrocious morally and unsound from a business standpoint to insist on that payment (into a depreciation fund) at that time, when all of the city's rights could be scrupulously preserved, and the claim in whole or in part enforced later on, as condition developed."

That was before October, 1922. More than two years have passed. The city's rights are still "preserved," rather "buried." The provision for the depreciation fund, which today should be in excess of $30,000,000 imposed an obligation on the I. R. T. It was for the city's benefit. In large part it would be the city's money on recapture. It was not for the Transit Commission to waive this obligation and surrender the city's rights. This false charity of which the Transit Commission is so proud, is nothing short of a betrayal of a public trust. Harkness calls it "a potent bit of help that it (the Transit Commission) gave in connection with the Interborough reorganization." This is the subject of Charges 4 and 5.

B. DETERMINATION OF COSTS

The contracts provide that from the pooled revenues, shall be paid interest to the city on its investment under Contracts 1 and 2, expenses of operation, maintenance and depreciation, the preferentials, and then a certain per cent. on the company's contribution to the cost of construction and equipment. So, too, upon recapture, the purchase price shall be such *cost of construction and equipment plus a bonus*. Of course, it was most important, as the construction and equipment proceeded, that the cost of the construction to the railroad companies be accurately determined. The contract fixed the procedure which was followed. The Chief Engineer of the Transit Commission and formerly of the Transit Construction Commissioner and the Public Service Commission of the First District, at the end of every three months determined the cost of construction and equipment, of both the city and companies, and these determinations came to be known as "quarterly determinations" (Harkness, pp. 650-652). A copy of each determination was forwarded to the Transit Commission and the companies, and they had the right to object. Upon objection the engineer had a right of re-determination, and upon such re-determination the Transit Commission and the Companies had a right of review, either by arbitration or to the court. The city had no right to object.

Prior to March, 1921, many of these objections to determination of costs had accumulated. I am annexing hereto Exhibit "O," a schedule of items which were the subject of determination and re-determination, and subsequent objection, by the Transit Construction Commissioner and his predecessors, under Contract 4. Besides, there was objection by the Transit Construction Commissioner to a charge, of a portion of $470,000 expenses of receiver, counsel, accountants, engineers, for printing and other purposes in connection with the receivership of the B. R. T.; that sum is in addition to the $254,500 already referred to—which was paid at the time of the reorganization of the B. R. T. This $470,000 was also the subject of an objection by Commissioner Delaney, because a part of it was included in the cost of *operation* to which reference will be made. Having failed to secure satisfactory disposition of these disputed items, Commissioner Delaney resorted to arbitration.

On March 21, 1921, the Transit Construction Commissioner named as his arbitrator Mr. Charles S. Hervey, and on April 18, 1921, the Brooklyn Company named Mr. Benjamin G. Paskus. The Transit Construction Commissioner then passed out of office and the

Transit Commission, his successor, abandoned the arbitration.

The explanation of the Transit Commissioners is, that after they came into office they agreed with the company to effect an adjustment of the disputed items, in conference, by a committee consisting of representatives of the Transit Commission and the railroad company. The representatives of the Transit Commission were: Mr. Cooper, the assistant chief accountant; Mr. Wilcock, the auditor of rapid transit costs, and Mr. Fullen, the counsel of the Transit Commission (Harkness, pp. 655-2326-2327).

Harkness says that all matters in dispute were adjusted; that the adjustment was in the nature of a recommendation to the Chief Engineer of the Transit Commission, that the Chief Engineer of the Transit Commission approved the recommendations and that the approval served as a re-determination of these determinations of cost; that before the conferences began, a written agreement was entered into, under which the Transit Commission and the companies agreed not to object to any adjustments of the Conference Committee.

The only parties having a right to object or to appeal to the court or to arbitration were the Transit Commission and the companies. *The City had no right to object to this adjustment.* Mr. Harkness conceded that after this adjustment was made, the Corporation Counsel objected thereto, and urged that the Transit Commission, on the city's behalf, press these objections, but that the requests and protestations of the Corporation Counsel were ignored, and that these objections of the Corporation Counsel were not forwarded because, to use the language of Mr. Harkness, it would be "upsetting an adjustment so laboriously worked out" (Harkness, pp. 2334-2335).

This adjustment in conference was made public on June 30, 1924. I call attention to the fact that on November 7, 1924 the Corporation Counsel wrote the members of the Transit Commission and stated:

> "On behalf of the City of New York I respectfully request that pursuant to articles 29 of chapter 5 of subway contract No. 3 you give written notice to the lesssee that you require such redetermination to be submitted to arbitration or to the court as provided by article XXX of chapter 6 of said contract. Will you kindly advise this department at your earliest convenience whether or not you will comply with the request herein and if so when such action will be taken."

and to another communication from the Corporation Counsel wherein is set forth specifically the items objected to, which concludes as follows:

> "In addition to the objections above set forth, further objection is made to the items so determined by the Chief Engineer by reason of the fact that they are deemed by the City of New York to be *excessive, improper and unauthorized.* I therefore respectfully request that you file on behalf of the City of New York with the Chief Engineer objections to his determinations and redeterminations."

Commissioner Harkness says that this adjustment committee disposed of "all the outstanding determinations of disputes between the city and the Interborough Company" (p. 656). There were two adjustment committees, one for the Interborough and the other for the Brooklyn Company.

An examination of these adjustments will disclose that in the largest measure they consist of a waiver and abandonment of the city's objections.

With respect to the $470,000 charged to cost of construction and cost of operation and maintenance, Commissioner Harkness explains that a portion thereof, amounting to $106,816.70 which represented the compensation of receiver and counsel during the years 1919, 1920, 1921 and 1922 (p 2334) *was charged to the companies' cost of construction and equipment.* It is difficult to conceive, *how an adjustment whereby over* $100,000 *paid to a receiver and counsel, in a proceeding brought about solely through the insolvency of the traction company as a charge to cost of construction and equipment of a subway, can be said to be a disposition of a dispute at all fair to the city.*

With respect to the seven items of objections in the annexed Exhibit "O," it will be found that only two were adjusted, namely, the sixth and seventh, and that the remaining five were practically ignored and nothing appears to have been done.

I call particular attention to the third of these objections. That has reference to the salary of Mr. Williams, the former president of the B. R. T. Notwithstanding that the company was suffering financial reverses, his salary as president of the New York Municipal Railway Corporation, the operating company under Contract 4, was increased from $50,000 to $75,000 a year. Curiously enough his whole salary was charged to cost of construction of our subways. Objection was made by the Transit Construction Commissioner to this $25,000 increase. After objection, the

Chief Engineer arranged with the company for a reduction of this $25,000 increase, as a charge against construction, the difference being charged to other companies in the B. R. T. system, but before that arrangement was made the $25,000 had already been included in the cost of construction, and the demand was made by Commissioner Delaney that it be removed—apparently the objection did not prevail in the adjustment conference.

The conduct of the Transit Commissioners in connections with these objections to determination of cost and the abandonment by them of the arbitration proceedings initiated by Transit Construction Commissioner Delaney constitutes the subject matter of Charge 8.

C. COST OF OPERATION AND MAINTENANCE

The dual contracts provide, that from the pooled revenues, there shall, among other things, be deducted the expenses of operation and maintenance and preferentials, and thereafter the interest due the company and city. Naturally the amount of such expenses determined the city's prospect of realizing anything on its investment. It was the claim of Commissioner Delaney that large items of expense were improperly charged against these pooled revenues. As was pointed out by Commissioner Harkness, provision was made in the dual contracts for objections to such charges, and in the event of disagreement, for arbitration, as in the case of objections to determinations of cost (Harkness, p. 650).

With respect to Contract No. 4 the principal objection, was, that there was included in the cost of operation and maintenance the large expenses of the receivership, to which reference has already been made.

This aggregate expense as Commissioner Harkness pointed out, was $470,000 for the years 1919 to 1922, and presumably in proportion, up to June 14, 1923 when the receiver was discharged. That does not take into account the final payments of $254,500 made to the receiver and counsel as per the statement of disbursements of Rushmore, Bisbee and Stern, elsewhere referred to.

On March 15, 1921 (302 R. T. 6922 of Transit Construction Commissioner record) Mr. Delaney filed his objection to such receivership expenses, as a proper charge to maintenance or operation, and on March 18, 1921, he designated as his arbitrator Mr. Edward Ward McMahon. On March 29, 1921 the receiver designated as his arbitrator Mr. Benjamin G. Paskus. So, too, similar objections were made to certain items charged to cost of operation and maintenance, under Contract No. 3 on January 27, 1921—principal of which was an item of $84,472.65, being 60 per cent. of $140,000, the cost of an investigation made in 1919 by a committee, acting solely in the interest of the bondholders of the Interborough Consolidated Company, as successor of the Interborough Metropolitan Company, *for the purpose of protecting the interests of those bondholders.* This item had been charged as deduction from revenue.

The Transit Construction Commissioner on March 3, 1921 named as his arbitrator Mr. George V. S. Williams and the Interborough on March 9, 1921, Mr. Frank R. Ford. Hon. Luke D. Stapleton was named as third arbitrator. Hon. Abel E. Blackmar succeeded him on April 5, 1923. Nothing has come of these arbitrations. They have apparently been abandoned.

The explanation of the Transit Commission is the same as that given with respect to the arbitrations upon objections to determinations of cost. ——"all disputes have been settled."

As already indicated with respect to the item of

$470,000, the expenses of the receiver for the years 1919-1920-1921 and 1922, $106,816.70 has been charged to cost of construction *and the balance was, to use the language of Commissioner Harkness, "absorbed by the company out of its own funds—receivership expenses—or it may eventually go into operating expenses."*

It is respectfully submitted that when the dual contracts were made it was contemplated, that there should be charged against the gross income the *usual and ordinary expenses* incurred in the operation of a transit line by a solvent carrier. The insolvency of the B. R. T. was not of the City's making. In no event should the City have been held accountable for its consequences, or be charged with any of the expenses of the receivership, either in computing the company's contribution to the cost of construction and equipment, or as an expense of operation or maintenance. Apparently the City has been so charged. That $470,000, or a major portion thereof, is reflected in the deficit from operation, which the company claims, and which must be paid before the City receives any return on its investment. But this has "all been adjusted," says Commissioner Harkness, and the adjustment is final and conclusive upon the City.

The City through the Corporation Counsel has requested that objections be filed, but, say the Transit Commissioners, these objections have been ignored and overruled, because to honor them would be to upset "an adjustment so laboriously worked out." It is submitted that the Transit Commission failed in its duties and sacrificed the City's interests by abandoning the remedy by arbitration which Commissioner Delaney set in motion. This matter is the seventh charge against the Transit Commissioners.

D. POOLING REVENUES

The City's chances of a return on its investment are dependent upon the revenue being large, or the expenses of operation being small. To safeguard the City's interest with respect to the revenue, it is provided in Article 49, Chapter 2, Part 3, of both contracts that

> "* * * *the gross receipts* from whatever sources *derived directly or indirectly* by the lessee or in its behalf in any manner from or out of or in connection with the operation of the railroad and existing railroad * * * *shall be combined* during the term of the contract and the City shall receive for the use of the railroad * * * a specified part * * * of the income, earnings and profits of the railroad and the existing railroad. The amount of such income, earnings and profits shall be determined as follows:"

It is thus clear that the gross income of the railroads for purposes of an accounting with the City, is its "combined income" derived directly or indirectly out of or in connection with the operation of our rapid transit lines.

Both companies have from time to time made public reports of their gross income from *all* sources whatsoever, and whether or not related to the dual contracts, and have also from time to time reported to the Transit Commission their alleged *gross revenue subject to accounting with the City under the dual contracts.*

A comparison of these reports had indicated that the companies withheld from their account with the City, their substantial revenues. The Commission has knowledge of this situation and concededly has done nothing to protect the City. This constitutes the subject matter of the Board of Estimate's sixth charge.

It appears that with respect to Contract No. 4 the Brooklyn Company has excluded and retained from the revenues an aggregate of at least one million dollars. The items thus improperly excluded and retained by the companies may for purposes of convenience be classified into four groups:

a. Payments received by the Brooklyn company from the Nassau Electric Railway Company for trains operated by the Nassau Company over the Brooklyn company's tracks;
b. Similar payments made to the Brooklyn company by the South Brooklyn Railroad Company;
c. Payments received by the Brooklyn company from the Long Island Railroad Company;
d. Interest received by the Brooklyn company on bank balances.

These moneys were collected by the Brooklyn company from the other railroad companies for use by the other companies of its cars and facilities.

These revenues, as already indicated, were reported by the Brooklyn company in its annual reports as *non-operating revenue* but were excluded by it from its income in its statements of "pooled revenues" under Contract No. 4.

As indicating to some extent the amount involved the following schedule of non-pooled revenues is given:

	1914	1915	1916	1917	1918
Nassau Elevated	$107,601	$116,120	$90,127	$67	....
South Brooklyn.	48,181	54,549	56,474	68,103	$58,630
Long Island....	8,948	3,404	34,892	28,236	9,056
Interest on Bank Bal....	10,058	12,303	16,186	9,807	9,800
Total......	$174,788	$186,376	$197,679	$106,213	$77,486

The aggregate of these amounts to June 30, 1918, is $752,542. It is assumed that this practice has continued to date. No explanation of the failure to assert the city's rights in respect to the non-inclusion of these revenues is furnished by the Transit Commission, except that Commissioner Harkness says that there is no "provision in the contract in respect to income, no way to object and force an arbitration on the part of the company to make credits to the accounts" (Harkness, p. 659); that in 1916 he was assistant counsel to the Public Service Commission; that the counsel to the commission had advised that no suit for an accounting against the companies would lie "until some amount, however small, was coming to the city. Therefore, he advised that there was no basis for an accounting action, that we have to wait until there was a right of participation—an actual participation" (Harkness, p. 660); that means "forever" according to the present outlook.

It hardly needs argument that the city is not without remedy. Without doubt an appropriate action will lie for an intermediate accounting between the city and the company, in which the question of the liability of the company to account for this revenue can be determined. According to Harkness the railroad company may withhold any portion of its income, until 1962 and 1964, when the leases expire, unless at some earlier time there is a balance due to the city. A mere statement of this claim is its own refutation.

CHAPTER IX

An Essay in Financial Jugglery

TRANSIT COMMISSION PLAN OF READJUSTMENT AND UNIFICATION OF TRANSIT LINES AND RAPID TRANSIT CONSTRUCTION PROGRAM

Much was said before Commissioner McAvoy about the "plan of readjustment" of our existing transit system, and the Transit Commission's program for construction of new subways, and the opposition which the city administration made to this plan and program. To a proper appreciation of this controversy it is necessary to refer to Chapter 134, Laws of 1921 (The Act which created the Transit Commission). That law was of most extraordinary character, without parallel in the history of legislation. It constitutes an affront to the people of the City of New York. It created the Transit Commission as a lordship over the municipal government of the City of New York. It was a grant of an unlimited agency to the Transit Commission, in the name of the city and jointly with the traction companies, to rehabilitate the traction companies at the expense, and without the consent of the city and over its objection—an objection which the Legislature knew would come, and which by express provision in the law, it permitted the Transit Commission to overide. *That law empowered the Transit Commission to negotiate with the traction companies and prepare a plan for the acquisition of their properties, to fix the price with them, to fix the rate of fare to be thereafter charged the public, and to lay down a plan for the control and operation of these properties so acquired; to nullify all existing contracts between the city and the traction companies, to strip the people of their vested right to be carried under the dual contracts at a five-cent fare and to make contracts for the use of the city streets—all without the consent and over the objection of the local authorities.*

The City authorities have contended and still contend that this power is in violation of Section 18 of Article III and Section 3 of Article XII of the Constitution of the State of New York, which vests exclusively in the municipal government the right to fix the terms and conditions of street railway franchises. That question, as elsewhere indicated, remains undetermined by the courts. The Transit Commission was not slow to commence the exercise of these great powers. The Commission went into office on April 25, 1921. By September 29, 1921, it had evolved a fantastic and gigantic scheme which has since been called the plan of "readjustment." It made it public. The railroad companies were requested to give a statement of their views thereon, which they did. The City was never asked to express any views with respect to it. The Transit Commission never finally adopted this plan, and never held any public hearing upon any "adopted plan" as the law requires. Commissioner O'Ryan says that the Transit Commission might have adopted it without the City's consent. Its reasons for failing so to do are not made public. It appeared as if it were abandoned. We are assured, however, by him, that the Commission will go ahead "at the proper time." When that will be, he does not say (O'Ryan, 2497-2498).

This plan provided for the organization of a consolidated company which would purchase all of the existing lines, subway, elevated and *surface, at prices to be fixed by agreement with each of the forty companies which own the* 1,000 *franchises existent in the City of New York.* It provides for the formation of three other operating companies, under the control of the consolidated company. The consolidated company would pay the purchase price for the existing lines, in bonds bearing interest at the rate of 5 per cent. plus 1 per cent. for amortization. After the consolidated company acquired these properties by the issuance of these bonds secured by purchase money mortgages it would transfer the property subject to the mortgages to the City of New York. The City would thus own all of our existing subway, elevated and surface cars, *charged, however, with the lien of the mortgage, in an amount equal to the purchase price of the lines to be fixed by agreement between the Transit Commission and the railroad companies.* The City would then lease the lines to and they would be operated by the operating companies.

In explaining this arrangement recently Commissioner O'Ryan said: "No state or city commission can roughly seize the property of these companies. Their property can only be obtained by purchase or due process of law." Of course that only means, that since there is no process of law by which these lines can be acquired, *that eventually the price to be paid would be what the companies ask.* It is also provided in the Plan that besides this 5 per cent., and 1 per cent. amortization, *not more than* 3 *per cent. of the amount of the bonds, payable out of the revenue, shall be applied annually for what the commission characterizes as reward for efficient management, to be divided* 1½ *per cent. to the bondholders and* 1½ *per cent. to the management.* The Commission caused valuations of the railroad companies' properties to be made. The companies do not agree with these valuations. They claim that they are worth about $190,000,000 more, not including the I. R. T. roads or Brooklyn Rapid Transit Lines under the Dual Contracts.

The total valuation which the Commission has placed on the Manhattan elevated, old B. R. T. elevated lines, B. R. T. surface lines and the other surface lines in Manhattan, Staten Island and Queens, was $225,627,621. The valuation claimed by the companies is *$416,000,000.* Besides there must be added the investment of the I. R. T. and the B.-M. T. under the dual contracts including their expenditures for third-tracking and extending existing elevated lines. The Commission's valuation of these investments is $174,000,000 for the I. R. T. and $88,000,000 for the B.-M. T., a total of $262,-000,000, but the companies claim at least $250,000,000 more—a valuation of *$512,000,000* making the grand total valuations claimed by the traction companies *$928,-000,000.* The purchase money bonds and mortgages according to the plan of the Transit Commission would be in this amount. Included in the valuations of the Transit Commission are the huge exaggerations intended to justify the capitalization of the I. R. T., B. R. T. and N. Y. Railways upon reorganization, elsewhere referred to.

It is provided in the plan of readjustment that after the expiration of one year from the time it becomes effective the rate of fare to be charged for a single ride by the consolidated service shall be determined as follows:

> "After payment of operating expenses and fixed charges (the fairness of the amounts of which is insured by the valuation of the properties by the Transit Commission and the control over expenditures by the Board of Control), the surplus moneys

> are to be paid into a contingent reserve or *barometer* fund. If the available surplus keeps this fund above a specified maximum, the fare is to be automatically lowered; if the fund falls below a specified minimum, *the fare is to be automatically increased* until the reserve is restored."

Of course it needs no argument that this barometer fund means a fare beginning at least at 8 cents and increasing to what amount no one can tell. Besides this $928,000,000 there will be represented the city's investment of $300,000,000, a total of roughly a billion two hundred million dollars. It was proposed in the plan that there be paid 5 per cent. interest on the outstanding bonds, 1 per cent. amortization and 3 per cent. for efficient management, a total of 9 per cent., or $108,000,000. Under municipal operation and with interest and amortization at 4¾ per cent. per annum, the charge would be $57,000,000. *In other words, the city could borrow more than another billion dollars for public improvement at no greater interest cost.*

Since the plan was made public it has been consistently opposed by the Mayor of the City of New York. His position is very tersely stated as follows:

> "The Transit Commission's plan provided, among other things, for the purchase of elevated railways and surface lines, which while rendering a public service at this time, are for the most part of an obsolete type of transportation, which the city will have to scrap for a better type as an aid in the solution of its acute traffic problems and as a measure of general public improvement. The

surface lines will ultimately have to give way to bus lines and the elevated lines to subway transit."

Realizing the force of this argument, and in the light of the overwhelming public disapproval which this plan received at the November election in 1921, when it was the real issue, and when the public supported the Mayor and his administration by their re-election to office, *Commissioner O'Ryan now for the first time insists that it was not part of the plan to include all of the surface lines.* He says that some were to be "discarded," "not included in the plan." Such was his testimony before Commissioner McAvoy (2474-2476).

It is too late to make such complete reversal of position. The Mayor's objections were made immediately after the plan was made public. There was then no disavowal by the Transit Commissioners of their intention to purchase *all* of the surface lines. In the plan it is stated that its purpose is as follows:

> *"All existing corporations and their franchises under leases and securities are gradually to be eliminated or extinguished except such underlying lines carrying a low rate of interest as the commission deems it advisable not to disturb. Existing securities with such exceptions are to be replaced by an issue of bonds of the consolidated company representing a fair and honest valuation of the properties."*

And as late as October 20, 1924, Commissioner O'Ryan said into the microphone at Station WNYC that

> "These are the fundamental features of the transit situation, namely, the great number of franchises

> that should be surrendered, the large number of operating companies whose activities should be consolidated," etc., and * * * "We have, therefore, caused expert engineers employed by the Transit Commission to make inventories of *all* of the property owned and used by all the companies now operating in the City of New York. * * * Our plan proposed that when the property values have been agreed upon, this city owned company will take over the properties and pay for them, not with money, but with its bonds equal in amount to the value of the railroad property taken over. * * *"

The valuation to which Commissioner O'Ryan refers includes the valuations of every single surface line in the city, including those which he now admits should be scrapped. Furthermore, "franchises cannot be extinguished and surrendered" without the agreement of the railroad company and as he has very clearly stated it, they will not agree to such surrender, except upon payment of what they believe is the value of their lines.

Furthermore, since the plan is dependent upon separate agreements with all the railroad companies (pp. 2471-2472) *they surely will not agree to sell what is good and keep what is to be scrapped, unless the price be so high for what is bought that they can afford to keep what is rejected.* The inclusion in this plan of those surface lines was one of the principal grounds of objection by the city administration.

Furthermore, it has been repeatedly pointed out by the Mayor that the claim of the Transit Commission that the purchase price would not be paid by the public, is a deceit. The plan provides that the railroad companies shall be guaranteed that the fares will be sufficient to pay the *interest and the principal* of the bonds, to be amortised annually. Since, as has already been pointed out, the great majority of the people of our city use our transit lines, in effect the Transit Commission's plan is, that the public pay in fares not only carrying charges, not only interest at 5 per cent. per annum, not only 3 per cent. for alleged efficiency, but the amortization annually of the entire principal of these bonds, to be given in payment of the purchase price of these lines.

The Mayor's position always has been and still is, that this is a deliberate attempt to deceive the public; that new subways are needed; that they should be built with public moneys, raised directly by the public at interest and amortization charges of 4¾ per cent. and not 9 per cent.; that when built they should be operated by the city; that the city should from time to time recapture the existing subways under the dual contracts, make necessary connections, changes and improvements, improve existing service to the standard that the law requires and to which the people are entitled, and that eventually the city will not only own on paper, but own and operate in fact, its own rapid transit system, and use the profits therefrom for construction of future subways. It is further the position of the Mayor that by a justifiable constitutional amendment all the money needed for these purposes will be available to the City.

It was pointed out at the hearings that repeated appeals have been made to the legislatures in recent years, for the adoption of a Constitutional amendment by which the bonds heretofore issued for rapid transit purposes, would be placed in the same class as water bonds, that is, they would not be counted against the 10 per cent. assessment debt limit, "provided they are not issued to an amount in excess of water bonds that are outstanding and self-supporting, which amount to $270,000,000" (Craig, 2164).

So, to use the language of Comptroller Craig, "the amount of transit bonds to be exempted from a charge against the debt margin, shall be measured by the amount of water bonds, that are outstanding at the time and are self-supporting out of water revenue" (p. 2161).

It has already been shown that if this $270,000,000 is released, there will be available at least $550,000,000 before January 1, 1928 when this Constitutional amendment can be made effective. The cost of recapture of all the subways is less than $200,000,000; leaving $350,000,000 available before January 1, 1928. The Board of Transportation's program for future construction involves an expenditure of only $254, 000,000, and with its extensions an additional $150,000,000.

Commissioner O'Ryan says that the consummation of the Transit Commission's plan of "readjustment" will mean that the city will receive interest on its $300,000,000 present investment in subways; that the city's outstanding rapid transit bonds will thus become self-supporting and not counted against the city's debt margin, and in that way that sum will be available to the city for future construction. *A much more simple remedy would be to give the railroad companies the increase in fares which they have sought.* I am quite confident that they would be willing to pay the 4 per cent. interest on the city's investment if the city administration permitted them to charge an 8 or 10 cent fare, and after all, that is what the Transit Commission proposes shall be done under its "plan of readjustment."

Commissioner O'Ryan speaks of honest valuations in connection with the plan of readjustment, but he forgets to state that it would involve the payment of **$38,000,000** to the New York **Railways** System; **$34,000,000** to the Third Avenue Railway System; **$59,000,000** for the B. R. T. and Brooklyn City Company lines and **$57,000,000** for the antiquated Manhattan Elevated lines.

Besides, the valuations of these obsolete systems, are full of over appraisals. They include power plant facilities at full original cost, with no deduction for depreciation. These power plants could not possibly be operated under the plan. They contain duplications which pile up the amount to be paid by the city.

In speaking of this plan the Mayor stated:

> "I was, am now, and always will be, opposed to such gigantic scheme to loot the public. I believe that the public should raise money * * * that when the money is raised it should be put into new subways, and that with respect to the present subways and other means of transit, they are here and everything should be done to compel safe and adequate service for the public as is required by law and contract."

To understand the City's opposition to the program of the ***Transit Commission*** for *construction* of new subways, *it is most important to bear in mind that all of these plans for future construction were supplementary to this plan of readjustment.* ***New*** *subways were suggested only as additions to and extensions of the existing lines which the* ***"Plan of Readjustment"*** *proposed that the city should purchase.*

Commissioner McAneny testified that the policy of the Transit Commission in relation to the construction of our future subways was "in favor of building extensions to the existing lines" (McAneny, pp. 2568-2570), and it is equally true that the Mayor, Comptroller and Mr. Delaney are opposed to the extension of private operation of our transit lines by our traction companies and are in favor of the construction of independent lines to be owned and operated by the City (see pp. 2050, 1025). *Having in mind these diametrically opposed policies and the fact that the Transit Commission until July, 1924, had exclusive power to initiate future construction and that the City was absolutely without power, it will be easy to understand the helplessness of the City Administration to relieve the transit situation in the City of New York until the advent of the Board of Transportation on July 1st, 1924*

The first subway contracts were made in 1900 and 1902. The Dual contracts were executed in 1913. The City grew, its traffic increased but nothing was done to build new subways until Commissioner John H. Delaney became Transit Construction Commissioner. His Chief Engineer was Daniel L. Turner. Under his directions Mr. Turner prepared a plan which was made public on July 29, 1920 and provided for a comprehensive program of rapid transit construction for 25 years, estimated to cost about $350,000,000 (p. 78). He was requested by Mr. Delaney to work out the details of routes for immediate construction. Before this could be done the Republican Legislature turned Comm. Delaney out of office. That was April 25, 1921. The Transit Commission was not concerned in the beginning with construction of new subways. It first wanted to insure the financial rehabilitation of the traction companies. It was not even concerned with improving the service on the existing lines as has been pointed out. It promptly made public its plan of readjustment in September, 1921, *and in May of 1922 it sent to the Board of Estimate plans for the construction of new subways* (p. 95.) The plans provided for four routes; two may be disposed of, the extension of the Fourth Avenue line to Fort Hamilton and of the Corona line to Flushing. That work was done. The other two were the so-called Washington Heights line and the Brooklyn Crosstown line. The Washington Heights line was intended to run from about 193d Street and Fort Washington Avenue down through Amsterdam Avenue to 64th Street and there to connect with the two-track line of the B.-M. T. which were already congested by traffic from lower Manhattan, about which so much was said before Commissioner McAvoy. It was proposed that the heavy traffic from Washington Heights be diverted into that two-track line of the B.-M. T.

Certain engineering objections developed because of the location of the water mains in Amsterdam Avenue and the large cost of changes, with the result that the Transit Commission withdrew and modified its plan and provided for the construction along Central Park West.

The Brooklyn Crosstown line was intended to run from the Queensboro Plaza to the central part of Brooklyn traversing seven subway and "L" lines operated by the I. R. T. and B.-M. T (McAneny, p. 2606).

It was proposed that this line should run to Fulton Street to a connection with the B.-M. T. subway at DeKalb Avenue (pp. 982-997), again adding to the congestion at DeKalb Avenue, the neck of the bottle.

The Mayor immediately opposed this plan. His position was, as it always has been, that he is opposed to linking up any new subways with the existing lines. His reasons therefor are as follows:

"I have vigorously opposed the Transit Commission's efforts to put into effect transit plans, similar to those foisted upon the people under the dual contracts, that will tie the City of New York for generations to the traction corporations now operating the City-owned subways.

Over ten years have passed; the money has been invested; the business has been more prosperous than was ever contemplated; the subways are more packed than was ever expected; more nickels are coming in than could possibly have been calculated, but the net result is that the City has not received one cent interest.

The City regards that as a poor business investment for the people and I regard those with whom the City had that investment as not good partners; and my point of view is that if the City is to continue in the same line of business, it certainly does not want to continue with the same partners, where it can expect the same results—in other words, more money and no return.

The proper attitude of a business man would be, after he has invested $300,000,000 with certain partners who promised him a return, which he never got, that for the future he would have no business with those partners; on the contrary, he would go in business on his own account, and especially is this so, when I am unable to reconcile the failure of the City to get any return with the extravagance, wastefulness and bad faith, both of the companies and the State Transit Commission, which was charged with the duty of supervising their affairs.

My position in this matter is, that as the business representative of the City of New York, it would be folly to put more money in an enterprise with partners who have promised a return which they have never made."

This program by the Transit Commission for future construction was claimed by it to involve an investment of $218,000,000 for construction and about $100,000,000 for equipment, a total of $318,000,000 with which it proposed to construct about 32½ miles of new rapid transit lines.

On September 6, 1922 the Mayor published his plan for future subways. It is to be borne in mind that neither the Mayor nor the Board of Estimate had any power to put that plan into effect. It operated at most as a suggestion to the Transit Commission. The law provides that the City may make such "suggestions" for new subways, but the Transit Commission refused to adopt those suggestions. That plan provided for the building of 111 miles of new rapid transit lines in The City of New York at a total expense of $600,000,000.

The Mayor was in favor of a Washington Heights line but he did not want it to end in 64th Street, and to connect with the line of the B.-M. T. His proposal was for a trunk line from Washington Heights down through Eighth Avenue to the end of the Island, with proper connections to Brooklyn and Queens.

He was also in favor of a crosstown line in Brooklyn. The line which the Transit Commission proposed would cost $44,000,000 and would not be serviceable except in partnership with the B.-M. T.

The Mayor proposed an independently operable crosstown line in Brooklyn, self-sustaining from beginning of operation, from Queens Plaza through the large industrial section of Greenpoint, to cross Fulton Street to Franklin Avenue, to Washington Avenue and eventually Sheepshead Bay and Coney Island and to cross the East River to connect with the sections of Manhattan, from the vicinity of Huron Street to the neighborhood of 23rd or 34th Street in Manhattan, and then crosstown to the Sixth or Eighth Avenues to connect with the Washington Heights line (pp. 1044-1045).

The result of the Transit Commission's submission of their plan to the Board of Estimate was its rejection in November 1922. Nothing further was done. The Transit Commission did not adopt any of the Mayor's proposals.

In June of 1923 a conference committee was appointed consisting of Messrs. Delaney, Tuttle, the City's Chief Engineer, and Mr. Murray Hulbert, Borough President; the Transit Commissioners and Engineers Turner and Ridgway. Fourteen of these conferences were held.

After five conferences, the Conference Committee reccommended generally the Brooklyn Crosstown and Washington Heights routes, upon the understanding that the details of these routes would be worked out in the Committee, and on August 3, 1923, the Board of Estimate and Apportionment approved these routes. Nine conferences were thereafter held by the Joint Committee representing the Board of Estimate and Apportionment, Transit Commission and the Engineers.

These two lines were the principal subjects discussed. There developed, as from the outset, disagreements based on the fundamental differences of policy. The proposals of the Transit Commission all looked to the construction of the new lines as additions to our existing subways. The suggestions of the City's representatives were all in the direction of independently operable lines. Commissioner Delaney very clearly stated his position with respect to the Brooklyn Crosstown line as follows:

> "I opposed the tie-up of routes and I was not in favor of the line laid down for the crosstown route" (p. 978).

In the conferences "the Transit Commission proposed that the lines should be run through Fulton Street to a connection with the B.-M. T. subway at DeKalb Avenue." The City's representatives favored the continuations of this line into Lafayette Avenue, having in mind its eventual operation as an independent line. Two separate reports, one favoring the Lafayette Avenue line and the other the Fulton Street line, were submitted to the Board of Estimate and Apportionment respectively by the Transit Commission and the City's representatives (pp. 993-994).

From the latter part of August, 1923, until March, 1924, and while these conferences were in progress, the Mayor was prevented from discharging his duties by serious illness. At the time of his return to office, the 1924 amendment to the transit laws by the creation of the Board of Transportation was in process.

It was clear from all that had transpired in the Committee, that the Transit Commission was determined to carry out its policy of "new construction only as extensions of the existing lines," thereby further binding the City to a joint venture which had proved so disastrous to the City, and that the Mayor's proposals for "independent lines" had been completely ignored. Accordingly the Mayor upon his return refused to lend himself to these policies of the Transit Commission and so announced, in a letter dated March 21, 1924, a copy of which is annexed, marked Exhibit "M," in which, among other things, he says in respect to the Brooklyn Crosstown line:

> "A connection of this kind will tie up a $44,000,000 subway proposition with the Brooklyn-Manhattan Transit Company (formerly the B. R. T), to be operated by that company. Such a connection and operation will provide nothing but deficits to be made up by the taxpayers in the yearly budget, in addition to the $10,000,000 which the taxpayers are now forced to provide in the budget under the present subway contracts" (p. 1044).

The 1924 amendment to the Transit Laws creating the Board of Transportation, was enacted May 1, 1924, but by its terms that Board did not come into office until July 1, 1924.

Notwithstanding the Transit Commission had due notice that its construction powers would end on July 1, 1924, apparently for purposes of embarrassing the new Board, it let a contract for the construction of one mile in the middle of the proposed Brooklyn Crosstown line, at a cost of $3,500,000, and submitted this contract for approval to the Board of Estimate and Apportionment (pp. 143, 1010-1018).

The matter was referred to Commissioner Delaney, who was about to become Chairman of the Board of Transportation, and he, in a letter dated June 3, 1924, addressed to the Mayor, recommended the disapproval of this contract (Delaney, 1016, et seq). A copy of Commissioner Delaney's letter to the Mayor, dated

June 3, 1924, is annexed and marked Exhibit "N." In it he said, among other things:

> "It seems to me that the new Board of Transportation should be given an opportunity to study the situation before your Board definitely adopts a policy. Otherwise the new Board will come into office on July 1st under conditions similar to those which prevented initiative in respect to the route by your recent Conference Committee" (p. 1017).

The matter which received the principal consideration of the Conference Committee in the Fall of 1923 was the Washington Heights line.

It will be remembered that the Transit Commission's plan for that route was, that it run under Central Park West (after it had been changed from Amsterdam Avenue), and *that it end at 64th Street,* there to connect with the B.-M. T. lines; that plan was rejected by the Board of Estimate in November, 1922.

On May 15, 1923, the Transit Commission presented to the Board of Estimate for its approval a route beginning at 59th Street and Seventh Avenue, proceeding under 59th Street, Central Park West, Manhattan Avenue, St. Nicholas Avenue, and terminating at 162nd Street. On June 1, 1923, it was the subject of discussion before the Board of Estimate. The result was the appointment of the Conference Committee to which reference has been made.

On June 15, 1923, the Conference Committee held its first meeting, and a report recommending the general approval of this route was submitted, as already indicated, and on August 3, 1923, the Board of Estimate and Apportionment formally gave its approval.

On October 2, 1923, the Chief Engineer of the Transit

Commission suggested to the Conference, that the route as adopted *be changed* so that it would proceed from 59th Street to 110th Street under Central Park; then to Eighth Avenue instead of Manhattan Avenue, to 121st Street, and then through St. Nicholas Avenue.

The suggestion that the line be constructed under Central Park, instead of under Central Park West, was made because of an alleged estimated saving of $5,-000,000. The matter was referred to the Board of Estimate, public hearings were held, and strong opposition developed to such use of the park. Then Commissioner McAneny suggested a modification *and a resubmission of the route through Amsterdam Avenue,* which had previously been rejected by the Board of Estimate. The Committee again took into account the existence of the extensive water mains and conduits under Amsterdam Avenue, the reconstruction of which would cost about $5,000,000, and reached the conclusion, that engineering and other difficulties which were the cause of the previous rejection by the Board of Estimate, were of sufficient magnitude to prevent concurrence in the proposed change of route, and the Committee notified the Transit Commission that it would not agree to the Transit Commission's recommendation of this Amsterdam Avenue route. That occurred on December 20, 1923.

A suggestion was then made for the first time that consideration be given to a substituted route in Columbus Avenue. The matter had not been previously discussed. Chief Engineer Tuttle then stated that before making any definite commitment as to this proposed route, he desired further information as to the character of the subsoil and structures, cost of underpinning the elevated railroad structure and probable land damages which would be involved in joining the portion of the road under Broadway with the stub ends of the Broadway-Seventh Avenue Line, and that he desired to consider other features of the proposition, and requested an adjournment until January 3, 1924, which was taken.

There was no agreement or understanding that the Columbus Avenue route would be accepted in place for the Central Park West route, which had been approved by the Board of Estimate. During the recess and on the eve of the publication of the Governor's message to the 1924 Legislature, *which recommended the abolition of the Transit Commission, there unexpectedly appeared from Chairman McAneny of the Transit Commission a public statement, in effect that the Columbus Avenue route had been agreed upon in the Committee, with, to quote the Hon. Murray Hulbert, "the presumptous declaration" on the part of the Chairman of the Transit Commission that "the other members of the Board of Estimate and Apportionment can hardly withhold their approval to start the shovels moving dirt."* It is to be borne in mind, that on August 3, 1923, the Washington Heights Line, proceeding along *Central Park West,* had been approved by the Board of Estimate on the Transit Commissioners' recommendation.

This statement by McAneny indicated clearly, that his participation in the conferences with the City's representatives was not in good faith, that it was never his intention to depart from the original policy of the Transit Commission, viz.: To embark upon such construction only, as would benefit the traction companies, and that his purpose was, if this could not be accomplished, at the appropriate time, to end the conferences, which he did by this public statement.

The Transit Commission did nothing further of a constructive character, in regard to either the Washington Heights Line or the Brooklyn Crosstown line, except that it expended $361,000, in preparing useless maps and drawings (p. 140), and except that it let, to use the language of Mr. McAneny, a contract for a "very fragmentary bit of that line which happened to come under the site of a proposed public school—at some thing like $240,000 which was sent to the Board of Estimate and approved". Besides, on June 3, 1924, with knowledge that the Board of Transportation would take hold of construction work on July 1, 1924, the Transit Commission suddenly developed a great activity and advertised for a bid on a section of the proposed Washington Heights route covering thirteen City blocks from 160th to 173rd Streets, St. Nicholas Avenue and Broadway. No beginning point and no ending point had at that time been determined for this route. Without "rhyme or reason" thirteen blocks of subway in mid-section were to be contracted for. On the 6th of June, 1924, upon learning of this advertisement, Mr. Delaney wrote Mr. McAneny to discontinue the same, which he did. There ended the "inactivities" of the Transit Commission in relation to construction of new subways.

The record in regard to proposed subway construction would be incomplete without a reference to the Ashland Place Connection. Under the dual contracts, no provision was made for any additional rapid transit service to the central part of Brooklyn. It was left dependent on the Fulton Street Line, which runs through downtown Brooklyn, over the Brooklyn Bridge to the Park Row terminal, but not through Manhattan (pp.

669-670). Under a "related certificate" granted with contract No. 4 this line was to be third-tracked. The third track was added from East New York to Nostrand Avenue, when opposition developed to further third-tracking down Fulton Street, the main business district of Brooklyn and, accordingly, the third-tracking ended in 1915 or 1916 (p. 670). Then there developed a movement to connect this Fulton Street line at Ashland Place with the Broadway-4th Avenue line, (p. 671). The B. R. T. was opposed to this connection because it involved an expense of several million dollars for new equipment; the old rolling stock of the Fulton Street line was not serviceable for subway operation (p. 671).

In 1917, it appears that the B. R. T. indicated its willingness to consent to this connection (p. 672). But nothing appears to have been done in that direction until Mr. Delaney, as Transit Construction Commissioner, took up the matter and worked out a new agreement with the B. R. T. for this connection, but at that time the B. R. T. was already in receivership (p. 672) and nothing, of course, could be done.

The matter was again taken up in the Conference Committee in the Fall of 1923 (pp. 673-674) and with the B.-M. T. in December of 1923 (p. 676). There had developed in November 1923 "a new agitation in Brooklyn for this line". The result of the negotiation with the B.-M. T. was that an agreement of modification of Contract No. 4 was drawn, in which the B.-M. T. proposed to consent to the construction of this Ashland Place connection *but upon conditions, however, among others, that the city build the Broad-Nassau Street line* (pp. 676, 678, 684).

Of course this proposal by the B.-M. T. was not made in earnest, because it well knew that the City would not consent to these conditions (p. 692). Furthermore, the proposal for the Ashland Place connection has always been regarded by those informed, as impracticable and not a solution of the transit problem of that locality, but rather, as tending to aggravate it.

The connection was proposed to be made with the 4th Avenue line above DeKalb Avenue, thus adding the traffic from the Fulton Street line to the congestion, already existing at DeKalb Avenue (p. 672).

The engineers of the railroad company "fought the proposal steadily" and pointed out that the introduction of additional trains into DeKalb Avenue would result in further congestion at that point and reduce the service for the outlying districts." Mr. Turner, the present Chief Engineer of the Transit Commission, was likewise opposed to this construction (p. 780).

CHAPTER X

Dawning Light

BOARD OF TRANSPORTATION'S SUBWAY CONSTRUCTION PROGRAM

This Board was created by Chapter 573, Laws of 1924, signed by the Governor, May 1, 1924, effective July 1, 1924. It transfers the power to construct rapid transit lines, from the Transit Commission to the Board of Transportation, named by the Mayor of the City of New York. The members of the Board are John H. Delaney, William A. DeFord and Daniel L. Ryan (p. 557).

The Transit Commission still retains its regulatory powers over our existing transit lines. It also has regulatory jurisdiction over all future extensions and additions to the existing lines (p. 82).

This law contains novel features. It provides that the city may operate all newly constructed lines, at a five-cent fare, for three years, but thereafter, they must be self-supporting.

It directs that, accompanying all proposed routes or general plans of constuction, for the approval by the Board of Estimate, shall be a statement, signed by at least two members of the Board of Transportation, and countersigned by its Chief Engineer, setting forth the estimated cost of construction and equipment of the proposed line, the estimated time required for its construction and equipment, together with an estimate for ten years, of the prospective results of operation of such rapid transit railroad (p. 1048).

This Board of Transportation has proceeded expeditiously with the construction of new subways. It is working in harmony with, and has the cooperation of the city administration. Its Chairman is, by reason of long and varied experience in transit and kindred service, and natural ability and fitness, highly qualified to carry forward the work of new construction. There remains no doubt that under the directions of this Board, the people will have the subways for which they have been clamoring, and which are sorely needed.

The legislation of 1924 gives only partial relief. The Board of Transportation has no authority to direct better service on our existing lines.

Immediately upon coming into office, the Board of Transportation proceeded to lay out a comprehensive new trunk subway line for the City, running from about 215th Street in the Borough of Manhattan, through Fort Washington Avenue, to Fulton or Wall Street, with projected tunnel connections under the East River, in the neighborhood of 53rd Street and Wall or Fulton Street, to Queens and Brooklyn respectively. Beginning at 193rd Street and Fort Washington Avenue, it will be a four-track line, except possibly for a short distance at the northerly end, down Fort Washington Avenue to Broadway, thence through St. Nicholas Avenue to Eighth Avenue, thence from 110th Street to 64th Street, along Central Park West, then as a six-track line from Eighth Avenue to Greenwich Avenue, down to Church Street, and then running east, under the river either at Fulton or Wall Street, with a connection west, across 53rd Street, to Sixth Avenue, and a two-track line down Sixth Avenue, and east through 53rd Street under the East River to Queens, and another connection crosstown at 139th Street to the Harlem River, a distance of 1½ miles, where there will be the terminal yards and shops for those lines, also a connection at Houston Street east to the Bowery with possible extension to Brooklyn (pp. 1052-1055).

Although it is generally conceded that it takes at least nine months to prepare plans for a subway construction, this comprehensive plan was proclaimed by the Board of Transportation on December 9, 1924 (pp. 1047-1048). The route in its entirety has not yet been validated by the Board of Estimate (pp. 1051-1052), but the Board of Transportation is proceeding to advertise for and let contracts for the portion of the line between 64th Street and 193rd Street, under prior validations (pp. 1054-1073).

The route from Pearl and Wall Street to 193rd Street and Fort Washington Avenue has already been laid out. Shortly, the details of the route from 193rd Street to Overlook Terrace will be completed. That will provide 18.53 miles of subway with 65.57 single track miles (Ridgway pp. 1880-1882).

The cost of construction of the routes laid out, will be about $181,000,000, and, together with equipment, in all, $254,000,000. It will take three years to build and one year to equip the subway (Ridgway, 1927-1928.) Attempted comparisons were made at the hearings between the estimated cost of this new construction, and the cost of construction under Contracts 1, 2 and 3, operated by the Interborough.

It appears that the old subway has 217.4 miles of single track. Its cost was $264,000,000 but of this construction 85.8 miles represents elevated structure, the cost of which is only one-fourth of subway costs (pp. 1920-1922). Engineer Ridgway explained that the new structure will not be a mere duplicate of the present I. R. T. subway. It will be a "modern" rapid transit line. The bore of the tunnel will be greater to accommodate wider cars; there will be emergency exits, and a proper system of ventilation lacking in the old subway. The stations will be longer and be adaptable for use of at least 12 car trains on both local and express lines (pp. 1924-1925), thereby adding not only to the comfort and convenience of the riders but to the passenger bearing capacity of the line.

These estimates of cost of construction and equipment, resulted in speculations by the Transit Commissioners and their specially employed public accountant Mr. S. Herbert Wolfe, as to how much will be lost annually from operation of the new line on a five-cent fare.

Mr. Wolfe and Commissioner Harkness, both concurred that the result of operations on this new line, on a five-cent fare will be an annual loss to the city of $7,500,000, according to the former, and $7,000,000 according to the latter (see Wolfe, p. 2283); (Harkness, pp. 2298, 2302, 2303).

Commissioner Harkness says that the cost of carrying a single passenger in the new subway will be eight and three-quarter cents; Commissioner O'Ryan says that the cost will be ten cents (p. 2461).

Notwithstanding, the Transit Commission apparently approves the line of the Board of Transportation, so that there is unanimity of opinion as to the necessity for this new subway, except that there is the disappointment by McAneny that it will not be linked up with the B.-M. T. and I. R. T. (pp. 2569,2606,2608).

It is difficult to conceive the purpose of the Transit Commissioners in venturing estimates of deficits from operation of the new line. Clearly it is necessary, and will serve to relieve the disgraceful congestion in our existing rapid transit lines. Are we to understand that the Transit Commission could construct new lines for less money?—no such claim is made. Is the city to continue the McAneny policy of only talking about new subways and not building them, which the Transit Commission pursued for four years, because standards of living have changed and cost of construction is higher than in 1913? Concededly there are deficits aggregating $100,000,000 under the dual contracts. Are we to understand that had the Transit Commission foreseen these deficits, the subways would not have been built? Is it not the fact that McAneny anticipated that there would be deficits from the operation of the subways under the dual contracts?

It is undoubtedly true, that if the new subway be operated by the traction companies, who pay exorbitant rates of interest, indulge every now and then in receiverships, suffer waste and extravagance, there will be more deficits on a five-cent fare. But the city, intends to operate the new subway itself, and these conditions will not obtain.

Reference has already been made to calculations, set forth in annexed schedules, which demonstrate that even on the basis of an increase of 125 per cent. in cost of construction and equipment, subways can be operated by the City of New York, on a five-cent fare, at a profit.

Comptroller Craig called attention before Commissioner McAvoy to the fact that past experience has proved that the cost of operation and maintenance, is about 60 per cent of the gross revenue, and he says:

> "If you have forty per cent of the gross on the new lines to cover interest and sinking fund charges, you will very likely be able to build some new lines out of the surplus" (p. 2244).

Besides, there is every expectancy that this 60 per cent. for operation, will be reduced by the elimination of unnecessary expenses and extravangances and substantial savings in the cost of power and other items of service (Craig, pp. 2250-2251).

BUSES

The bus problem has been the subject of discussion and litigation. The "bus" has come to be recognized as a satisfactory means of transportation. Repeated attempts have been made to secure from the legislature in recent years the power for the City of New York to purchase and operate its own bus lines, without success. The Fifth Avenue Coach Company operates buses, on a ten-cent fare, at a cost of operation it is claimed of 8.4 cents per passenger (p. 2264). Our bus operation has been the subject of litigation in certain cases resulting in injunctions secured by surface line companies (p. 2669). The buses in operation in the city, are privately owned and operated, upon temporary permits issued by the Commissioner of Plant and Structures of the City of New York (p. 2667). There are 36 of such bus lines carrying approximately 188,710 passengers per day (p. 2669).

It was suggested at the hearings that the city's traffic problems have become aggravated by the large increase in the number of taxicabs on the city streets. A record of the number of taxicabs in operation is as follows:

1918— 4,700
1922—13,449
1923—15,000
1924—17,550

It is estimated that the gross revenue from taxi operation is about $5,000,000 a year, as against $52,000,000 from all of the surface trolley lines operating in the city.

The city is about to embark upon the program of acquiring and operating its own bus lines. Difference of opinion has arisen, as to the power of the city under the recent Home Rule law to undertake this municipal operation. Undoubtedly that question will be speedily determined and then the way will be open for an extension and enlargement of that service.

CHAPTER XI

SUMMARY AND CONCLUSIONS.

The hearings before Commissioner McAvoy were closed on January 8, 1925. I have attempted to set forth in this report a summary of the principal subjects of the inquiry amplified by evidence essential to a proper understanding of the problem. Owing to lack of space and time, many of these matters have received but skeleton presentation. I have felt that it is urgent that at the earliest moment you be advised of the outstanding factors in the situation, because immediate relief must come to the public by appropriate legislation, vesting in a single body, complete control over both new subway construction and the service on our existing lines.

"Shameful" and "disgraceful" have been the words used in the inquiry, as descriptive of the treatment of the riders on our rapid transit lines. Undoubtedly a full measure of relief could have been given during the last four years, when the Legislature first declared the emergency, but none has come.

Our present intolerable conditions of service are due primarily to the persistent refusal of the Legislature to vest in the city the power to build its own subways with its own money. Until July 1, 1924, the State Transit Commission had the exclusive power to lay out new lines. subject only to veto by the local authorities. As the Governor well stated in his January, 1924 message:

> "Division of power divides responsibility, and in the case of the City of New York has resulted in a

deadlock which can only be broken by placing the statutory powers in the municipality already vested with the constitutional powers necessary for authorizing construction."

There is a promise of relief by the creation of the Board of Transportation appointed by the Mayor of the City of New York, but that relief will come only in the future when the subways which that Board has laid out are completed. For the present the people are helpless.

The Transit Commission's failure to direct and secure better service was due entirely, as it admits, to financial consideration, and the insolvency of the traction companies, brought about by over-capitalization upon organization and reorganization, wastes, extravagances, costly and embarrassing receiverships, and the diversion of about $100,000,000 in swollen dividends which should have been used for development and improvement of service. The Transit Commissioners approached every proposal for the alleviation of the public's suffering with a tender solicitude for the balance sheets of the traction corporations.

That these things happened, and that these causes brought about the collapse of the traction companies, is not disputed by the Transit Commissioners. They say, in effect, we found those conditions, when we came into office, and it was our "duty" to rehabilitate these companies even at the expense of the public. The I. R. T. is still financially embarrassed and unable to make necessary capital expenditures, according to the testimony of its own President. The B.-M. T. persists that it cannot give good service on a five-cent fare, but it can and does pay dividends on its preferred stock. The stock speculators have profited.

The remedy is plain. The regulatory and construction powers should be vested in a single Board named by the local authorities, and that Board should immediately order necessary changes and improvements, such, among others, as the lengthening of the stations on the I. R. T. line, the addition of new cars, the furnishing of more guards and conductors, revision of schedules by increasing the number of trains during non-rush hours and the maintenance of full service before and after the commencement of the rush period. By Constitutional amendment our rapid transit bonds should be exempted from charge against the city's debt limit, thereby releasing nearly $275,000,000 for future construction; the proceeds, together with amounts from time to time otherwise available, should be applied to carry out the general plan of construction of the Board of Transportation, and for a recapture of all of our rapid transit lines under Contracts 3 and 4.

The remedy will come only by less talking and more building of new subways, and by securing more and better service on our existing lines.

New York, January 29, 1925.

Respectfully submitted,

HARRY A. GORDON.

EXHIBIT A

CHARGES

Hon. ALFRED E. SMITH,
Governor of the State of New York.

Honorable Sir—The Board of Estimate and Apportionment of the City of New York hereby prefers charges of wilful neglect and failure to discharge duty, and misconduct in office, and inefficiency, against George McAneny, Leroy T. Harkness and John F. O'Ryan, as Transit Commissioners appointed pursuant to Chapter 134 of the Laws of 1921, and respectfully request and demand that each of them be removed by you from such office by reason thereof and by reason of the matters and things hereinafter set forth:

First Charge—That in and by Section 26 of the Public Service Commissions Law of the State of New York it is provided that

> "Every corporation, person or common carrier performing a service designated in the preceding section, shall furnish, with respect thereto, such service and facilities as shall be safe and adequate and in all respects just and reasonable."

That in and by the Rapid Transit Contract No. 4 entered into by and between the City of New York and the Railroad Company, for the unification, consolidation and extension of then existing subway, street and elevated car lines, and for the construction of additional subways, it was, among other things, provided (substantially same provisions in Contract No. 3):

> "The principal object of the City in making this contract is to secure for the public convenience an adequate, comfortable and rapid transit system of passenger transportation in the portions of New York which will be served by the Railroad and the Existing Railroads. By the foregoing provisions of the Lease the Lessee has covenanted, among other things, to operate the Railroad and Existing Railroads carefully and skillfully, according to the highest standards of railway operation; to supply adequate equipment; to run trains so as to furnish adequate service; to use the best safety devices; to keep the Railroad and Equipment and Existing Railroads clean, dry, well lighted, heated and ventilated; and to do other things, as hereinbefore set forth, for the convenience and accommodation of the public. These covenants on the part of the Lessee are among the principal moving considerations to the City in making this contract, and any breach thereof will entitle the City to the remedies provided in this contract. If at any time Additions to the Railroad or Equipment or to the Existing Railroads or any change in the mode of operating the Railroad or the Existing Railroads or conducting the business thereof are necessary in order to carry out the purposes of the Lease in securing service and facilities as shall be safe and adequate and in all respects just and reasonable the Commission may direct the provision or construction of such Additions and the making of such changes in the mode of operation of the Railroad or Exist-

ing Railroads or in the conduct of the business thereof as may be necessary to accomplish such purposes."

That in and by the Act, to wit, Chapter 134 of the Laws of 1921, Messrs. McAneny, Harkness and O'Ryan, as Transit Commissioners, succeeded to powers and duties of the former Transit Construction Commissioner, and as such were charged with the duty of planning and building of rapid transit railways in the City of New York, and of completing the subway work then remaining unconstructed under such contracts, and of securing compliance by the Railroad Companies with all of the terms and conditions of the aforementioned Rapid Transit Contracts Nos. 3 and 4, and as successor of the Public Service Commission for the First District, as well as of the Transit Construction Commissioner, of regulating, and insuring to the public, the safety, and convenience and operation of structure, equipment and track of all rapid transit lines in the City of New York, and of securing the performance and observance by all Rapid Transit Railroad Companies, of all their duties and obligations imposed by law and contract, and of making a study and investigation, and preparing a plan, for the relief of the intolerable transit conditions and emergency existing at the time of the appointment of said Commissioners, and of effecting a radical and permanent readjustment of the then existing transit system.

That said Commissioners entered upon the discharge of all their duties in or about the month of April, 1921, and that at all times since, said Commissioners have failed, neglected and refused to secure for the public rapid transit service and facilities such as are safe and adequate, have failed, neglected and refused to secure from the Railroad Companies performance of and compliance with the provisions of Contracts Nos. 3 and 4, but on the contrary, have permitted the said Railroad Companies to breach said contracts, and to evade and avoid the performance thereof, the construction of work and the rendition of safe, adequate and convenient transportation thereunder; and have permitted the structure, cars and equipment to become and remain dangerous and unsafe, and the public to be jammed, crowded and inconvenienced in the service thereof, and have permitted, through their gross culpable negligence, said dangerous and defective conditions to be and remain unabated, and that as a result thereof, various and divers persons have been killed and large numbers severely injured by said railroad Companies.

That on or about June 25, 1923, a train operated by the Brooklyn-Manhattan Transit System was wrecked at the curve of the elevated railroad from Fifth Avenue into Flatbush Avenue; that two wooden cars which said Commissioners permitted to be and remain in the service and in operation, fell from the elevated structure into the street, and as a result thereof seven persons were killed and seventy injured. Said wreck occurred and said lives were lost and injuries sustained, by reason of the rotten and defective guard rails and wooden ties, and because the spikes holding the running rails to the ties were not in contact with the rails, and many of the bolts holding the ties to the steel structure were loose, and because the said Commissioners failed and neglected to abate said nuisance and dangerous condition. That as a result of said accident, and at a meeting of the Board of Estimate and Apportionment held on July 13, 1923, of which said Commissioners had knowledge, a resolution was adopted under which a Committee on

Transportation Facilities was appointed by said Board, to investigate and report as to the condition of the cars and road equipment then in use on all of the elevated railroad lines in the City of New York, giving first consideration to the older structures in the Borough of Brooklyn, and next to the older ones in the Borough of Manhattan.

That upon the appointment said Committee, there was organized by said Committee a Joint Commission consisting of three persons, representing the Board of Estimate and Apportionment, the Transit Commission and the Railroad Company, as follows: Robert Ridgway, Chief Engineer of the Transit Commission, Dr. George F. Swain, Professor of Civil Engineering at Harvard University, representing the Board of Estimate and Apportionment, and Eugene Klapp, of the firm of Parsons, Brinckerhoff & Klapp, representing the railroad. That thereafter the said Joint Commission was directed to investigate and report on the then condition of the cars and road equipment in use on all of the elevated railroads of the Brooklyn-Manhattan Transit Corporation, and it commenced its work on July 26, 1923 and concluded the same on January 4, 1924. That a copy of the Report of said Commission was duly forwarded to the Transit Commissioners of the City of New York, together with a Supplemental Report made by the aforementioned Committee on Transportation Facilities to the Board of Estimate and Apportionment on or about April 21, 1924.

That in and by said Report of said Joint Commission it was, among other things, found, that the tracks of the Brooklyn-Manhattan Transit Corporation elevated lines were and had for a long time been in respects defective, unsafe and required replacement and repair;

that many of the guards and rails, the purpose of which was to guide a derailed car, and to prevent the same from falling from the elevated structure in the event it was derailed by reason of defective equipment or track, were defective on almost all of the Brooklyn-Manhattan Transit Corporation elevated lines; that the safety of the traveling public required the replacement of the inner guard timbers by steel rails, and the removal of the many defective outside guard timbers; that the structure of the Brooklyn-Manhattan Transit Corporation elevated lines lacked necessary automatic signal stops or other means of insuring safety; that the method and system which for all time had been in force on the Brooklyn-Manhattan Transit Corporation elevated lines, for the inspection and removal of railroad ties, was nondependable and did not insure safety of carriage; that the elevated structure upon which the Commissioners tolerated and permitted the elevated cars to be operated, was insufficient and inadequate to sustain the load, required steel bracing and supporting, was corroded, unpainted and unclean, and dangerous to life and limb; that there were operated and maintained on said Brooklyn-Manhattan Transit Corporation elevated lines obsolete and unsafe wooden cars; that the danger was augmented and increased by the absence from said cars of the usual "dead man's button," a device by which if the motorman is rendered unconscious and his hand removed from the master controller, the power is automatically shut off and the brakes applied; that the absence of said automatic device, coupled with the use of said obsolete wooden cars, rendered transportation of the public on said lines unsafe, and that said Joint Commission did recommend the installation of said modern automatic "dead man's button."

That in and by the Report of the Committee on Transportation Facilities dated April 21, 1924, to the Board of Estimate and Apportionment, of which said Commissioners then had due notice, the attention of said Transit Commission was called as follows:

> "The Board of Estimate and Apportionment has no power to take action to enforce compliance with any of these recommendations, such power being vested by law in the Transit Commission. As the report of the Joint Committee of Engineers is unanimous, it is to be inferred that the Transit Commission and the operating company itself will recognize the justice of all the recommendations made and will co-operate to carry them out." * * *
>
> "It is recommended that the Transit Commission be requested to give its immediate attention to the elimination of defects reported by the Joint Committee of engineers and to the need for a general improvement of the elevated railroad facilities as disclosed by this investigation, giving particular attention to the report of the Equipment Committee of the Joint Committee of Engineers, contained in Appendix VI of the Joint Committee report."

That the Brooklyn-Manhattan Transit System's elevated and subway rolling stock consists substantially of 907 wooden cars and 900 steel cars; that substantially all of said wooden cars were constructed many years ago and are obsolete, inadequate and insufficient for the safe, adequate and convenient transportation of passengers. That in and by the Rapid Transit contract No. 4 it is provided that the Railroad Company shall, and the Railroad Company, a party thereto, has agreed to, provide money for new cars and to commence the retirement of such wooden cars not later than January 1, 1924. In said contract, among other things, it is provided:

> "On the dates given in the following schedule, the Lessee shall pay out of its own resources into the Depreciation Fund for the Existing Railroads provided for in paragraph 5 of Article XLIX the following amounts representing depreciation accrued upon the properties stated in the schedule prior to January 1, 1914.

SCHEDULE OF ROLLING STOCK OF EXISTING RAILROADS INCLUDING DATES OF ESTIMATED RETIREMENT AND ACCRUED DEPRECIATION

Item No.	Date of Retirement	Accrued Depreciation						
1	Jan. 1, 1924	$240,058.00	Bodies and	trucks	of	Group	A
2	" 1, 1929	526,249.00	" "	"	"	"	B
3	" 1, 1929	622,904.00	" "	"	"	"	D
4	" 1, 1934	240,263.00	Equipment		"	"	A
5	" 1, 1936	388,951.00	"		"	"	B
6	" 1, 1936	338,711.00	Bodies & Trucks		"	"	C
7	" 1, 1936	499,724.00	Equipment		"	"	C
8	" 1, 1946	35,680.00	"		"	"	D

Group A comprises 118 converted motor cars bearing the following numbers:

No. 1000—1078 inclusive
No. 1080
No. 1082—1119 inclusive

Groups B comprises 236 rebuilt motor cars bearing the following numbers:

No. 600—683 inclusive
No. 700—743 "
No. 745—758 "
No. 800—816 "

No. 818—820 inclusive
No. 822—859 "
No. 900—935 "

Group C comprises 306 motor cars bearing the following numbers:

No. 684, 817, 936, 998, 1079, 1081.
No. 1200—1499 inclusive.

Group D comprises 268 trailer cars bearing the following numbers:

No. 1— 6 inclusive
No. 8— 81 inclusive
No. 83—125 inclusive
No. 127—271 inclusive

The dates cited in the above schedule represent the estimated dates of retirement of the car bodies, trucks and equipment named in the schedule.

That the Transit Commissioners have failed, refused and neglected to secure compliance by the Railroad Company with the aforementioned provisions of said Contract No. 4, and have failed, refused and neglected to secure the retirement, prior to January 1, 1924, of the 118 wooden cars embraced in Group A; that all of said cars are wooden and are old, obsolete, dangerous and unsafe, and that said Commissioners have permitted said cars to be and remain in operation and in the service of the Brooklyn-Manhattan Transit Corporation, and the operating companies whose stocks it holds and controls, after January 1, 1924, and at the time of the wreck hereinafter set forth.

That among said wooden cars required by Contract No. 4 to be retired prior to January 1, 1924, and permitted by said Commissioners to be and remain in service and in operation, was car No. 1080 hereinafter referred to. That said Commissioners failed, neglected and refused to require the removal and replacement of the dangerous cars, structure and equipment in use in the Brooklyn-Manhattan Transit System, reported by the aforementioned Joint Committee and the Committee on Transportation Facilities, and failed to secure the retirement of the aforementioned wooden car in pursuance of the provisions of Contract No. 4, and that such conditions continued and remained in force at the time of the wreck hereinafter mentioned.

That on July 30, 1924, a wreck occurred at the Sunnyside Yards of the Long Island Railroad, as a result of which one human being was killed and many others were seriously injured. The Grand Jury of Queens County that made inquiry into the circumstances and causes of this wreck and the responsibility therefor, found that the direct cause thereof was the throwing by hand of a switch under a moving train which caused the derailment of the last three cars of this train; that there was no excuse for the operation of this switch by hand; that the operation of said switch should have been included in the interlocking system of the railroad which was in operation within ten feet of the switch. The Grand Jury, among other things, made its presentment as follows:

> "The Transit Commission has a large number of experts and the operation of the Long Island Railroad in the Greater City of New York is under its jurisdiction. The control and operation of this switch at the time of the wreck is now condemned by the engineers of the Transit Commission. As the Commission now condemns the switch and its operation as antiquated and obsolete, it must have

been antiquated and obsolete before the wreck and that being so it was the duty of the Commission to have ordered and required the removal of the switch and the installation of the safe method of operation it now recommends.

"The criminal responsibility for the wreck must be placed on the railroad company and its employees, but that does not relieve the Transit Commission for its failure to properly and adequately function in its control of the railroad.",

and concluded as follows:

"We condemn the failure of the Commission to take proper action for the removal of this condition before the disaster and for its very evident policy that 'anything is good enough' until the contrary is proven by a disaster costing human lives, and we also condemn the officials of the railroad company above named for their neglect to take the initiative in the adoption of ways and means for the protection of human life and for their total disregard of their responsibilities."

That said wreck was due to the culpable negligence of said Commissioners in failing to properly inspect the properties used at the place of said wreck by said Long Island Railroad, and in failing to require the installation of necessary automatic switching, interlocking and other automatic safety devices.

That on August 5, 1924, a wreck occurred at the Ocean Parkway Station of the Brighton Beach Line of the Brooklyn-Manhattan Transit Corporation operating under Contract No. 4 with the City of New York. A train, consisting of six wooden cars, crashed into a train of seven steel cars which were at a standstill, with the result that the roof of the first car of the wooden train telescoped over the roof of the last car of the steel train and the after part of the roof of the same first wooden car telescoped over the forward part of the second wooden car. The forward platform of the second wooden car was crushed, and as a result of said wreck, one human being was killed, and thirty passengers were injured, fifteen of whom were removed to hospitals. That said train of wooden cars was composed of wooden cars numbered as follows: The first and colliding car, No. 1080; and the following, Nos. 845, 1051, 47, 1078, 904. None of said cars was equipped with the modern "dead man's button" for the automatic cutting off of power and application of brakes.

The first car, No. 1080, was built in 1903, and it, together with cars Nos. 1051 and 1078, both built in 1902, were included in Group A required by Contract No. 4 to be retired prior to January 1, 1924, but permitted by the Commissioners to continue in operation. Car 845, built as a steam coach in 1887, Car. No. 47 likewise built as a steam coach in 1884, and Car. No. 904 built in 1898, were likewise of wood, old, obsolete, dangerous and unsafe. Cars Nos. 1051 and 904 were the subject of the aforementioned investigation by the Joint Committee and by the Committee on Transportation Facilities, following the aforementioned disaster of June 25, 1923. That at the time of said accident, the brake handle, controlling the brakes of the first Car. No. 1080, failed to function, and the brakes were not applied, and that said accident would not have happened had said car the modern "dead man's button."

That said wreck was due solely and only to the culpable negligence of the executives and officials of the Brooklyn-Manhattan Transit Corporation, and the operating companies which it controls, in maintaining, and the culpable negligence of the Transit Commissioners in permitting the use, continuance and operation of, and failing to abate and remove, the aforementioned wooden, dangerous and unsafe cars, and in failing to require the installation of the modern automatic "dead man's button."

Second Charge.—That among other things, the Transit Commissioners were by law charged with the duty of effecting a radical and permanent readjustment of the entire transit system in the City of New York, with a view to its enlargement, extension and improvement, and for the purpose of providing the public with adequate, safe and convenient transportation. That in the year 1919 and prior to the appointment of said Commissioners, the lines of the Brooklyn Rapid Transit System and of the New York Railways Company were in receivership by reason of general insolvency and so continued until 1923. It was generally regarded and understood that said receiverships and the failure of the Railroad Companies to operate successfully, from a financial viewpoint, and to furnish safe, adequate and convenient transportation to the public, was due to waste, mismanagement and in a large measure to overcapitalization of the operating Railroad Companies, and it was the duty of the Commissioners to approve only a reorganization of the Railroad Companies in receivership at the time of their appointment, as would proceed upon an economic basis and would effect an elimination from the new capitalization of what was generally regarded as "water" and the product of corporation stock manipulation, and presented no real investment, and to require that said reorganization be upon a sound financial basis, and that the activities and operations of the reorganized companies, both financial and transit, be conducted solely for the purpose of promoting the interests of said companies and the traveling public, and not for the purpose of stock promotion or manipulation, or with a view to influencing the action of the securities and stocks of said reorganized companies upon any stock exchange. It was also the duty of said Commissioners to require and insist that the management and control of said reorganized companies be vested in directors, officers and managers primarily and solely, interested in the welfare of said companies and the efficient operation and enlargement of their lines, and the safety, security and convenience of the traveling public, and not in persons interested solely in the manipulation upon any stock exchange of the corporate stock or securities of any holding or operating companies. That it was the duty of said Transit Commission to require and insist that adequate financial provision be made in said reorganization, for the immediate remedying and removing of the dangerous and defective condition that had been found to exist in the cars, structure and equipment of the rapid transit lines in the City of New York and failing which, to require and insist that the net income and surplus be applied to said purposes. That said Transit Commissioners failed, refused and neglected to carry out and discharge any of the aforementioned duties, but on the contrary, the said Commissioners permitted the New York Railways Company to be reorganized along the lines of its predecessor organization and upon the basis of an inflated capitalization, dividends and returns on which capitalization, in a large measure not represented by any real investment, can and will come only by the imposition of unwarranted and illegal burdens upon the public. That said Commissioners have likewise permitted the Brooklyn Rapid Transit Company to be reorganized into the Brooklyn-Manhattan Transit Corporation, a holding company for principally the New York Rapid Transit Corporation (the successors upon reorganization of the New York Municipal Railway Corporation), and other subsidiaries, and permitted the over-capitalization of its predecessor, the Brooklyn Rapid Transit Company, to be continued and concealed by the issuance of both common and preferred stock, without fixing a par value therefor, and by permitting said Brooklyn-Manhattan Transit Corporation to issue of said authorized stock, 249,468 shares of Preferred Stock, and 769,911 shares of Common Stock, and by permitting said Brooklyn-Manhattan Transit Corporation immediately after said reorganization, to set up said Preferred stock on its books as of the value of $100 per share, and its Common Stock as of the value of about $54 per share, thereby laying a foundation for prospective dividend distributions upon said stock upon the basis of said alleged fictitious values, and the diversion of the earnings of said corporation, from its legitimate purposes, of making safe, adequate and convenient the operation of its transit lines.

That in truth and in fact said stocks are of a value equal to but a small fraction of said amounts so set up as their value upon the books of said corporation; that in truth and in fact, within one year prior to the date hereof, said Common Stock sold as low as $9.25 per share, and Preferred Stock under $35 per share, upon the New York Stock Exchange where said stock is listed for trading; that the difference between the value of said outstanding capital stock as the same has been entered upon the books of said Brooklyn-Manhattan Transit Corporation, and their value based on sales thereof as aforementioned in the open market, is about $50,000,000, representing water and fictitious investment, which the said Commissioners have tolerated and permitted to be carried upon the books of the Brooklyn-Manhattan Transit Corporation, to the injury of the public of the City of New York, and as a basis for a false cry that has been raised that the rapid transit lines cannot be operated successfully in the City of New York on the existing five-cent fare, and for the purpose of accelerating a movement for the raising of such fares; that in truth and in fact, upon the elimination of its watered capitalization, the said Brooklyn-Manhattan Transit Corporation can successfully operate its lines and remedy and remove the defects in its structure and equipment, and afford a fair and reasonable return upon its real investment upon the basis of a five-cent fare; that in fact the Brooklyn-Manhattan Transit Corporation is governed by a directorate and officers some of whom are serving in dual, antagonistic and incompatible capacities; that certain of said parties are primarily and principally interested in the actions, manipulations and courses of prices and sales of the stocks and bonds of said corporations, and that said Brooklyn-Manhattan Transit Corporation is being managed and controlled largely with a view to the favorable action of the stock market on the stocks and securities of the said Company, and not in the interest of said Company or the traveling public.

That the Transit Commissioners have permitted the said officials, directors and mangers, some of whom are engaged in stock brokerage, jobbing and manipulation business, to make public, facts and figures with respect to income, expense and surplus of the Brooklyn-Manhattan Transit Corporation since its reorganization, for the purpose of enticing an innocent and unsuspecting public into the purchase of the stocks and bonds of said corporation, at prices largely in excess of their real value, by said means, and by means of unwarranted distributions to stockholders of moneys properly applicable to the operation, improvement and development of its lines. That it was the duty of said Transit Commissioners, with knowledge that said Railroad Company represented and claimed the existence of said income and surplus to require and insist, that the same be applied towards remedying and removing the defective conditions in the cars, structure and equipment, which had been found to exist, thereby preventing the wrongful diversion of said funds, and that the Transit Commissioners failed, refused and neglected to direct and require such application of said alleged income or surplus.

That it has been reported that for the year ending June 30, 1924, the Brooklyn-Manhattan Transit Corporation earned a net surplus, after payment of all operating expenses, interest, rent, sinking fund accruals and amortization, of $4,922,065. Notwithstanding the matters and things hereinbefore set forth, and the dangerous and defective condition of the car, structure and equipment of said Brooklyn-Manhattan Transit Corporation, and its failure to comply with the provisions of Contract No. 4, the directors of said corporation, among other things for the purposes of influencing thereby the action of prices of its securities on the stock exchange, commencing May 1, 1924, and ever since, have paid dividends at the rate of $6 per annum on each share of Preferred Stock, an aggregate of about $1,500,000 per annum, or at the rate of 18 per cent. per annum, upon the basis of the low price at which said stock sold within one year prior to the date hereof. That the Transit

Commissioners have permitted said dividend to be paid and to continue, and the funds of the corporation and its operating companies to be thus improperly diverted from the legitimate uses and purposes of the coropora-tion and its controlled companies, to wit, for the purposes of removing its dangerous and defective cars, structure and equipment. That said Commissioners have permittted the said officers of the corporation to represent to innocent and prospective purchasers of stock of the Brooklyn-Manhattan Transit Corporation, that after deducting the amount paid as dividend on the Preferred Stock, that there was earned during the year ending June 30, 1924, about $3.50 per share, on the Common Stock, or at the rate of about 40 per cent. per annum, on the low price at which said Common Stock sold during the period of one year prior to the date hereof.

That contrary to law and in violation of the letter and spirit of the Rapid Transit Contract No. 4, the Transit Commissioners have permitted the officers and directors of the New York Rapid Transit Corporation to divert, unlawfully use and employ its moneys and funds and to charge the same as an operating expense under Contract No. 4, for purposes of the advertisement and acceleration of its aforementioned movement to impose upon the public an increased fare, and have tolerated and permitted the use of its cars by the said corporation for the display of posters and advertisements calculated by misrepresentation and deceit to advance and further said movement for an increased fare, and to wrongfully arouse an unwarranted public indignation against the administration of the City of New York, and to wrongfully shift the responsibility for the present intolerable traction conditions in said City, from the

Brooklyn-Manhattan Transit Corporation and operating companies to the City of New York.

Third Charge—That the Transit Commissioners have failed and neglected, and are still failing and neglecting, to direct and require that sufficient railroad cars, and adequate, efficient and proper train crews and other equipment, be furnished by the railroad companies under Contracts Nos. 3 and 4, as a result of which the traveling public, especially during the so-called rush hours, receives inadequate and insufficient accommodation upon the cars, and are crowded, packed and jammed beyond the capacity thereof, into the cars of the railroad companies and into more or less solid masses, to the detriment of the morals, health, decency and comfort of the traveling public, and in violation of the provisions of the Public Service Commissions Law, the Rapid Transit Act, and contrary to the provisions of Contracts Nos. 3 and 4. That said Commissioners have likewise tolerated and permitted said condition of jamming, crushing and packing of the public to prevail as well as during the so-called non-rush hours, without even pretense at an excuse from said railroad companies, and under conditions which border on indecency and danger to health and morals. That said Commissioners have tolerated said railroad companies to deliberately embarrass, maltreat and inconvenience the traveling public by wilfully and without reason or cause, decreasing the number of trains and cars operated after the passing of the so-called peak-hour, with the result that the aforementioned conditions of crowding, jamming, packing and crushing continue throughout the day and into the late hours of the night.

Fourth Charge—That said Commissioners have failed to properly administer and secure compliance with the terms, obligations and duties placed upon the rapid transit railroad companies under Contracts Nos. 3 and 4, and have failed to protect the rights and interests of the City of New York in said contracts.

In Chapter 2, Article XLIX, paragraph 5, of Contracts Nos. 3 and 4, it is specifically provided as follows:

> "Within thirty (30) days after the 30th day of June following the beginning of such temporary operation and annually thereafter the Commission and the Lessee shall determine the classification and amount of depreciation, and excess maintenance not covered by the amount set aside under paragraph 4 of this article, during the preceding fiscal year, and the deduction for such year shall thereupon be adjusted to conform with such determination."

It was the purpose of said contracts to set aside systematically at the close of each year the amount of depreciation applicable to the properties operated under said contracts during the preceding fiscal year, and to accumulate such depreciation funds for the retirement and renewals of all units of properties. Said provisions were inserted specifically for the purpose of preventing the gradual disintegration of the properties of the railroad companies, such as had taken place during prior operation on the various street railway properties in the City of New York through the neglect of adequate provision for depreciation and proper renewals and maintenance of property.

That the Commissioners permitted the operating companies and particularly the Interborough Rapid Transit Company operating under Contract No. 3, to continue charging such inadequate sums for depreciation, that they are practically negligible for the purposes set forth in said contracts. That as a result, the financial integrity of said rapid transit properties has not been adequately safeguarded, insufficient funds for renewal and replacements have been provided, and the properties permitted to deteriorate, with a resultant deterioration in service and a consequence that in the event of recapture by the City of New York, said properties will be in an impaired condition requiring large expenditures of money for repairs.

Fifth Charge—That the Transit Construction Commissioner, the predecessor of the Transit Commissioners, had taken active steps to secure compliance by the operating companies with the provisions in Contracts Nos. 3 and 4 for depreciation allowance. Upon failure to agree with the Interborough Rapid Transit Company as to the amount of depreciation to be provided annually under said Contract No. 3, said Transit Construction Commissioner, under the provisions of Contract No. 3, demanded that the question be arbitrated, and named as his arbitrator the Hon. Milo R. Maltbie on March 16, 1921. In April 1921, the Interborough Rapid transit Company designated as its arbitrator Mr. Charles F. Uebelacker, and the two arbitrators then selected ex-Judge Luke D. Stapleton. Said arbitration commenced, but no steps have been taken to consummate said arbitration since the abolition of the office of the Transit Construction Commissioner and the appointment of the Transit Commissioners. That said Transit Commissioners have failed, refused and neglected to proceed with said arbitration, and thereby to secure adequate allowance for depreciation under the provisions of Contract No. 3.

Sixth Charge.—That said Transit Commissioners are responsible for the administration in the City of

New York of the rental provisions contained in Contracts Nos. 3 and 4. Under said contracts each Company is required to pool all revenues directly or indirectly derived from the operation of the properties, and then to pay out of the amount so pooled all necessary operating charges as fixed in the paragraphs in said contracts defining the cost of operation.

That said Transit Commissioners have failed and refused to secure observance by said railroad companies of said last mentioned provisions contained particularly in Contract No. 4. That said entire revenues derived from the operation of the properties have not been pooled. That said Commissioners have permitted the said operating companies to exclude and retain from said revenues large sums received as rentals from cars temporarily leased to other corporations, as well as the proper share of joint revenues with other companies, and the amount received as interest upon bank balances on current cash used in operation, the aggregate amount of moneys so improperly excluded being approximately $1,000,000.

Seventh Charge.—That said Commissioners have, contrary to and in violation of the provisions of the said Contract No. 4, permitted the railroad companies to include large, exorbitant and unwarranted charges for the maintenance of the receivership in the cost of operation. That said Commissioners have permitted unjust, unwarranted and unlawful methods of apportionment of joint operating costs incurred in operation with outside properties. That the Commissioners have failed and refused to provide an adequate examination of the operating accounts of the lessees under Contracts Nos. 3 and 4, and have failed and refused to exclude from the cost of operation of the railroad properties, all items of expense which should not be properly charged against operation under said Contracts Nos. 3 and 4.

Eighth Charge.—That the Transit Construction Commissioner, the predecessor of the Transit Commissioners, had made objections to the inclusion of a number of substantial and important items in the Twelfth and Nineteenth Quarterly Determination of Cost by the Engineers under Contract No. 4. Upon failure to reach an agreement with the railroad company and in pursuance of the provisions of Contract No. 4, said Transit Construction Commissioner resorted to the arbitration provision contained in said contract and appointed Hon. Charles S. Hervey, a previous Public Service Commissioner, as the City's representative on the Board of Arbitration, and that the Railroad Company likewise appointed as its representative, Benjamin G. Paskus, but upon the abolition of the office of said Transit Construction Commissioner, and the appointment of the Transit Commissioners, said Transit Commissioners failed and neglected to proceed with said arbitration, to the detriment of the City's rights and interests under said contract.

That prior to the abolition of the office of Transit Construction Commissioner, said Commissioner objected and excepted to a number of important and substantial charges which the railroad companies had included among the operating expenses under Contracts Nos. 3 and 4, but that his successors, the Transit Commissioners, have failed to urge such objections and exceptions, and have done nothing to cause the removal of said unjust and unwarranted charges against the rights and interests of the City of New York under Contracts Nos. 3 and 4.

Ninth Charge.—That the Transit Commissioners have violated their duties to the public by creating and maintaining expensive and useless positions in the appointment of officers who by previous training and experience were unfitted for the duties and responsibilities of their positions.

That said Transit Commissioners in creating useless positions filled the same with appointees who secured their office solely because they were favorites of the Commissioners.

Notwithstanding that valuation reports have long since been completed and hearings of the Commission on such valuations have been discontinued, the large organization which said Transit Commissioners created has been continued without the accomplishment of any object in the public interest. The said Transit Commissioners have, in connection with said organization, employed and continued to retain useless and high-priced employees, as well as a large clerical force, at the expense of the City of New York.

That the total cost to the City for salaries and expenses of the Commission has been about $7,500,000; that said sum is almost entirely a waste of the City's funds, and that the Transit Commissioners have failed and neglected to accomplish anything of a constructive character to relieve the emergency, and the danger and inconvenience in the transportation facilities of the City of New York.

Tenth Charge.—That the Transit Commissioners have failed and neglected to discharge the duty resting upon said Commissioners under the Public Service Commissions Law of restoring unified service which had been temporarily split up during the period of receivership of the Railroad Companies in New York and

Brooklyn, and of reinstating a universal five-cent fare as it existed prior to these reciverships. The Legislature, in the Transit Law of 1921, which created the Transit Commission, had specifically, in connection with the proposed plan for the relief of the emergency then existing in the transit situation, made provision looking to a unification and betterment of the street railway lines with a view, as far as possible, for the maintenance of the five-cent fare.

That contrary to the spirit and intent of said Law and against the insistence of the Corporation Counsel of the City of New York, that the Brooklyn City Railroad Company be included in the newly organized B.-M. T. system, so that all of the surface lines in the Borough of Brooklyn could be operated as a unified system for the service of the public, the Transit Commissioners permitted the Brooklyn Rapid Transit Company to be reorganized into the Brooklyn-Manhattan Transit Corporation without the inclusion of the properties of the Brooklyn City Railroad Company, thereby continuing the splitting up of the lines caused by the receivership, on an arbitrary basis and a duplication of fares, and other interference with reasonable service, to the injury of the public.

That the Transit Commissioners, against the insistence of the Corporation Counsel of the City of New York, refused to direct and require, in connection with the reorganization of the Brooklyn and New York Companies, that provision be made for the restoration of transfers on all points of intersection as they had existed prior to the dissolution, following the receiverships.

That the Transit Commissioners have failed and neglected to require the Brooklyn City Railroad Company to furnish proper service, nothwithstanding that the said corporation is conducting its operations on a profitable basis since the receivership, to wit, for the fiscal year ending June 30, 1923, it reported a net return of 18% upon its $12,000,000 capital stock outstanding, and that the said Commissioners have likewise failed and refused to direct said Railroad Company to restore the transfers in effect prior to the receivership.

Eleventh Charge.—That the Transit Commissioners have permitted the officers and managers of the Brooklyn-Manhattan Transit Corporation, to nullify, avoid and evade the provisions of Contract No. 4. That in and by said Contract No. 4 specific provision was made for the retirement from service, prior to January 1, 1924, of 118 wooden, obsolete and dangerous cars; that said Transit Commissioners wrongfully and contrary to the provisions of said Contract, permitted said cars to remain in operation in the servce of the Railroad Companies after January 1, 1924, and to the date hereof; and contrary to the express provisions of said Contract No. 4 and its clear purpose and intent that ultimately the Brooklyn public should be transported in steel cars only, and to that end, that from time to time as fixed in said contract, the wooden cars be retired, the said Transit Commissioners, for the purpose of perpetuating and continuing in operation said wooden cars, have agreed with the Brooklyn-Manhattan Transit Corporation and its operating company, the New York Transit Corporation upon a policy of alleged reconstruction of about one-half of the present wooden equipment of said Railroad Company into 150 three-car units, each consisting of two motor cars with a trailer car between, permanently connected together and operated as a single three-part "articulated unit." That the continuance in use of said wooden cars so reconstructed, is contrary to the provisions of Contract No. 4. That the Transit Commission, on June 10, 1924, approved the reconstruction of 50 of such wooden cars contrary to and in violation of the provisions of Contract No. 4, thereby perpetuating to the people of the City of New York the danger from said wooden cars.

Dated, New York, October 24, 1924.

EXHIBIT B

LETTER—GORDON TO SHERMAN

January 6, 1925.

In re management and affairs of the Transit Commission before the Hon. John V. McAvoy.

Mr. Henry L. Sherman,
42 West 44th Street,
New York City.

Dear Sir:

I imagine that the investigation into the affairs and management of the Transit Commission is nearing its close.

In view of Commissioner McAvoy's ruling at the outset of the hearing, that the representatives of The City of New York would not be permitted to introduce evidence, examine or cross-examine witnesses, Mr. Steuer and I, who were retained to make such proof and conduct such examination, withdrew from participation on the second day of the hearings and I have refrained from attempting, in any way, to interfere with the course of the investigation so determined by Commissioner McAvoy. The charges which the Board of Estimate and Apportionment made to Governor Smith against the Transit Commission remain unheard. I assume that at the appropriate time the Board of Estimate and Apportionment will be afforded the opportunity of proving them.

I have read the testimony thus far adduced before Commissioner McAvoy. Although I have only been studying the Transit situation less than three months it is clear to me that at least ninety per cent of the evidence thus far presented is but a repetition of matters many times previously stated and restated, and now to be found in public records.

Apparently it was not your purpose to attempt, in this proceeding, proof of the Board of Estimate's charges against the Transit Commission. Notwithstanding, however, many of the allegations of neglect and failure to perform duty, charged against the Transit Commission, have been sustained in the investigation before Commissioner McAvoy, principally through the admissions of the Transit Commissioners, their associates and representatives.

It hardly needs extended argument that many of the essential allegations of the first charge are already proved. By your questioning you showed from the mouth of McAneny that although an emergency existed in the Transit situation in 1921 when the law was passed which created the Transit Commission, and athough the Transit Commission was ostensibly created for the purpose of remedying these conditions, and although the Transit Commissioners came into office in April, 1921, they took no steps to even conduct any public inquiry into the service of both the I. R. T and B. R. T. until March 15, 1922, and that no order affecting that service was made by the Transit Commission until May, 1922, as to the I. R. T., and July, 1922, as to the B. R. T.

It is needless to refer to the report of the Joint Committee of Engineers made in January 1924; the result of the investigation made into the cause of the Flatbush and Fifth Avenue wreck of June, 25, 1923. Mr Mc-Aneny testified that that report had the approval of the Transit Commission. In it attention was called to the imperative necessity of immediately replacing 19000 ties, 2590 outer guard timbers, 15000 joints and 77000 inner guard timbers, and of installing the modern "dead man's button", and to the necessity of painting over the corrosions which prevailed in the elevated structure of the B. M. T., and to the fact that notwithstanding the Transit Commission has never made an order requiring the remedying of these defects with the resultant accident at Ocean Parkway station on August 5, 1924, which might have been avoided and human life might have been saved if the modern "dead man's button" had been installed.

I direct your attention to the fact that Mr. McAneny testified that no order was even made requiring the B. M. T. to paint its corroded structures, because, to use his own language, the company had no money with which to buy paint, and yet, that during that very month of April, 1924, the B. M. T. declared a dividend at the rate of 6 per cent per annum on its preferred stock, an outlay of about $1,200,000 per annum,—only nine months after the reorganization of the B. M. T. which occurred in June, 1923; although in the certificate of incorporation of the B. M. T., it is provided that the preferred stock shall not be cumulative as to dividends until July 1, 1926. Besides for the year ending June 30, 1924, the B. M. T. reported a net earning from subway and elevated operation of $2,492,982.42, or at the rate of about 30 per cent. of the price at which the common stock of the B. M. T. sold within nine months prior to the date of that report.

I note from the testimony of Mr. Harkness that he claims that some water was squeezed out of the capitalization of the B. R. T. upon the reorganization when "R" was changed into an "M." He states the capitalization of $164,000,000 as follows: $139,000,000 bonds and $25,000,000 preferred stock. He places no value upon the common stock because he says that it has "no par value". It is singular that he should fix "no value" on the B. M. T. common stock and at the same time fix $100, as the value of the preferred stock which is also of "no par value". He forgot to state that in the balance sheet which the B. M. T. issued immediately after the reorganization the common stock was valued at $40,000,000 which added to the amount of capitalization which Harkness figured makes a total of $204,000,000. I confidently feel that at least $100,000,000 of that is unadulterated water, and of the remaining $104,000,000 a substantial part is represented by obsolete and about to be scrapped property.

You will remember that I directed your attention, over the telephone, to the fact that in the plan of reorganization of the B. R. T. on pages 6 and 7, it is recited that "power plants, repair shops, car barns common to the use of both surface lines and the subway and elevated lines were *operated* by the Brooklyn Rapid Transit Company itself, and the power plants are also *owned* by the Brooklyn Rapid Transit Company" and to the fact that under Section 2, of Subdivision 8, Article I, of the Public Service Commissions Law, it is provided, that a railroad corporation includes "every corporation * * * owning, operating or managing any railroad or other equipment used thereon or in connection therewith." Surely power plants, car barns, repair shops are equipment, and yet the Transit Commission permitted the organization of the B.-M. T. as a business corporation, not subject to control or supervision by the Transit Commission.

You will remember that I called your attention to the fact that it is provided in Section 55 of the Public Service Commission Law, that the capital of a consolidated or merged corporation shall not exceed the capital of the corporations consolidated at par value thereof and any additional sum actually paid in in cash, that necessarily this section contemplated that a reorganized company could only be incorporated with "par value" stock, because otherwise, it would be impossible to apply this section, and that apparently the Transit Commission approved a reorganization of the B. R. T. with "no par value" stock, both common and preferred, that so section 55 could not be applied. How well the B.-M. T. succeeded, in creating a situation where for the purposes of the Transit Commission the capitalization would be one amount, and for the purposes of stock manipulation another amount, may be inferred from a comparison between Mr. Harkness' testimony before Commissioner McAvoy, where he fixes the capitalization at $164,000,000, and the records in Wall street which show the capital at $204,000,000, not taking into account earnings and surpluses since reorganization.

The third charge needs but brief reference, namely: the charge of intolerable service and undue crowding and jamming in our subways. No better proof in support of this charge need be offered than the testimony of Mr. McAneny as to the inactivity of his commission for one year after its appointment, and the character of the service given today by the traction companies. Besides there might be taken into account the testimony of the Transit Commissioners and the traction companies, that under Contracts 1 and 2 involving a joint expenditure by the City and the I. R. T. of $100,000,-000, 1,140 cars were bought and used in the operation of the subways, whereas under Contract No. 3 which involved twice the expenditure, namely, $200,000,000, only 795 cars were bought until July, 1923, and since, only 100 additional in 1923 and another 100 cars within recent months, and, that the total equipment for subway operation under Contracts 2 and 3 to date, is only 2,135 cars, when, on the basis of 1140, as necessary under Contracts 1 and 2, there should be at least 3,500 cars today.

Charges 4 and 5 need not be commented upon. No depreciation reserve has been up under Contract 3. Commissioner Delaney attempted to secure such reserve, the Company failing to comply, he resorted to arbitration. The Transit Commission has conceded that it has abandoned that arbitration. It claims that that reserve amounts to about $12,000,000. Please bear in mind that that would be the City's money on recapture. Commissioner Harkness says that the reason the arbitration was abandoned was that every body was good to the poor old I. R. T.; it needed financial assistance; that the Manhattan Railway Company agreed to reduce the rent it was charging; that the bondholders agreed to defer payment of sinking fund requirements, and it was for the City to make a gift to the I. R. T. of this $12,000,000, at least temporarily. Of course it needs no argument that it was not within the power of the Transit Commission to do charity with the City's money, but in any event the amount was not $12,000,000, but nearly $30,000,000, payment of which, these charitable gentlemen have waived.

The sixth charge namely, that the Company has not accounted fully for its receipts from operation is likewise substantially admitted. The alibi of the Transit Commission is that the contract with the City does not provide that objections may be made against such withholding of income by the railroad companies, until there is in effect, a final accounting between the City and the Railroad Companies. I am not, and surely you are not in agreement with this interpretation of the law. Surely the rights of the City to participate in this income could be determined upon an interlocutory accounting. I am not ready to believe that the City is without remedy.

The charges that the Transit Commission failed to prosecute objections, which Commissioner Delaney had urged, to improper and unwarranted expenses of the railroad companies and to the inclusion in the determination of costs of improper items, are answered by the Transit Commission, by the omnibus statement that an adjustment has been made of all the matters which were the subject of the objections. I am rather surprised that the inquiry was not pursued for the purpose of determining what the objections were and how they were "adjusted." I think you will find upon inquiry that in the largest measure the alleged adjustments consisted of the withdrawing of the objections and waiver of the City's claims.

Of course I need say nothing about the Brooklyn City Railroad situation. The unified transfer system between the Brooklyn Heights and Brooklyn City was conceded disrupted. The reorganization of the B. R. T. was approved on that basis. The point is not, as the Transit Commission would have it, that the Brooklyn City could not be compelled to lease its lines to the Brooklyn Heights, but that under the provisions of the Public Service Commission Law, the Transit Commission could have compelled these separate companies to issue transfers to each other upon appropriate terms.

I have referred to the foregoing matters because I realize that in the great mass of the detail contained in the two thousand pages of testimony already taken within a comparatively brief period of time, the significance of certain of the evidence and its relationship to the basic questions presented in the inquiry, may have been lost, and in the hope that by my references suggestions may come to you for further inquiry from witnesses already examined along the lines that I have indicated.

I am writing this letter principally because there has crept into the record matters emanating from both the Transit Commission and the Railroad Companies tending to execuse the intolerable service, on our rapid transit lines, because of alleged large deficits from operation, on a five cent fare basis.

Of course from the time when figures first came into existence, there were always some who were able to distort them, and so it has been in this proceeding. The fact is that from the very commencement of operation under Contracts 1, 2, 3 and 4 the subways and elevated lines operated under those contracts, always brought a profit to the railroad companies, except during the years 1920 and 1921 of the receivership of the B.-M. T., when besides there was an extraordinary cost of operation, due to strikes.

I am sending you certain data which I have caused to be prepared to which I shall make references as exhibits. Exhibit A shows that during every year, commencing 1915 and ending 1924, excepting 1920-1921, the Brooklyn Company operating under Contract No. 4 realized a net profit from operation of its rapid transit lines after paying all expenses of operation, maintenance, interest, rentals and making provision for sinking funds and other contractural deductions. The profits in 1924, 1923 and 1922 are respectively as follows: $2,492,982.43; $1,038,939.65; $1,106,623.12. The interest deductions include all the interest on all of the obligations of the Brooklyn Company *including its watered bonds on the old elevated lines.*

Exhibit B shows that the I. R. T. during every year without exception commencing 1912, made a substantial profit from operation of its lines under Contract No. 3, after likewise paying all interest, maintenance, operating expenses, etc., the profits for the last three years being likewise as follows, respectively: $3,359,259.73; $2,002,854.82; $2,012,587.36. Please bear in mind that these are the company's figures, that none of the items of expense or income have been questioned, including the extravagance and wasteful and unbusinesslike expenditures, which should not be under municipal operation. They include what brokers and money-lenders exacted on loans, also charges which belonged to other and less profitable properties of the companies and not operated as part of Contracts 1, 2, 3 and 4.

As against the results of these operations I am submitting to you two schedules which I am sure you will find very illuminating. You will bear in mind that in the computation made in Schedules A and B no account was taken of interest on the City's $250,000,000 investment under Contracts Nos. 3 and 4.

If the City, instead of the Company, had operated the lines under Contract No. 3 and the City paid only the 4 per cent. interest, which it does, without in any way disturbing any of the expense items reported in Schedule A, there would have been earned from the operation of the I. R. T. subway lines during the year ended June 30, 1924, *a sum sufficient to pay the interest on the entire investment of both the City and the Company and besides a net profit of $4,390,000.* If the computation of interest is made upon the basis of the investment of City and Company, properly depreciated as it should be, namely, on $250,000,000, after payment of all operating and maintenance expenses and interest there would have been a profit of $5,950,000 during the same year.

Exhibit D will also disclose to you the true situation with respect to the B.-M. T. under Contract No. 4. Upon the basis of the operations of the B.-M. T.'s subsidiary, for the first three months of the current fiscal year that corporation will earn from rapid transit lines after payment of interest of 4 per cent. per annum on the Company's as well as the City's investment, a total of $240,000,000, a net profit of $1,390,000.

I also in conclusion desire to direct your attention to another matter. You will remember that there is some evidence in the record as to what the cost of construction of new subways will be, in comparison with costs under Contracts Nos. 3 and 4. I believe there is some testimony to the effect that future construction would cost about 125 per cent. more than the cost of construction under Contracts Nos. 3 and 4. There appears to be documentary proof which shows that the cost of construction will be much lower.

I am sending you Exhibit E. That is a copy of a valuation report, made by the present Transit Commission, of properties of the Brooklyn Rapid Transit system as of June 30, 1921; showing both the original cost and the 1921 bases. You will note that the New York Consolidated Railway Company then had invested under Contract No. 4 about $75,000,000. Its total investment to date is $82,000,000, so that in 1921, 90 per cent. of its investment under Contract No. 4 had been made, and you will note that the 1921 price basis for this investment, was only $106,000,000, in other words, that the 1921 value was about 42 per cent. in excess of the original cost. I understand that costs in 1921 were fully as high, if not higher, than they are today.

In connection with these figures you should also bear in mind that the so-called cost of construction set forth in this schedule represents a mass of items aggregating a substantial part of the whole, not representing real cost of construction, namely, losses from delay, duplications, renewals charged as additions, commissions, excess interest, loan brokerage fees; and other extravagant overheads, and that the 1921 values were adjusted in relationship to these exaggerated costs.

Lastly may I be permitted to again suggest, as I did on the day Mayor Hylan testified, that the names of the persons who shared in the $6,484,000, in part incurred as an expense of a reorganization of the B. R. T., and the amount which they received should be the subject of inquiry.

Very truly yours.

HARRY A. GORDON,
Special Counsel.

INTERBOROUGH RAPID TRANSIT COMPANY

SUBWAY DIVISION

Results of Operation Years Ended June 30, 1912 and 1915 to 1924

	1924	1923	1922	1921	1920	1919	1918	1917	1916	1915	
g revenues:											
enger	$35,746,659.35	$33,830,663.35	$32,248,773.70	$31,969,289.00	$29,299,777.05	$23,043,791.27	$20,898,226.47	$20,689,282.42	$18,550,564.65	$17,256,315.31	$15
er	2,645,975.26	2,513,595.11	2,394,067.17	2,858,125.85	2,323,195.99	1,588,416.69	942,221.43	765,610.33	806,687.99	587,479.58	
Total operating revenues	$38,392,634.61	$36,344,258.46	$34,642,840.87	$34,827,414.85	$31,622,973.04	$24,632,207.96	$21,840,447.90	$21,454,892.75	$19,357,252.64	$17,843,794.89	$15
g expenses:											
ntenance of way & structures (actual)	2,586,152.82	2,495,030.09	2,446,130.28	2,378,855.53	1,974,783.59	1,645,634.53	1,012,147.82	881,809.19	807,377.56	848,435.42	
ntenance of way & structures (depreciation)	350,883.73	285,305.68	Cr 90,416.98	Cr 10,591.32	175,578.57	Cr 146,548.36	Cr 23,325.64	57,907.00	89,846.03	Cr 22,999.07	
ntenance of equipment (actual)	4,065,310.55	3,535,870.95	2,714,368.52	2,686,592.44	2,463,654.07	2,556,166.69	1,396,756.80	1,118,472.74	1,042,654.52	977,137.03	1,
ntenance of equipment (depreciation)	Cr 475,599.22	Cr 137,682.79	819,201.28	865,803.84	761,889.18	Cr 238,527.90	Cr 21,393.94	239,540.96	301,894.84	294,472.32	
ration of power plant	5,358,138.15	5,794,640.30	5,006,603.34	5,148,486.61	3,754,419.16	3,457,097.13	1,986,508.54	1,595,778.56	1,354,955.13	1,190,411.25	1,
ration of cars	8,489,661.31	8,406,687.93	8,205,235.69	9,488,772.33	7,758,184.33	6,070,658.07	3,939,386.87	3,277,000.29	2,491,394.66	2,248,870.89	2,
ries to persons and property	718,694.53	635,780.99	417,900.45	432,886.77	502,236.80	446,917.96	390,482.51	475,177.95	428,604.26	309,971.50	
eral & miscellaneous (incl. traffic expenses)	863,391.22	939,505.57	845,401.61	838,497.49	770,741.65	586,500.87	478,619.22	471,915.59	358,464.71	356,770.78	
Total operating expenses	$21,956,633.09	$21,955,138.72	$20,364,424.03	$21,829,303.69	$18,161,487.35	$14,377,898.99	$9,159,182.18	$8,117,602.28	$6,875,191.71	$6,203,070.12	$6,
crued	595,262.71	450,976.39	447,260.15	435,403.59	436,765.37	882,175.29	1,649,411.54	801,511.50	503,629.70	442,371.86	
Total revenue deductions	$22,551,895.80	$22,406,115.11	$20,811,684.18	$22,264,707.28	$18,598,252.72	$15,260,074.28	$10,808,593.72	$8,919,113.78	$7,378,821.41	$6,645,441.98	$6,
g income	15,840,738.81	15,938,143.35	13,831,156.69	12,562,707.57	13,024,720.32	9,372,133.68	11,031,854.18	12,535,778.97	11,978,431.23	11,198,352.91	8,
rating income	318,492.42	492,969.53	581,677.85	579,451.49	534,845.81	494,944.16	495,424.54	483,486.84	467,450.25	484,504.49	1,
ome	$16,159,231.23	$14,431,112.88	$14,412,834.54	$13,142,159.06	$13,559,566.13	$9,867,077.84	$11,527,278.72	$13,019,265.81	$12,445,881.48	$11,682,857.40	$10,
ns from gross income:											
rest	8,343,197.91	8,128,522.55	8,228,001.39	7,939,445.83	7,050,485.50	5,931,802.86	3,329,524.64	2,872,165.06	2,744,364.62	2,670,072.97	2,
tals	2,637,173.46	2,611,273.96	2,501,085.29	2,435,793.09	2,429,987.52	2,424,237.70	2,396,957.57	2,389,024.80	2,381,419.76	2,360,865.95	2,
ing fund and other contractual deductions	1,694,884.64	1,688,461.55	1,671,160.50	1,637,372.10	1,448,139.36	1,218,685.80	366,326.84	18,897.36	....	....	
Total deductions	$12,675,256.01	$12,428,258.06	$12,400,247.18	$12,012,611.02	$10,928,612.38	$9,574,726.36	$6,092,809.05	$5,280,087.22	$5,125,784.38	$5,030,938.92	$5,
me	3,483,975.22	2,002,854.82	2,012,587.36	1,129,548.04	2,630,953.75	292,351.48	5,434,469.67	7,739,178.59	7,320,097.10	6,651,918.48	4,
income 1918 to 1924 .... $16,986,740.34											
Depreciation adjustment (a)											
reciation credits (net) included operating expenses detailed ove	124,715.49	....	....	....	....	385,076.26	44,719.58	....	....	....	...
income adjusted according to tual expenditures	3,359,259.73	2,002,854.82	2,012,587.36	1,129,548.04	2,630,953.75	D 92,724.78	5,389,750.09	....	....	....	...
justed net income 1918 to 1924. 16,432,229.01											

SOURCES: 1912 to 1921 transcribed from Report of T. C. Bureau of Valuation, dated Feb. 15, 1922; 1922 to 1924 from Company's annual reports to T. C.

(a) The actual maintenance expenses in 1918, 1919 and 1924 exceeded the percentage of operating revenues which the Company provided under its depreciation rules. It therefore credited depreciation account by the amount of the excess. In restoring the maintenance total to the actual expenses incurred, no depreciation whatever has as yet been provided for. The net income adjusted is therefore still overstated by an amount required as a depreciation charge for the given period.

EXHIBIT D

New York Rapid Transit Corporation (a)

Results of Operation Years Ended June 30, 1912 and 1915 to 1924

	1924	1923	1922	1921	1920	1919	1918	1917	1916	1915
ting revenues:										
assenger	$26,859,741.47	$24,045,043.51	$22,237,362.67	$20,250,842.06	$18,842,994.31	$15,255,720.12	$12,685,497.35	$11,100,527.19	$9,703,384.31	$8,370,004.24
ther	792,689.52	605,320.27	750,101.03	744,384.51	676,083.24	411,378.25	344,304.92	247,530.73	187,115.23	183,240.98
Total operating revenues	$27,652,430.99	$24,650,363.78	$22,987,463.70	$20,995,226.57	$19,519,077.55	$15,667,098.37	$13,029,802.27	$11,348,057.92	$9,890,499.54	$8,553,245.22
ting expenses:										
[aintenance of way & structures (actual)	2,184,408.59	1,600,722.47	1,473,042.15	1,413,333.82	1,204,414.05	735,372.82	528,718.10	558,624.37	494,863.49	443,199.14
[aintenance of way & structures (depreciation)	120,000.00	114,666.67	120,000.00	430,506.22	395,320.46	121,828.69	252,568.28	122,807.06	98,026.43	69,608.89
[aintenance of equipment (actual)	3,443,124.53	2,667,572.11	2,619,606.31	2,750,461.78	2,991,202.26	1,893,703.37	1,191,552.25	1,022,239.33	807,681.83	718,881.44
[aintenance of equipment (depreciation)	180,000.00	172,000.00	180,000.00	645,759.34	Cr 881,731.67	Cr 408,753.71	Cr 18,870.06	Cr 914.15	82,463.11	50,910.60
peration of power plant	4,289,012.77	5,168,687.45	4,372,381.25	4,444,864.33	3,973,837.67	3,114,094.48	2,213,243.16	1,744,965.04	1,553,417.29	1,363,326.92
peration of cars	6,610,944.82	6,095,976.01	6,193,243.64	7,961,883.85	6,245,742.31	4,219,960.37	2,681,640.90	2,240,063.62	1,946,310.29	1,623,902.33
ijuries to persons & property	801,176.71	435,160.51	340,466.30	364,053.53	407,813.68	492,390.53	284,434.11	230,558.41	190,857.49	150,382.67
eneral & miscellaneous (incl. traffic & paving)	683,323.24	656,876.50	570,022.72	732,879.78	740,930.30	438,134.62	340,221.07	303,978.04	308,044.04	259,708.15
Total operating expenses	$18,311,990.66	$16,911,661.72	$15,868,762.37	$18,743,742.65	$15,077,529.06	$10,606,731.17	$7,473,507.81	$6,222,321.72	$5,481,663.97	$4,679,920.14
accrued	1,414,394.73	1,344,287.40	1,221,153.03	1,080,773.01	972,854.79	864,451.10	793,054.55	734,362.03	545,403.98	541,007.61
Total revenue deductions	$19,726,385.39	$18,255,949.12	$17,089,915.40	$19,824,515.66	$16,050,383.85	$11,471,182.27	$8,266,562.36	$6,956,683.75	$6,027,067.95	$5,220,927.75
ting income	7,926,045.60	6,394,414.66	5,897,548.30	1,170,710.91	3,468,693.70	4,195,916.10	4,763,239.91	4,391,374.17	3,863,431.59	3,332,317.47
perating income	331,021.33	993,183.98	722,669.75	451,708.33	374,387.18	343,381.02	287,000.01	308,474.77	398,702.98	392,632.98
income	$ 8,257,066.93	$ 7,387,598.64	$ 6,620,218.05	$1,622,419.24	$3,843,080.88	$4,539,297.12	$5,050,239.92	$4,699,848.94	$4,262,134.57	$3,724,950.45
tions from gross income:										
iterest	5,460,262.01	$2,075,331.21	$1,238,684.23	2,072,481.27	1,958,908.48	1,978,701.44	1,984,870.80	1,981,339.98	1,998,280.62	1,976,531.04
entals	292,930.50	4,262,499.78	4,263,852.66	4,200,918.08	2,954,836.24	2,373,233.84	1,745,606.90	1,188,288.31	746,563.14	184,933.71
inking fund and other contractural deductions	10,892.00	10,828.00	11,058.04	16,757.00	6,046.50	17,467.02	4,511.00	6,763.30	4,094.01	3,838.75
Total deductions	$5,764,084.51	$6,348,658.99	$5,513,594.93	$6,290,156.35	$4,919,791.22	$4,369,402.30	$3,734,988.70	$3,176,391.59	$2,749,937.77	$2,165,303.50
rporate income	2,492,982.42	1,038,939.65	1,106,623.12	D 4,667,737.11	D 1,076,710.34	169,894.82	1,315,251.22	1,523,457.35	1,512,196.80	1,559,646.95

SOURCES: 1912 to 1921 transcribed from report of T. C. Bureau of Valuation, dated Feb. 15, 1922; the other figures transcribed from annual reports to the Commission.
(a) The New York Rapid Transit Corporation became the latter part of 1923 the successor to the New York Consolidated. The latter was organized in 1912.

EXHIBIT E

B.-M. T.—NEW YORK RAPID TRANSIT COMPANY (SUBSIDIARY) RESULTS OF OPERATIONS FOR 1924 AND 1925—ELIMINATING TAXES

Return—Assuming complete municipal ownership and not questioning operating expenses as reported by the company

The first annual report of the Brooklyn-Manhattan Transit Corporation contains (page 6) the following summary statement showing the results of its operations under Contract No. 4 for the year ending June 30, 1924.

	Year Ended June 30, 1924
1. Revenue	$27,707,951.76
2. Operating deductions and company's first Preferential	23,463,470.97
3. Balance available for return on new money invested under contract	4,244,480.79
4. Company's Second Preferential representing interest and sinking fund on Company's contribution to construction and equipment under contract	5,316,510.00
5. Deficit representing amount by which revenue failed to equal interest and sinking fund on company's contribution to construction and equipment under contract	1,072,029.21

	Year Ended June 30, 1924
6. City's Preferential representing interest and sinking fund on city's contribution to construction under contract, unearned and unpaid	4,076,918.95
7. Deficit representing amount by which revenues failed to equal company's and City's interest and sinking fund on contributions to construction and equipment	5,148,948.06

RESTATED TO REFLECT MUNICIPAL OWNERSHIP AND OPERATION

The above statement shows that during 1924, net revenue failed by $5,148,948.06 to meet the amount necessary for annual interest and sinking fund requirements under the contract. If the lines operated under Contract No. 4 had been constructed exclusively and entirely with the aid of city credit and were operated during 1924 by the city so as to exempt them from taxation and other public charges, what would have been the result?

Item 3 in the table above shows as a balance available for return on new money invested under the contract..............	$4,244,480
To this should be added, the company's first preferential, which had been deducted in reaching said Item 3, namely............	3,500,000
Making a total earned by the company during 1924 of..........................	$7,744,480

This amount however reflects the deduction of taxes (local, state and federal), amounting to $1,414,394 (see report of New York

Rapid Transit Co. for 1924 to Transit Commission). No taxes would have been levied against the rapid transit properties or earnings therefrom had they been operated by the city. Hence, to determine earnings under the assumption of municipal operation, there should be restored to income 1,414,394

Making a total available for interest on City bonds and other purposes $9,158,874

The determined cost and cost of property in operation, as of June 30, 1923, were as follows:

	Determined Costs	Cost in Operation
City's contribution	$149,494,970	$125,095,798
Company's contribution.	82,829,150	81,570,287
Original elevated lines*..	28,534,060	28,534,060
Total	$260,858,180	$235,200,145

Included in the company's contribution under Contract No. 4 are the following items of cost:

Debt discount and expense............	$2,310,000
Taxes	405,014
Interest	11,058,025
Total	$13,773,039

If the city had financed the complete project, debt discount and taxes would have been saved and interest cost would probably have been reduced by about one-third. So on the hypothesis of complete city construction, there may be eliminated from cost:

* Original cost as of December 31, 1922, as estimated by Transit Commission's engineer.

Debt discount and taxes..............	$2,715,014
Interest	3,686,008
Total	$6,401,022

So from the cost of property in operation, as of June 30, 1923..................	$235,200,195
there may be deducted..............	6,401,022
Making a total assumed investment on which interest should be earned.......	$228,799,173

Assuming a rate of 4% to meet the interest on city bonds, earnings for 1924 should have been	$9,151,967
The amount available, as recomputed above was	9,158,874
Leaving an excess of	$7,107

This excess leaves no margin for sinking fund payments or for more generous payments to depreciation funds.

RESTATED TO REFLECT INCREASED REVENUE FOR 1925

Taking due recognition of operating rentals and restoring "taxes" to revenue, we find that for the first three months of the fiscal year 1925, there was a net revenue of $2,517,300 as compared with a revenue of $2,024,765 for the corresponding three months of 1924—an increase of $492,535 or over 24 per cent. Assuming, however, that the annual increase will be only 20 per cent., revenue for 1925 should exceed that for 1924 by $1,831,775, making a total of $10,990,649. This would provide a return of 4 per cent on about $275,-

000,000 of investment. But it is not likely that the average amount in operation during 1925 will exceed $240,000,000.

Accordingly.

With assumed earnings of................	$10,990,649
and interest requirements of 4 per cent on $240,000,000....................	9,600,000
There will be an excess for sinking fund or for increased depreciation contribution or for increased service	$1,390,649

EXHIBIT F

I. R. T.—Adjustments For Depreciation-Interest Computed At 4 Per Cent.

EARNING POWER OF SUBWAYS OPERATED UNDER CONTRACT NO. 3 BY THE INTERBOROUGH RAPID TRANSIT COMPANY

For the year ended June 30, 1924, the Interborough Rapid Transit Company reported an operating income for the Subway Division amounting to $15,840,738.81. This consists of the gross revenues derived from subway operation, aggregating $38,392,634.61, less operating expenses and taxes incurred in subway operation, aggregating $22,551,895.80. These expenses include high salaries of I. R. T. officers as well as royalties paid to Hedley and Doyle and other items which would be saved by municipal operation.

To the operating income thus reported there should be added something over $100,000 for interest on bank allowances and miscellaneous rentals derived from the various operating properties. This is classed as non-operating income. If it is added to the operating income, we have, in round numbers, a net income of $15,950,000 available as interest or return on the entire subway investment, both city and company, under the three contracts.

For the operating period in question, the Company's investment under Contracts Nos. 1 and 2 was $36,011,000 and under Contract No. 3, $103,401,000, total under the three contracts $139,412,000, while the city's investment under Contracts 1 and 2 was

$62,676,000, and under Contract No. 3, $86,900,000 total under the three contracts $149,576,000. These figures represent the cost of property in operation, excluding cost of property not yet placed in operation. They represent actual cost, except for the company's investment under Contracts 1 and 2, which is placed at the net valuation recommended by the Transit Commission valuation report of February 15, 1922. The entire investment, company and city, was $288,988,000.

ESTIMATED ACTUAL INTEREST ON INVESTMENT

To represent approximately actual conditions of the several groups of investments, we should allow 5 per cent. return on the company's investment under contracts 1 and 2, and 6 per cent. on the company's investment under Contract No. 3. The difference of one per cent. in the rate represents the amortization of the company's investment under Contract No. 3 during the life of the contract, while the property under Contracts 1 and 2 belongs to the company at the termination of the contract. On this basis the total interest on the company's investment in operation for the year 1923 amounts to $7,805,000.

The city's investment was made, naturally, at varying rates of interest. But if we allow 4 per cent. on the total investment of $149,576,000 we have a total interest charge of $5,983,000. Adding this to the company interest, we have a total interest burden against the entire investment, aggregating

Company interest	$ 7,805,000.
City interest	5,983,000.
Total company and city	$13,788,000.

For the sake of round figures, we may thus place the total interest against the entire subway investment in operation in 1924, at $13,800,000. Deducting this amount from the operating income of $15,950,000, we have a surplus of $2,150,000.

This surplus represents, on the basis of the company's own report, a return above interest on the entire investment operated under Contracts Nos. 1, 2 and 3, City and Company. This result shows the error of the claim, commonly made, that the subways are not paying their own expenses and fixed charges. This, it must be understood, includes full interest, not only on the Company's, but also on the City's investment made under the three contracts.

PROVISIONS FOR DEPRECIATION

It should be stated, however, that the net operating income of $15,950,000 did not make any provision for currently accrued depreciation. Instead of a charge in operating expenses for depreciation, there was a credit of $124,715.49, so that the expenses as stated were less than actually incurred without providing anything for depreciation. If, then, adequate depreciation were made, the surplus of $2,150,000 would be consumed almost altogether for depreciation.

INTEREST COMPUTED AT 4 PER CENT.

It is to be noted that the interest on company investment was figured at 5 per cent. on $36,011,000 and 6 per cent. on $103,401,000, with a total interest charge of $7,805,000 on company investment. But if the entire property had been constructed and equipped by the city, at the interest rate available to the city, the rate would not have been 5 or 6 per cent., but on the average, probably less than 4 per cent. If, then, on the basis of the entire city investment and operation we were to allow 4 per cent. on the entire investment, we would have, in round figures, a total interest burden of only $11,560,000 on property in operation for this fiscal year ended June 30, 1924. If we deduct this amount from the net operating income of $15,950,000, we have a surplus of $4,390,000. This, then, would be available not only for the accumulation of an adequate depreciation reserve, but also for the establishment of a real surplus and for the improvement of service.

PAST ACCRUED DEPRECIATION

The investment figures used, for Company and City, under the three contracts, aggregate $288,988,000. This, as already explained, represents the actual cost of property in operation for the fiscal year in question, with the exception of Company investment under Contracts Nos. 1 and 2, where the recommended valuation of the Transit Bureau was used. As to this latter figure, both the original cost as used by the Bureau valuation of the Transit Commission was excessive and the deduction for depreciation was inadequate. Otherwise, it includes all of the properties provided under Contract No. 3, Company and City, at full original cost without deduction for depreciation. Moreover, the cost in the case of the company investment under Contract No. 3, was excessive as to various items, particularly for interest, discount and superintendence during construction.

If, then, we were to make an adjustment for the actual net investment, including actual reasonable cost of the properties, less depreciation for past wear and tear and obsolescence, we should have a total of about $250,000,000 for the property in operation during the fiscal year in question. If, on this amount, the interest is computed at 4 per cent. on the basis of the city credit, we would have a total interest charge of $10,000,000. If this is deducted from the operating income of $15,950,000, we have a surplus of $5,950,000.

The last computation is unquestionably the proper one to show the profitableness of the subway operation under Contract No. 3 on the basis of the city credit and municipal operation. There would thus be nearly $6,000,000 available for accumulation of adequate depreciation reserve, as well as for surplus and improved earnings. These figures show, without any doubt, that the five cent fare on the subways operated under Contract No. 3 has been sufficient.

The so-called deficits were due to the excessive fixed charges imposed on the subways by the extravagant financial methods of the Company. But even under the actual conditions, the company has shown a substantial surplus above fixed charges for every year of operation.

The deficits as to the company preferentials under the contract are due entirely to the unreasonable returns allowed to the company prior to any return to the city on investment under Contract No. 3. The remedy is not to increase the fare, but an equitable revision of the contract.

Incidentally, it should be stated that while the subways have furnished a surplus to the Interborough every year during the operation under Contract No. 3, the elevated lines, with which the city has nothing to do, have been operated at a large deficit. For the fiscal year ended June 30, 1924, the subway surplus of

$3,483,975.22, as reported to the Transit Commission, was balanced by a reported elevated deficit of $2,412,-798.39.

For the period of 1918 to 1924, inclusive, the subways operated under Contract No. 3, as reported, showed a surplus above all fixed charges amounting to $16,986,741,34; but against this subway surplus there was an aggregate elevated deficit, as reported, amounting to $24,662,419.17.

Here is the real difficulty of the Interborough, that profitable subway property is hopelessly burdened with the unprofitable elevated lines. As conditions are now, the prospect is that for the future there will be an annual elevated deficit of about $2,500,000 to eat up the subway surplus, and will thus prevent the accumulation of adequate reserves and the rendering of proper service, as required under Contract No. 3, with the city.

Earnings of Subways Operated Under Contract No. 3 by the Interborough Rapid Transit, Calculated on Four Different Bases, Year Ended June 30, 1924

	Fixed charges as reported by the Company (1)	Interest Computed at 5% and 6% for Company and 4% for City investment (2)	Interest Computed at 4% on entire investment Company and City (3)	Interest Computed at 4% on depreciated investment of $250,000,000 (4)
Gross earnings	$38,392,634.61	$38,392,634.61	$38,392,634.61	$38,392,634.61
Operating expenses and taxes	22,551,895.80	22,551,895.80	22,551,895.80	22,551,895.80
Operating income—				
as reported by Company	$15,840,738.81	$15,840,738.81	$15,840,738.81	$15,840,738.81
adding $110,000 interest on bank balances and rentals (round figures)	15,950,000.00	15,950,000.00	15,950,000.00	15,950,000.00
Interest on investment (or fixed charges)	12,675,000.00	13,788,000.00	11,560,000.00	10,000,000.00
Surplus above interest (or fixed charges)	$3,275,000.00	$2,162,000.00	$4,390,000.00	$5,950,000.00

EXPLANATIONS: The gross earnings, operating expenses and taxes are taken from the Company's 1924 report to the Transit Commission. The adjustment of $110,000 to operating income is to include interest on bank balances and rentals received from operating property, so that in round numbers the net income available as return on subway investment is $15,950,000.

In column (1) the interest deductions include the fixed charges as reported by the Company; rentals to City under Contracts Nos. 1 and 2, plus interest and sinking fund charges on Company's bonds and other obligations issued for subway purposes. The charges do not include interest on City investment under Contract No. 3; nor are they based on the Company's preferentials under the contract.

In column (2) the interest is computed for Company investment at 5% on $36,011,000 under Contracts Nos. 1 and 2, and 6% on $103,401,000 under Contract No. 3; for City investment at 4% on $149,576,000 under all three contracts.

In column (3) the interest is computed at 4% on entire investment, Company and City, aggregating $288,988,000 under all three contracts.

In column (4) the interest is again computed at 4%, but is based on total depreciated investment estimated at $250,000,000, City and Company, under all three contracts. In columns (2) and (3) the investment is taken at full original cost, without deduction for past depreciation; except that Company's investment under Contracts Nos. 1 and 2 is taken from recommended valuation of the 1921 Transit Commission valuations, and these represented original cost, less depreciation, but the recommended value of $36,011,000 is excessive by about $10,000,000. The entire net present investment, original cost of the properties less all past depreciation, does not exceed $250,000,000.

All the investment figures relate to property in operation during 1924. For Contract No. 3 they were taken from the 41st quarterly determination.

The operating expenses made no provisions for depreciation, but on the contrary had a credit of $124,715.49 instead of a charge; thus the indicated surplus would be reduced by proper depreciation charges.

EXHIBIT G

B. M. T.—New York Rapid Transit Co.,

SUBSIDIARY OPERATIONS FOR 1924

Return, adjusting operating expenses and taxes assuming complete municipal ownership and operation

In an earlier memorandum, it was shown, assuming City ownership and operation of the B.-M. T. subway and elevated lines, that earnings for 1924 would be increased to $9,158,874, merely by eliminating taxes. On a 4 per cent. basis, this would provide for year ending June 30, 1924, a small excess ($7,107) on about $228,000,000, the estimated cost of the entire system, assuming the use of City credit throughout. Taking into account the increase reflected by operations for the first quarter of the current fiscal year, it was estimated that operations for 1925 will pay 4 per cent. on an average investment of $240,000,000 and provide an excess of about $1,400,000, available for depreciation, sinking fund or improved service. *This—without questioning operating expenses, as reported by the Company.*

In the following, reported operating expenses will be scrutinized with a view to pointing out abnormalities and suggesting amounts that may reasonably be substituted therefor—continuing the assumption of municipal ownership and operation of the existing system, with the added supposition that the City has constructed and operates a new power plant.

OPERATING STATISTICS AND EXPENSES—1922, 1923 AND 1924

Below is a table giving significant reported figures of operation for a three year period:

Statistics	1924	1923	1922
Fare passengers	537,194,829	480,900,870	444,747,229
Passenger car hours	5,341,538	4,801,634	4,267,812
Revenue car miles—number	75,001,252	66,973,552	58,909,210
annual increase	8,027,700	8,064,342	3,534,583
%—increase	12%	14%	7%
Cents per car mile:			
Operating revenue	36.87	36.81	39.02
Operating expenses	24.42	25.25	26.94
Operating ratio	66.22%	68.61%	69.03%

Expenses	1924	1923	1922
Maintenance expended	$5,627,533	$4,254,961	$4,093,054
Operation of power plant	4,289,013	5,168,687	4,372,399
Operation of cars	6,610,945	6,095,976	6,193,244
Injuries and damages	801,176	435,161	340,466
General expenses	683,323	656,877	570,122
Total (excl. depreciation)	$18,011,990	$16,611,662	$15,569,285

The five main groups of operating expense will be discussed in the order listed in this table.

Maintenance expenditures during 1924 may be classified as follows:

Superintendence	$250,470
Ties, rails, roadway and track labor, etc	724,563
Tunnels	94,066
Elevated structures, bridges, crossings, etc	292,769
Signal, telegraph and distribution system	506,841
Buildings	355,305
Cars and car equipment	2,819,585
Shop expenses and machinery repairs	557,257
Cleaning track, etc	26,677
Total	$5,627,533

The amount expended during 1924 exceeds that spent on maintenance during 1923 by $1,372,572—an increase of over 32 per cent. Revenue car mileage increased in that period by only 12 per cent. During the four years prior to 1924, maintenance expenditures were slightly over $4,000,000 per annum. During 1919, it it was $2,628,000 and during 1918, $1,720,270.

However viewed, maintenance expenditures for 1924 are abnormal and burden 1924 operations so as to bar the use of the reported income figure as representative for present purposes. A normal figure for maintenance may be reached by any of the following methods:

(1) Averaging last five years (including 1924) this gives $4,467,000.

(2) Taking preceding year (1923) as normal and adding a percentage increase, equal to the increase of car mileage, during current year over preceding year; this is 12 per cent. and gives a resultant of $4,765,000.

(3) By eliminating from the reported figure some amount, identifiable as "deferred" maintenance.

The Transit Commission valuation as of June 30, 1921, recognized "deferred" maintenance of $2,357,117 on the old elevated properties. Its system of valuation did not call for a similar figure with respect to construction under Contract No. 4; but it is fair to assume that there was some, let us say such an amount as to make the total on the entire system, $3,000,000. Assuming further, that the company's program called for the making good of "deferred" maintenance within three years, $1,000,000 may be eliminated from the 1924 maintenance figures.

Of the three suggested methods, that based on increased mileage gives the highest figures, namely, $4,765,000 and that will be used in the revised income figures.

Another possibility not considered in the preceding is that wholesale changes in the equipment (such as the installation of the "dead man's button") were in process during 1924 and charged to "maintenance" instead of in whole or in part to capital account.

POWER

The NewYork Rapid Transit Co., purchases most of its power from the Williamsburgh Power Plant Co., an affiliated company. Total cost of generating power plus percentages for profit and interest on power plant investment, are prorated among the B. M. T. subsidiaries. It is suspected that the rapid transit lines are burdened with more than their due share. The 1924 figures show that the rapid transit company paid 5.72c. per car mile (both subway and elevated operation) as compared with 3.45c. for the Interborough Company. (subway and elevated operation averaged.)

The point is frequently made that the Interborough and Manhattan power plants are not of the most modern and efficient type; but notwithstanding, it will be assumed for present purposes that the hypothetical plant that the City is operating will not produce power at less than 3.45 cents per car mile, a total for 1924 of $2,587,543.

Although the Williamsburg plant is not of the most modern type and supplies most of the power necessary to run the rapid transit and all the Brooklyn surface lines, including those of the Brooklyn City R. R. Co., it will be assumed that the City would in effect have to reproduce that plant for its exclusive use in operating these rapid transit lines.

On a 1921 price basis, it would cost as follows:

Land		$463,000
Power Plant Buildings		
Total owned by B. R. T. Co.	$5,930,900	
Deduct for central Power Plant included—est. 25%)	1,475,225	4,455,675
Power Plant Equipment		8,968,319
Total physical		$13,886,994
Add for interest, engineering, etc., (company's figures for interest reduced one-third and brokerage fees eliminated—8½%)		1,080,000
Total		$14,996,994
Add for material and coal, etc		1,000,000
Total		$15,996,994
Round		$16,000,000

Recognition of this additional investment will be given at another point, in its appropriate place.

OPERATION OF CARS

This covers salaries of motormen, guards, station and car house employees and operators of the signal systems. These employees are presumably paid on an hourly basis. The rate per passenger car hour is $1.24 as compared with Interborough (elevated and subway) of $1.37, but per car mile it cost the N. Y. Rapid Transit 8.81 cents as compared with the Interborough cost of 8.04 cents. This is due to the fact that the latter gets more mileage per car per hour.

No suggestion can be made on present data for reducing this class of expenses.

INJURIES AND DAMAGES

During 1924, the total outlays made in this connection were $801,176, made up as follows:

Claim dept. and medical expense	$88,367
Injuries to employees	125,100
Other injuries and damages	494,809
Law expenses in connection with damages	92,900
Total	$801,176

This amount is the largest in the history of these rapid transit lines and is more than double the average in the last many years. It certainly is not typical and probably can be reduced by at least one-half—to $400,000.

GENERAL EXPENSES

This includes items for law expenses, insurance and general officers which under municipal operation can be reduced—it will be assumed, to $600,000.

OPERATING EXPENSES REVISED

The following table compares operating expenses, as reported, with revised figures and indicates the reduction:

	As Reported	Revised	Reduction
Maintenance	$5,627,533	$4,675,000	$952,533
Power	4,289,013	2,587,543	1,701,470
Car Operation	6,610,945	6,610,945	....
Injuries and damages	801,176	400,000	401,176
General expenses	683,323	600,000	83,323
Total	$18,011,990	$14,873,488	$3,138,502

RETURN FOR 1924 REVISED

The company reported a return of	$7,744,480
To which was restored in previous memorandum—for taxes not payable by a municipality	1,414,394
Total	$9,158,874
To which may be added for reduced expenses, as per preceding discussion	3,138,502
Making total available for interest on investment, etc.	$12,297,376
Deduct interest—4% on $244,000,000 ($228,000,000 as per previous memorandum *plus* $16,000,000 for power plant)	9,760,000
Leaving for additional depreciation, sinking fund and improved service	$2,537,376

EXHIBIT H

Transit Commission's Valuation—Cost on 1921 Basis

BROOKLYN RAPID TRANSIT SYSTEM

Summary Statement Showing by Companies the Valuation of the Property in Operation as of June 30, 1921

	Original Cost Basis	1921 Price Basis
	Original Cost	Estimated Cost
Brooklyn Rapid Transit System		
Brooklyn Rapid Transit Surface Lines		
(a) Brooklyn Heights Railroad Company..........	$791,076	$1,474,469
Brooklyn, Queens County & Suburban R. R. Co.;......	4,420,881	9,858,646
Coney Island & Brooklyn Railroad Co. (Owned & Leased).................	4,870,186	9,989,712
Nassau Electric Railroad Company................	10,183,007	22,476,116
Total Receivership Surface Companies......	$20,265,150	$43,798,945
Coney Island & Gravesend Railway Co..............	456,670	1,001,058
South Brooklyn Railway Co. (Owned & Leased)........	5,965,274	9,411,074
Total B. R. T. Surface Lines...............	$26,687,094	$54,211,075

	Original Cost Basis	1921 Price Basis
	Original Cost	Estimated Cost
Brooklyn Rapid Transit Elevated & Subway Lines		
New York Consolidated Rail-Road Co.—Original Property	28,534,060	49,725,332
(b) Contract 4. Construction & Equipment	41,672,294	59,758,985
Reconstruction of Existing Railroads	19,302,187	26,885,801
Additional Tracks	8,194,726	11,403,191
Elevated Extensions	5,161,568	7,933,762
Undistributed Costs	691,128	589,588
Total Elevated & Subway Lines	$103,555,963	$156,296,659
Brooklyn Rapid Transit Company	23,411,944	38,419,518
GRAND TOTAL, BROOKLYN RAPID TRANSIT SYSTEM	$153,655,001	$249,927,252

NOTES—(a) Includes Bridge Operating Company.
(b) Includes Company Investment Only.

STATE OF NEW YORK—TRANSIT COMMISSION
BUREAU OF VALUATION
April—1923

EXHIBIT I

Adjustment to Municipal Operation—Investment Assumed at 125% Above Cost

I. R. T. Subway

Operating Results for 1924 Adjusted

	As reported by company (1)	Adjusted to municipal ownership & operation (round figures) (2)
Operating revenue:		
Passenger	$35,746,659.35	$44,683,000.00
Other	2,645,975.26	3,969,000.00
Total	$38,392,634.61	$48,652,000.00
Operating expenses:		
Maintenance of W. & S. (actual)	2,586,152.82	2,586,000.00
Maintenance of equipment (actual)	4,065,310.55	3,233,000.00
Operation of power plant	5,358,138.15	4,500,000.00
Operation of cars	8,489,661.31	8,490,000.00
Injuries to persons & property	718,694.53	500,000.00
General (incl. traffic expense)	863,391.22	500,000.00
Total operating expenses	$22,081,348.58	$19,809,000.00
Taxes accrued	595,212.71	....
Total revenue deductions	$22,676,561.29	$19,809,000.00

	As reported by company (1)	Adjusted to municipal ownership & operation (round figures) (2)
Operating income..............	15,716,073.32	28,843,000.00
Add $110,000 for bank balances & similar items not included by co. in op. revenue (round figures)	15,826,000.00	28,953,000.00
Deduct return on investment, @ 4% on $250,000,000 in col. (1) and $565,000,000. in col. (2)...	10,000,000.00	22,600,000.00
Net available for depreciation, amortization and improvements	5,826,000.00	6,353,000.00

Explanation: Figures in col. (1) transcribed from I. R. T. annual report to the Transit Commission. The operating conditions assumed in col. (2) are: A subway system of the same extent of modern build, owned and operated by the City. Under such conditions, passenger revenues were calculated at a 25% increase, and other operating revenues at a 50% increase. The actual maintenance of Way and Structures were left unchanged although up to date operating conditions are assumed, because we assume 25% increase in passenger traffic. Maintenance of Equipment, according to years 1914 to 1918 average about 25% above 1924. Power costs were based on 3c. per car mile, with the car mileage assumed to have increased 25%. Operation of cars were left unchanged. Each of the items Injuries and Damages and General Expenses was rounded out to $500,000, because of the assumption that many law expenses, salaries of general officers, office expenses, and various bonuses would be eliminated. Interest was assumed in both cases at 4%, but the investment to date was adopted as being the remaining undepreciated cost of the properties, believed to be in round figures $250,000,000, for the modern system an increase of 125% of this remaining cost was taken as the basis.

OPERATION OF THE NEW CITY SUBWAYS AT A FIVE CENT FARE

The question has been raised at the transit hearings before Judge McAvoy whether the new city subway system, at present construction costs, can be operated at a five-cent fare, so that the revenues will be adequate to pay all operating costs as well as interest on the investment in construction and equipment.

There are so many hypothetical factors involved in the answer to this question, that the best course is to consider the present subways operated under the existing contracts with the City, and figure the return from operation on the basis of municipal credit and present day cost of construction and equipment.

I. R. T. SUBWAYS ON BASIS OF PRESENT CONSTRUCTION COSTS

Let us assume the present lines operated by the Interborough Rapid Transit Company, constructed under Contracts Nos. 1, 2 and 3 and operated under Contract No. 3. Could these lines be operated now by the City at a five-cent fare if the investment throughout for construction and equipment were made at present day prices?

This question assumes investment at present day prices and operation at present day range of operating expenses. Consequently the answer must assume also present day or modern facilities which would be provided if the properties were installed under present conditions.

MODERNIZING THE INTERBOROUGH FACILITIES

The existing investment in the properties operated under Contract No. 3 amounts to about $300,000,000, including company and city money under all three contracts. This represents the official cost determinations under Contract No. 3 and the costs as reported by the Transit Commission in the 1921 valuations for investment under Contracts Nos. 1 and 2. Not all of these properties are in operation, but for our purpose we assume that the entire investment is in operation.

In hearings before Judge McAvoy John H. Delaney, Chairman of the Board of Transportation, stated that the present construction costs are about 125 per cent. higher than the general range of actual installation cost under the existing contracts. This 125 per cent. increase was roughly assumed by Mr. Delaney, and presumably did not represent a carefully established figure of how the present day costs throughout would compare with actual costs under the existing contracts.

For our purpose, however, we shall assume a rough 125 per cent. increase in investment compared with the actual figures under Contracts Nos. 1, 2 and 3. As already stated the original cost of all the properties under Contracts Nos. 1, 2 and 3 may be stated at $300,000,000. This is without any deduction for depreciation and present physical condition of the various facilities. The property under Contract No. 1 goes back mostly to 1905 and is about 20 years old and is therefore subject to heavy depreciation. This is especially true as to equipment but applies also to construction. Even the properties installed under Contract No. 3 are subject to considerable depreciation. Roughly, we may assume therefore that the net investment, original cost less depreciation for past wear and obsolescence, is $250,000,000. If this amount is increased by 125 per cent. to represent present range of investment requirements, we have an equivalent present investment of $565,000,000.

But if we figure the present equivalent investment cost and adopt $565,000,000 as the present day capital equivalent, we must realize at the same time that the existing lines and the equipment would not be laid out at the present time as they actually exist. For example, the Broadway subway above 96th Street would now be constructed as a four track line to its destination instead of the three track line which makes express service beyond 96th Street impossible. But the additional cost of putting in a four track subway instead of a three track would be negligible, while the additional service, the carrying capacity and the earning capacity would be tremendously increased.

Likewise instead of putting in the existing short platforms for the local trains which makes 10-car trains impracticable, we could install the longer platforms with very little additional expense and provide 10-car trains which could be used as semi-express during rush hours. In this way with very little additional cost we could increase the service, the carrying capacity and the earnings tremendously. Again, instead of the existing power house and power plant equipment we would have modern design throughout, which corresponds to present actual requirements of service. Without any additional cost we could have modern power facilities througout, which would mean a reduction in operating expenses.

As to cars we could design the road throughout so that we could use the most economical and modern 1925 design, instead of being committed to the relatively heavy car with small carrying capacity and high operating costs. With no additional investment we could have modernized equipment throughout, which would permit the most economical operation and much better service.

This would mean greater carrying capacity, greater earnings and lower operating expenses.

1924 OPERATING RESULTS ADJUSTED TO PRESENT INVESTMENT AND MODERNIZED PROPERTIES

For the purpose of our problem, therefore, let us take the 1924 actual operating results as reported by the Interborough Rapid Transit Company under Contract No. 3. Let us see what actual return there was on the $250,000,000 net investment as compared with the required 4 per cent. under present city credit and consequently let us consider what would have been the corresponding result of operation of modernized plant and equipment as to the same routes but at an investment cost of 4 per cent. on the basis of present day cost of construction and equipment.

The total gross revenues for the fiscal year ended June 30, 1924, were reported at $38,392,634.61. The actual operating expenses, without any provision for depreciation, amounted to $22,081,348.58. The taxes were $595,212.71.

Deducting the sum of the operating expenses and taxes from the gross revenues we have a net operating income of $15,716,073.32. To this figure, however, should be added about $110,000, for interest on bank balances and miscellaneous rentals. This would bring the net operating income, in round figures, to $15,826,-000. This would be the sum available for interest on investment, without, however, any allowance for depreciation.

The actual net investment as stated at $250,000,000 and interest requirement at 4 per cent. is therefore $10,-000,000 a year. Deducting this from the net operating income of $15,826,000 we have a net surplus of $5,826,-

000 above operating expenses, taxes and interest on the actual entire net investment. This sum would be available for depreciation, amortization and improvements.

ADJUSTING THE 1924 FIGURES TO MODERNIZED PROPERTIES

We now assume that the same lines have been operated in 1924 at an investment of $565,000,000 but with thoroughly modernized properties as already indicated.

With this assumption we believe that the passenger revenues would have been at least 25 per cent. greater than those reported and that the miscellaneous other operating revenue would have been at least 50 per cent. greater. On this basis we should have in round figures gross operating revenues amounting to $48,652,000 instead of the actual reported $38,392,634.61. The increase would have resulted from the express tracks on Broadway, the longer stations permitting longer local trains and semi-express service, as well as cars with greater carrying capacity and better service.

Let us emphasize that we believe the present investment of $565,000,000 would have provided a plant and equipment which would meet present requirements and would furnish proper service. On this basis the 25 per cent. increase in passenger revenues is obviously an understatement of the receipts that would have been realized under such conditions.

OPERATING EXPENSES

With the modernized plant and equipment, properly proportioned throughout, there would have been an economy in operating expenses throughout especially with municipal operation. The comparative computation of revenues and operating expenses and charges is given in the statement attached hereto. This statement shows that as to the maintenance of way and structures, we have left the amount the same under adjusted operation as under the actual, assuming that it would cost no more to maintain a modernized structure than the existing lines, but that otherwise no particular economy would be realized.

MAINTENANCE OF EQUIPMENT

As to maintenance of equipment we believe that under existing conditions the expenses are far too high because of inadequate cars as well as insufficient inspection and shop facilities. The company has been enormously handicapped throughout in the equipment maintenance, which is reflected in the high range of expenses for maintenance of equipment. This is due, hovever, even more to inadequate number of cars, leaving an insufficient margin above the necessary service requirements for regular inspection and systematic overhauling. Under modernized conditions we assume that there are enough cars and enough shop facilities to provide for regular inspection and repairs under modern favorable circumstances. Under such conditions, with larger and modern cars, the expense in proportion to traffic, would be less, which would be a further factor in addition to the uneconomical present layout.

For our purpose to determine the proper charge for equipment we have taken the five-year period prior to 1917 when presumably a reasonable proportion between service cars and shops existed. We found that during that period the average annual cost for maintenance of equipment was 25 per cent. greater than for the maintenance of way and structure. For our purpose, therefore, we assume that normally, under proper proportion of service cars and shops, the cost of maintenace of equipment would be 25 per cent. greater than the maintenance of way and structure.

POWER COSTS

The actual power costs were reported at $5,358,138.-15. We believe these are excessive, due partly to the lack of thoroughly modern power facilities and partly to excessive charges to the subways as compared with the elevated lines. The Interborough's 1924 report shows that on the average the power charge per car mile on the elevated lines was 1.9c. while for the subway it was 4.5c. While unquestionably the power consumption per car on the subway is greater than on the elevated, there can be no such disproportion as is indicated by these figures.

For the purpose of our problem we have assumed a modern power plant and modern operation, with larger cars, greater amount of express service, and consequently a better distribution of traffic. Under these conditions we believe that 3c. per car mile for power would be adequate and probably the lower cost would be realized. We therefore have computed the power costs at 3c. per car mile and have increased the assumed mileage by 25 per cent. The reason for this increased assumed mileage is to provide relief from the existing congestion, so that the 25 per cent. additional car mileage with the larger cars would give proper relief for reasonable service.

OTHER OPERATING EXPENSES

As to other operating expenses we have assumed that there would be a considerable saving in injuries to persons and property and general expenses. We have eliminated excessive salaries, legal expenses and various overheads that would be avoided under City operation. There would of course be a complete saving as to taxes.

The total operating costs under the assumed modern conditions are stated at $19,809,000. Deducting this amount from the $46,652,000 operating revenues and adding $110,000 for bank balance and miscellaneous, we have a net operating income of $28,953,000.

This sum would be available for interest on the $565,000,000 investment. At 4 per cent. the interest charge would be $22,600,000. Deducting this from the operating income we have a surplus above operating expenses and interest amounting to $6,353,000. This amount would be available for depreciation, amortization and improvements. These figures represent conservative estimates as to results of a modernized plant operated under present range of operating expenses and present investment costs. There is no doubt that the operation could be profitably conducted at a 5c fare, giving reasonable service, paying all operating expenses, as well as interest on the investment, and leaving a sufficient surplus for depreciation, amortization and improvements.

EQUIVALENT PRESENT INVESTMENT

For the purpose of this problem we have increased the net actual investment of $250,000,000 by 125 per cent. to an assumed present equivalent of $565,000,000, to take into account the higher present cost of construction and equipment.

In reality, however, the 125 per cent. adjustment to present day costs is excessive, even if we assume a thoroughly modernized layout. In the first place, costs of construction and equipment have not increased on the average 125 per cent. above the actual costs incurred under Contracts 1, 2 and 3. At the present time materials entering into construction are about 108 per cent. higher than in 1913 and 1914; but this is not 125 per cent. Further, not even all the construction contracts were let at the pre-war prices, so that the average construction cost under Contract No. 3 was probably less than 100 per cent. above 1914 prices. But, as to equipment, most of the installation was at a much higher level than in 1914, and much of it at a much higher range than prevails today. Altogether, it is doubtful whether today the construction and equipment costs would be more than 75 per cent. higher than the average actual costs under Contracts Nos. 1, 2 and 3. This relates merely to the matter of price changes.

A second point should be considered in taking $565,000,000 as the equivalent present investment in modernized properties provided under the three contracts. While the basic prices of materials are much higher than the average actual costs under the contracts, in many respects, especially as to equipment, the net installation per unit *in terms of capacity* has increased much less and in some important matters not at all. Thus, in the case of power plant and power plant equipment, the net investment cost per k. w. capacity is not greater today than prior to 1914; probably less. The cost per car is much greater, but the modern car is larger and more convenient of operation, so that the net investment per passenger mile capacity today is probably not over 25 per cent. greater than before the war. The same principle applies to other equipment and construction.

A third point establishing present equivalent investment, relates to the huge overheads which were incurred under the existing contracts, but which would be avoided if the City were to build the same lines now as a modern system.

Under construction, Contract No. 3, the various overheads, including interest, superintendence, discount, etc., averaged over 33 per cent. on top of the cost of labor and materials. This represents the costs of delay, duplications and extravagance. There is no reason why these overheads should exceed 15 per cent. if the City is given full power to proceed with construction and installation of equipment. This would provide 8 per cent. for interest on the basis of two full years for the average investment prior to operation, and 7 per cent. for engineering and other superintendence.

RETURN ON $400,000,000 INVESTMENT

If the City were given full power to proceed, there is no doubt that at present costs and with present knowledge and experience, it could build and equip a modern subway system in place of the actual subways operated under Contracts Nos. 1, 2 and 3, for probably less than $400,000,000, instead of the $565,000,000 assumed in our computation. On this basis the annual interest at 4 per cent. would be only $16,000,000 instead of $22,600,000 in our computation. And accordingly the surplus above operating expenses and interest would be $12,953,000 instead of the stated $6,353,000; or about double. This is the proper basis of judging city operation at present day costs of construction and equipment, compared with the Interborough operation under its contracts with the City. This is more accurately the amount that would be available for depreciation, amortization and improvements.

EXHIBIT J.

LINES WHERE SERVICE SHOULD BE INCREASED—DEC. 9, 1924.—MAYOR HYLAN

"Lexington-Fourth avenue subway. Increase in the express service during the non-rush hours, with a corresponding increase in the local service during these periods of time past Grand Central station. Midday express service from Woodlawn extended beyond its present termination point at South Ferry to Brooklyn. Extension of all service on this line now terminating at Atlantic Avenue, Brooklyn, to Utica Avenue, as express service.

"Extension of the local service now terminating at Hunts Point Road, on the Pelham Bay branch of the above line, through to Pelham Bay Parkway during all hours, at an interval not greater than operated by the shuttle service now in operation between these points and the abolishment of the shuttle service.

"The extension of the service during the rush hours on the East 180th Street branch of the Lexington Avenue subway, through to 241st Street, on at least the same interval as now operated during these hours by the shuttle service, and the abolishment of the shuttle service during these hours.

"The extension of the present midnight service now terminating at Bronx Park, West 180th Street, through to 241st Street, and the elimination of the shuttle service during these hours between 177th street and 241st Street. This will necessitate the establishment of one car shuttle service between Bronx Park, West 180th

Street and the 177th Street station. This should prove a comfort and convenience to the patrons of this line.

"Ninth Avenue 'L'. Part of the present rush hour service on this line terminates at Fordham Road. Alternative service should be extended through to Woodlawn, to which point this service was operated prior to December 1, 1924.

"Third Avenue 'L'. On the Webster Avenue extension of the above line, the present through service during the rush hours is operated to 241st Street—should be augmented by additional service to enable the abolishment of shuttle service between Fordham Road and 241st Street during these hours. Extension of the shuttle service now operated during the non-rush hours beween Fordham Road and 219th Street, north to 241st Street.

"B. M. T. Corporation—Lexington Avenue 'L' line. The extension of the Park Row branch of this service during the A. M. and P. M. rush hours to 11th Street and Jamaica, the service to divide equally to and from each point.

"Myrtle Avenue 'L'. Operate all trains to and from Park Row during all hours of the day. Extend the present service originating at Wyckoff Avenue durin the morning rush hour, so as to go into service from Fresh Pond Road, reconstruction of the Metropolitan Avenue station. Through service during the P. M. rush from both Chambers Street and Park Row.

"Fifth avenue 'L'. Bay Ridge extension of the service now terminating at Sand Street, through to Park Row at all hours. The extension of this service should have a beneficial effect in relieving traffic on the Fourth Avenue subway during rush hours.

"Broadway-Manhattan subway. Service on above line now operated during midday hours should be resumed about 7.30 p. m. and continued in operation until about 12.30 a. m. This service should be short line from Whitehall Street during these hours, in order to take the place of the Brighton Line which is operated over the Manhattan Bridge, and on the express rails in Manhattan during the above period of time, during the hours, a suggested operation of but one local service. The Fourth Avenue local is operated north of Whitehall Street, while three branches of the express service are in operation between Canal Street and Times Square.

"West End line. The extension of service beyond Bay Parkway station to Coney Island during rush hours, and the abolishment of shuttle service between these points.

"Sea Beach line. Inauguration of a short line service say from Kings Highway to Chambers street, during rush hours, via the south roadway of the Manhattan Bridge, while on the lines of the B.-M. T. Corporation, it may be well to call attention to the fact that on a number of lines of this company, one car trains are in operation during midnight hours. This method of operation has proved a serious complaint on many occasions, as usually one car trains have been heavily loaded at times, and if there is any time of day where adequate service can be supplied, it is surely at these hours.

"Following is a short description of the time during which one car trains are scheduled:

"Sea Beach line, from 3:14 a. m. to 5: 14 a. m.

"Brighton Line, 2:32 a. m. to 5:23 a. m.

"West End Line, from 1:47 a. m. to 5:24 a. m., leaving Times Square Station.

"Fourth avenue local, from 12:58 a. m. to 4:47 a. m., leaving Queens Plaza.

"Culver line, from 12:55 a. m. to 5:23 a. m., leaving Park Row.

"Bay Ridge, from 12:55 a. m. to 5:23 a. m., leaving Park Row.

"Broadway-Jamaica, from 1:39 a. m. to 4:51 a. m.

"14th street-Eastern line, from 12:50 a. m. to 6:01 a. m., leaving Broadway.

"Astoria-Queens-Corona line, from 2:10 a. m. to 4:07 a. m., leaving Queens Plaza.

"It may be interesting to note that two car trains were operated during the midnight hours above quoted on the Sea Beach, West End, Culver, Bay Ridge, Brighton and Broadway lines, 22 years ago.

"Lines where service can be increased. I. R. T. Company. On all lines of the above company during the non-rush hours on both local and express service.

"White Plains Avenue extension, rush hour service can be increased to meet the traffic demands for same.

"Ninth Avenue L rush hour service can be alternated from Fordham Road and Woodlawn.

"Third Avenue 'L' service can be increased on Webster Avenue extension during rush hours and shuttle service can be extended from 219th Street to 241st Street during the non-rush hours. The extension of service suggested in different branches of the above companies' lines beyond their present terminating point can be made at the present time.

"B.-M. T. Corporation. All the service increases mentioned and answered in No. 1 can be made and cars should and can be added to one-car trains during the midnight hours.

"The Transit Commission and the operating companies claim maximum operation on East and West side subway trunks passing Grand Central and Times Square respectively has been reached during the traffic rush hours.

"Third Avenue L. Maximum operation is in effect between 129th Street and Chatham Square during a. m. and p. m. traffic rush hours.

"Sixth Avenue L, maximum operation has been reached during a. m. and p. m. traffic rush hours south of 9th Avenue and 53rd Street.

"Eastern Parkway extension, operation over local trunks between Atlantic Avenue and Franklin Avenue reaches maximum point from 8 a. m. to 9 a. m. and 5 p. m. to 6 p. m.

"B.-M. T. Corporation. Maximum operation has been reached during the peak of the rush hours on the Broadway-Canarsie, Broadway-Jamaica, Broadway-Myrtle Avenue and Broadway-Short line, owing to the fact that the Williamsburg Bridge, the point of control in this operation, reaches the limits of its track capacity between 7.30 a. m. and 9 a. m. past Marcy Avenue Station."

EXHIBIT K

Brooklyn Rapid Transit System

ESTIMATED COST OF ACQUIRING PROPERTY BY SECURITY PURCHASE AND DEBT SETTLEMENT, ABOUT JUNE 7TH, 1923

On June 7, 1923, the United States District Court approved the sale of the properties of the B. R. T. System. The accompanying schedule ("A") shows that on or about that date, the securities of that system owned by the public had a total valuation (at then prices) of $112,113,507. As explained by foot-notes, the prices used in that statement were derived, wherever possible, from the Financial and Commercial Chronicle and the Standard Bond Book. Where no quotations as of June 7, 1923, or thereabouts could be found, the highest figure in the 1923 price range was always taken. And where not derived from the sources above mentioned the par value of the security was used or the equivalent of market value (maximum in 1923) of the B.-M. T. securities given in exchange for said security upon reorganization was adopted.

To become the free and clear owner of all the assets of the various companies as of June 7, 1923, besides purchasing the outstanding securities, it would have been necessary to pay for or assume the debt not represented by these securities (such as trade and tort claims, unpaid taxes and interest, receivership expenses, etc., etc).

Whereas in the reorganization, cognizance was taken of and settlement made for unpaid interest on bonds and bank loan of over $27,000,000 (Schedule "B") the purchase of the defaulted bonds in the market would have rendered unnecessary the payment of any back interest on such bonds. In the absence of default, bonds are quoted in the market at a price *plus interest;* but where there has been default, they are quoted *flat.* Thus in acquisition no sum would need have been added for accrued or past due interest. On underlying bonds, however (which had not been disturbed by the receivership) and receiver's certificates, interest accrued up to June 30, 1923 and payable by bond purchaser, totalled $872,-164 (see Schedule "C."). In reorganization, settlement was also made with banks, general and tort creditors, by payment of cash and B. M. T. securities, which had a combined maximum market value in 1923 of $7,057,-265 (see Schedule "D").

As of the date of this assumed purchase, most of the companies in the system were in receivership and, to discharge the same, additional outlays would have been unavoidable. The reorganization plan (page 10) provided for disbursements of $6,484,119 on account of receivership expense, foreclosures, past due taxes, reorganization expenses, syndicate commission, etc., etc. By avoiding the reorganization and refinancing that was effected by the plan, a large portion of this could no doubt have been saved. For present purposes, it will be assumed that $3,000,000 at the extreme outside would have been necessary.

Thus—to acquire the complete ownership of the B. R. T. system, including its current assets and to discharge liabilities of every nature the following investment would have been necessary.

To purchase securities in open market..	$112,113,507
Plus interest on underlying bonds, etc., accrued to date of purchase..........	872,164
To pay general and tort creditors......	7,057,265
To discharge receivership	3,000,000
	$123,042,936

In approving the B. R. T. reorganization plan, the Transit Commission had before it the following values for physical properties, reached by the Engineers of the Transit Commission.

Estimated original cost, less cost of reconditioning as of Dec. 31, 1922........	$164,992,589
Cost to reproduce at 1921 prices, less accrued straight line depreciation, as of June 30, 1921	184,116,678

The Commission's opinion (p. 11) refers also to $34,-235,293 of current assets, but includes in its computations only $11,989,033 without deciding, however, that the remainder was worthless. This figure for current assets is probably as of March 31, 1923. By June 30, 1923, it should have increased, because of earnings before interest by about $2,800,000 (see Company's 1922 figures—plan p. 41). On June 30, current assets would, therefore be somewhere between $18,000,000 and $37,000,000. It will be assumed for present purposes that they aggregated $25,000,000.

Without considering physical property, additions from June 30, 1921, or December 31, 1922 (the dates as of which the Transit Commission valuations were made), we find that assets (physical and current) which could have been acquired, by the purchase of securities and a settlement with creditors, for about $123,000,000 had been valued by experts of the Transit Commission at about $190,000,000 *net* on an original cost basis and about $210,000,000 *net* on a 1921 price basis. These values are in excess of the above calculated aggregate market value of securities and other debt of the B. R. T. system as of June, 1923, by $67,000,000 and $87,000,000 respectively.

EXHIBIT K—Schedule A

B. R. T. System Securities Held by Public, About June 7, 1923

Approximate Total Market Valuation

Security	Amount	Quotation on or about June 7, 1923*	Price Range 1923** Low	Price Range 1923** High	Price used herein	Total Market Value
Receivers' certificates and car lease warrants (Total System)	$12,397,044	$....	..	..	100	$12,397,044
Brooklyn Rapid Transit Co.						
First gold 5s—1895-1945	6,963,000	76¼–78	..	..	78	5,431,140
First refunding gold 4s—1902-2002	3,433,000	63½–65	..	..	65	2,231,450
Three year secured gold notes—7s—1918-1921	57,253,700	93½	..	..	93½	53,532,210
Six year secured gold notes 5s—1912-1918	465,000	....	..	..	74 (a)	344,100
Common stock	74,422,959	2–2–½	..	..	2½	1,860,574
Brooklyn Heights R.R. Co.						
First mortgage bonds 6s—1891-1941	250,000	....	..	..	50 (b)	125,000
Bridge Operating Co.						
Common stock (owned by N. Y. Ry. Co.)	50,000	....	..	..	100 (c)	50,000
Brooklyn Queens Co. & Suburban R.R. Co.						
First mortgage bonds—5s—1894-1941	1,497,000	80½	..	..	80½	1,205,090
First Consol. bonds—5s—1894-1941	2,803,000	66	..	..	66	1,849,980
Jamaica and Brooklyn R.R. Co. 5s—1889-1930	231,000	....	68	68	68	157,080

Security	Amount	Quotation on or about June 7, 1923*	Price Range 1923** Low	High	Price used herein	Total Market Value
Coney Island and Brooklyn R.R. Co.						
Real estate mortgages	231,200	....	..	..	100 (c)	231,200
First Consol. gold 4s—1898-1948	1,986,000	....	50	60	60	1,191,600
Consolidated gold 4s—1904-1955	1,500,000	....	..	..	47 (d)	705,000
Bklyn. City & Newtown 1st gold 5s—1889-1939	1,988,000	....	66	70	70	1,391,600
Common stock	297,400	....	..	..	100 (e)	297,400
Nassau Electric R.R. Co.						
First consol. gold 4s—1898-1951	10,337,000	60	..	..	60	6,202,200
First consol. gold 5s—1894-1944	660,000	....	..	..	85 (e)	561,000
Atlantic Av. gen. con. gold 5s—1891-1931	2,241,000	....	72	86	86	1,927,260
Atlantic Av. impr. gold 5s—1894-1934	215,000	....	72	80	80	172,000
Bklyn. Bath & West End 5s—1893-1933	118,000	....	75	90	90	106,200
Preferred stock	105,225	....	..	..	100 (c)	105,225
Brooklyn & North River R.R. Co.						
Common stock (owned by N. Y. Rys. & 3d Av. R.R. Co.)	50,000	....	..	..	100 (c)	50,000
New York Consolidated R.R. Co.						
Brooklyn Union 1st mort. 5s—1899-1950	15,956,000	81½–82½	..	..	82½	13,163,700
Kings County El. 1st mort. 4s—1899-1949	6,980,000	70.7–71	..	..	71	4,955,800
Preferred stock	214,015	....	..	..	32 (f)	68,485
Common stock	469,169	....	..	..	29 (g)	136,059

Security	Amount	Quotation on or about June 7, 1923*	Price Range 1923** Low	Price Range 1923** High	Price used herein	Total Market Value
NEW YORK MUNICIPAL RY. CO.						
First mortgage 5s—1912-1966	1,997,000	83	..	..	83	1,657,510
PROSPECT PARK AND CONEY ISLAND R.R. CO.						
Income bond 6s—1880-1920	7,600	....	..	..	100 (c)	7,600
Total						$112,113,507

(a) Value based on exchange in reorganization for B.-M. T. 6% bonds, (Price Range 1923½ 65-74).
(b) Value based on exchange in reorganization for B.-M. T. preferred stock (Price range, 1923:34½-49⅞).
(c) No quotations or other basis for valuation found; placed at par notwithstanding the fact that, in view of condition of companies, stock was worth considerably less.
(d) No quotation found; price based on $13 margin between 1898-1948 issue and 1904-1955 issue existent on Sept 1, 1922, as per Transit Commission Valuation Report, p. 340.
(e) No quotation found; price based on $25 margin between 1898-1951 issue and 1894-1944 issue, existent on September 1, 1922, as per Transit Commission valuation report, p. 340.
(f) Value based on exchange in reorganization of one share of N. Y. Consolidated preferred stock for $50 of preferred stock and ½ share of common stock of B.-M. T. Co.:

	Low	High	Low	High
$50 Pfd.	34½	47⅞	17¼	25
½ share	9¼	14½	4¾	7¼
			22	32¼

(g) Value based on exchange in reorganization of one share of New York Consolidated Common stock for $40 of preferred and 6/10 shares of Common of B.-M. T. Co.:

	Low	High	Low	High
$40 Preferred	34½	49⅞	14	20
6/10 shares Common	9¼	14½	5½	8.7
			19½	28.7

*From Financial and Commercial Chronicle, June 9, 1923.
**Standard Bond Book.

EXHIBIT K—Schedule B

B.-M. T. Reorganization

Settlement With Creditors and Arrears in Interest—Reduced to Market Value Equivalent

	Amount of debt	SETTLED BY Cash	Preferred Stock	Bonds	Common Stock
Interest in Arrears					Shares
B. R. T. 3-yr. 7% notes	$20,038,795	$4,007,759	$10,305,666	$5,725,370	.....
B. R. T. 6-yr. 5% notes	116,250	23,250	46,500	46,500	.....
B. R. T. 50-yr. 5% bonds	1,653,712	348,150	174,062	....	11,315
B. R. T. 1st refunding 4% bonds	617,940	137,320	....	....	4,806
N. Y. Municipal 5% bond	499,250	99,850	199,700	199,700	.....
Bk. Hts. 5% bonds	53,125	....	53,125	....	.....
B. R. T. bank loans	937,166	937,166	....	....	.....
Bklyn. Bath Beach & West End—5%	23,600	23,600	....	....	.....
Atlantic Av. Impr. 5%	43,000	43,000	....	....	.....
Nassau Elec. 1st mort. 5%	132,000	132,000	....	....	.....
Nassau Elec. 4%	1,860,660	413,480	1,447,180	....	.....
Coney Is. & Bklyn. 4%	270,000	270,000	....	....	.....

	Amount of debt	SETTLED BY Cash	Preferred Stock	Bonds	Common Stock
INTEREST IN ARREARS					Shares
Bklyn. Queens Co. & Sub. First 5%	336,825	336,825	....	....	.....
Bklyn. Queens Co. & Sub. First Con. 5%	560,600	140,150	420,450	....	.....
Total interest	$27,142,923	$6,912,552	$12,646,693	$5,971,670	16,121
Bank loans	3,300,000	1,054,302	254,230	1,991,468	.....
General creditors (5/1/24—$1,411,245)	1,600,000	898,689	732,613	....	.....
Total creditors	2,200,000	2,200,000	....	....	.....
Total	$34,242,923	$11,065,543	$13,633,526	$7,963,038	16,121

SUMMARY

	AMOUNT	HIGHEST PRICE 1923	MARKET VALUE
Cash	....	....	$11,065,543
Preferred stock	$13,633,526	@ 50	6,816,763
Bonds	7,963,038	@ 74	5,892,646
Common stock	16,121	@ 14½	233,754
Total			$24,008,706

EXHIBIT K—Schedule C

B. R. T. SYSTEM

Interest Accrued on Underlying Bonds, June 30, 1923

	Interest Dates	Outstanding	Interest accrued June 30
Kings Co. Elev. 4% bonds	Feb. & Aug. 1	$6,980,000	$116,333
Brooklyn Union Elev.	Feb. & Aug. 1	15,956,000	332,417
Atlantic Ave. 5% bonds	Apr. & Oct. 1	2,241,000	28,013
Coney Island & Brooklyn 4% Bonds	Jan. & July 1	1,500,000	30,000
Brooklyn City & Newtown 5% Bonds	Jan. & July 1	1,988,000	49,700
Jamaica & Brooklyn 5% Bonds	Jan. & July 1	231,000	5,775
Total			$562,238
Receivers' certificates 6%	Feb. & Aug. 1	$12,397,044	309,926
Total Interest accrued			$872,164

EXHIBIT K—Schedule D

B. R. T. System Bank Loans and Other Debt

(EXCLUDING BOND DEBT)

Settlement in Reorganization—Market Value Equivalent

		New 6% Bonds	6% Pfd. Stock	Cash
Bank loans	$3,300,000			
Plus unpaid interest	937,166			
	$4,237,166	$1,991,468	$254,230	$1,991,468
General creditors	1,600,000	....	732,613	898,689
(May 1, 1924—$1,411,245)				
Tort Creditors	2,200,000	....	....	2,200,000
Total in settlement		$1,991,468	$986,843	$5,090,157
MARKET VALUE EQUIVALENT				
Bonds	....	$1,991,468	$74	$1,473,686
Preferred stock	....	986,843	50	493,422
Cash	....	5,090,157	...	5,090,157
Total	....	$8,068,468		$7,057,265

EXHIBIT K—Schedule E

B. R. T. Reorganization

Values Considered by Transit Commission

		Original Cost December 31, 1922*	1921 Price Basis June 30, 1921
Property under Contract No. 4....		$82,600,000	....
Other property..................		86,452,523	....
Total property.............		$169,052,523	$249,927,252
Less—Straight line depreciation (Contract No. 4)	1,330,536		
Less—reconditioning cost—other property........	2,729,398	4,059,934	
Less—Straight line depreciation....		....	65,810,574
Net valuation................		$164,992,589	$184,116,678
Current assets (as per books—$34,235,923.) Included only.....		11,989,033	11,989,033
New Capital—to be paid in.......		5,000,000	5,000,000
Total....................		$181,981,622	$201,105,711

Property additions to June 30, 1923 not included.

In their valuation report, the Commissioners' engineers concluded "That a fair valuation for the existing properties of companies other than that included under Contracts 1, 2, 3 and 4 and their related certificates would consist in allowing the original cost less the expenditures necessary to put the property in first class operating condition. Valuation of the property paid for by........The New York Municipal Railway Corporation under Contract 4 and........certificate for extensions........should be based on the determination of costs by the Chief Engineer of the Commission as provided in such contracts with the deduction therefrom of the accrued depreciation also therein provided for."

EXHIBIT L

Disbursements on B. R. T. Reorganization

B. R. T. REORGANIZATION

Cash payments made to date by Reorganization Committee to Consummate Reorganization and terminate Receivership lasting approximately five years

Paid to Trustee under First and Refunding Mortgage of N. Y. R. T. Corporation as Improvement Fund to be drawn down from time to time to pay for additional cars and equipment	$5,000,350,000
Paid to holders of Receiver's Certificates	11,845,000.00
Paid to B. M. T. Corporation as working capital	1,000,000.00
Paid to N. Y. R. T. Corporation as working capital	1,000,000.00
Paid in settlement of tort claims for personal injuries	1,759,000.00
Paid in adjustment of general contract claims	836,000.00
Paid to syndicate consisting of over 170 banks, financial institutions and individuals the 5½% commission provided in Plan for underwriting provision of $26,048,015 of new money	1,432,640.82
Paid to holders of $3,000,000 B. R. T. Bank Loans, on account of adjustment of claims as provided in Plan	1,977,815.57
Paid to holders of $250,000 B. R. T. Bank Loans, secured by special collateral in adjustment of claims including interest	281,165.59
Paid to holders B. R. T. 7% Notes on account of adjustment of claims as provided in Plan in respect of $57,253,700 face amount of notes with $20,038,795 of interest in arrears	4,007,759.00

Paid to holders of B. R. T. 5% Notes on account of adjustment of claims as provided in Plan in respect of $465,000 face amount of notes with $116,250 of interest in arrears..	23,250.00
Paid to holders of N. Y. Mun. Ry. Corporation 5% Bonds on account of adjustment of claims as provided in Plan in respect of $1,997,000 face amount of Bonds with $499,250 of interest in arrears	99,850.00
Paid to holders of B. R. T. 5% Bonds on account of adjustment of claims as provided in Plan in respect of $6,963,000 face amount of Bonds with $1,653,712.50 of interest in arrears	348,150.00
Paid to holders of B. R. T. 4% Bonds on account of adjustment as provided in Plan in respect of $3,433,000 face amount of Bonds, with $617,940 of interest in arrears........	137,320.00
Paid to holders of B. B. & W. End R. R. Co. 5% Bonds in adjustment of $23,600 of interest in arrears on $118,000 face amount of bonds	23,600.00
Paid to holders of Atlantic Avenue R. R. Co. 5% Bonds Improvement Bonds in adjustment of $43,000 of interest in arrears on $215,000 face amount of Bonds...........	43,000.00
Paid to holders of Nassau Electric Railroad Co. First Mortgage 5% Bonds in adjustment of $132,000 of interest in arreas on $660,000 face amount of bonds	132,000.00
Paid to holders of Nassau Electric Railroad Consolidated Mortgage 4% bonds on account of adjustment as provided in Plan in respect of $10,337,000 face amount of Bonds with $1,860,660 of interest in arrears	413,480.00
Paid to holders of B. Q. & S. Co. First Mortgage 5% Bonds in adjustment of $336,825 of interest in arrears on $1,497,000 face amount of Bonds	336,825.00

Paid to holders of B. Q. Co. & S. R. R. Co., Consolidated Mortgage 5% Bonds on account of adjustment as provided in Plan in respect of $2,803,000 face amount of Bonds, with $560,600 of interest in arrears	140,150.00
Paid to defray cost of foreclosure proceedings extending over five-year-period of receivership, including expenses, and compensation of trustees and counsel and bondholders' committees and counsel, in connection with defaulted bond issues (with defaulted interest) as enumerated below:	

Bonds and Interest	*Issue*	*Cost*
$8,616,712.50	B. R. T. 5% Bonds.......	$138,794.06
4,050,940.00	B. R. T. 4% Bonds.......	142,011.90
4,237,166.00	Loans secured by B. R. T. 4% Bonds	
29,000,000.00	B. R. T. Consolidated Bonds, (all pledged)	39,015.43
581,250.00	B. R. T. 5% Notes	10,000.00
77,292,495.00	B. R. T. 7% Bonds*	652,654.54
2,496,250.00	N. Y. M. R. Co. 5% Bonds.	80,000.00
303,125.00	Brooklyn Heights R. R. Co. 5% Bonds	9,306.74
141,600.00	B. B. & W. End R. Co. 5% Bonds	12,289.43
12,197,660.00	Nassau Electric R. R. Co. Cons. 4% Bonds	69,203.66
1,833,825.00	B. Q. Co. & S. R. Co. 1st Mtge. 5% Bonds	36,964.26
3,363,600.00	B. Q. Co. & S. R. Co. Cons. Mtge. 5% Bonds	38,973.02

*Includes representation of B. R. T. 5% Notes and New York Municipal 5% Bonds by Note holders' Committee.

Paid to defray cost of representation of stock and general claims during five years of receivership, including expenses and compensation of committees and counsel:

$74,422,959.00	B. R. T. Stock...........	$242,008.33
2,200,000.00 (Est.)	Tort claims for personal injuries against N. R. Consolidated R. R. Co., B. R. T. Co. and surface companies	155,000.00
1,600,000.00	General Contract Claims against B. R. T. V. Co., N. Y. Mun. Ry. Co., and surface companies	43,500.00

Paid to defray cost of depositing old securities and distributing new, including expenses and compensation of Depositaries and Registrars in respect of the issues enumerated below:

Amount	Issue	Cost
$6,963,000	B. R. T. 5% Bonds .... Depositary Charges still unadjusted)	1,035.85
3,433,000	B. R. T. 4% Bonds.........	8,078.77
3,300,000	Bank Loans secured by B. R. T. 4% Bonds	
465,000	B. R. T. 5% Notes	465.00
57,253,700	B. R. T. 7% Notes	45,431.95
1,997,000	N. Y. Mun. Ry. Co. 5% Bonds.	1,997.00
250,000	Brooklyn Heights R. R. Co. 5% Bonds	1,782.80
118,000	B. B. & W. End. R. R. Co. 5% Bonds	560.00
10,337,000	Nassau Elec. R. R. Co. Cons. 5% Bonds	12,445.15
1,497,000	Brooklyn Q. Co. & S. First Mtge. 5% Bonds	2,000.00
2,803,000	Brooklyn Q. Co. & S. Cons. Mtge. 5% Bonds...........	2,803.00
74,422,955	B. R. T. Stock	33,646.34

Paid to defray organization and mortgage recording taxes, documentary stamps and filing fees in connection with organization of new companies and issuance of securities.... **784,013.73**

Paid to defray cost of printing and stationery	51,793.84
Paid to defray cost of publication of official notices	50,875.17
Paid to defray cost of printing and executing new securities issued under Plan...........	18,920.29
Paid to defray cost of engineering and accounting services	51,500.00
Paid to defray cost of receivership proceedings of B. R. T. and all subsidiary companies, including expenses and compensation of Receiver and his solicitor, Special Master and record parties in creditor's marshaling suit..............................	254,500.00
Paid to defray cost of stenographic services, minutes of hearings, clerical help, incorporation incidental expenses and other miscellaneous expenses	15,060.94
Paid to defray Reorganization Committee's compensation, including subcommittees, secretary and counsel, as follows:	
Committee	40,000.00
Sub-Committee in charge of details of reorganition	85,000.00
Purchasing Committee	45,000.00
Counsel	225,000.00
Secretary	5,000.00
Paid to defray cost of expenses incident to securing deposit of securities under Plan and distribution of new securities, including expenses and compensation of Reorganization Committee's depositaries	92,885.21
Total cash payments by Reorganization Committee to December 15, 1924......	$34,336,642.39

NOTE.—The cost of the foreclosure proceedings listed above related to bond issues, including defaulted interest, aggregating $144,114,623, and the total cost of such foreclosure proceedings averaged approximately 8/10ths of 1% of such issues.

The cost of representation of stock, tort claims and general contract claims listed above related to stock and claims of an agregate face amount of $78,222,959, and such cost averaged approximately 5/10ths of 1% of such face amount.

The cost of depositing the old securities and distributing the new, as listed above, related to $162,830,655 aggregate face amount of securities, and such cost averaged approximately 7/100ths of 1% of the face amount of such issues.

EXHIBIT M

LETTER—MAYOR HYLAN TO BOARD OF ESTIMATE

"CITY OF NEW YORK, OFFICE OF THE MAYOR

March 21, 1924.

To the Honorable the Board of Estmiate and Apportionment.

Gentlemen:

In accordance with the suggestion made at the meeting of the Committee of the Whole on Monday, March 17, 1924, I present the following communication.

The Brooklyn Crosstown Subway, as now proposed, will connect with the Queensborough (60th Street) Tunnel operated by the Brooklyn-Manhattan Transit Company through Queens Plaza and Jackson avenue in Long Island City, through Manhattan avenue and Roebling street in Greenpoint and through Bedford avenue in Williamsburg, with a connection from Bedford avenue to the Fourth Avenue Subway in Flatbush avenue now operated by the Brooklyn-Manhattan Transit Company.

A connection of this kind will tie up a $44,000,000 subway proposition with the Brooklyn-Manhattan Transit Company (formerly the B. R. T), to be operated by that company. Such a connection and operation will provide nothing but deficits to be made up by the taxpayers in the yearly budget, in addition to the $10,000,000 which the taxpayers are now forced to provide in the Budget under the present subway contracts.

A Brooklyn crosstown route, self-sustaining from the beginning of operation, could be provided by the construction of a line through the large industrial section of Greenpoint, crossing the East River to connect with the mercantile sections of Manhattan, for example, from the vicinity of Huron street, Brooklyn, to the neighborhood of from 23d to 34th streets, Manhattan.

This independent line would likewise give access to larger residential areas along the greater portion of the route than would the proposed route. On the Manhattan end, running crosstown from 23d street and the East River, it could connect with either of the proposed 6th or 8th avenue Subways in Manhattan for operation into the Central Park West-Washington Heights Route. The Brooklyn end need not turn down Fulton street from Bedford avenue, but could be continued across Fulton street to Franklin avenue to Flatbush avenue and eventually to Sheepshead Bay and Coney Island , operating through territory which has no adequate transit facilities at the present time. This route is possible because the Ashland place connection will link up the Fulton Street Elevated with the Fourth Avenue subway in Flatbush Avenue Extension for direct operation into Manhattan and thus provide a subway connection to Manhattan for central Brooklyn.

The Layfayette Avenue Subway should continue from a connection in downtown Brooklyn easterly in Lafayette avenue to Broadway, then through the Ridgewood section into Queens Borough. This route would be a self-sustaining line and provide direct access to downtown Brooklyn and Manhattan for Ridgewood and communities of Queens entirely without rapid transit facilities.

The Brooklyn crosstown trains should not be operated through the Queensborough (60th Street) Tunnel. That tunnel should be reserved in its full capacity for the demands of the Borough of Queens. The next logical rapid transit route for Queens Borough should traverse Queens Boulevard to provide transit facilities for the people of Jamaica and points beyond, and hasten the development of a large area of Queens Borough tributary to the Queens Boulevard. With such a route connecting into the 60th Street Tunnel no particular purpose would be served in constructing a subway connection for the Brooklyn Crosstown Line costing $10,000,000 across Newtown Creek, under the network of Long Island Railroad tracks, to Queens Plaza and the 60th Street Tunnel.

It is requested that this communication be referred to the Transportation Facilities Committee for consideration and report.

Very truly yours,

John F. Hylan,
Mayor."

EXHIBIT N.

Letter—Commissioner Delaney to Mayor Hylan

"June 3, 1924.

Hon. John F. Hylan,
Chairman of the Committee of the Whole,
Board of Estimate and Apportionment

Dear Sir:

Responding to the request of the Committee of the Whole for an expression of my view in respect to the pending contract with the Oakdale Contracting Company, Inc., for the construction of a section of the Brooklyn Crosstown Subway Route which was submitted by the Transit Commission, the situation appears to be about as follows:

1. Approval of the contract before you would definitely commit your Board to the construction of the next Brooklyn subway along Bedford Avenue and Roebling Street. The funds available will permit the immediate construction of only one Brooklyn line and therefore I suggest that the Board should consider the comparative advantages of more than one route before committing itself to any construction.

2. The action of the Legislature in continuing the State Transit Commission in control over the existing City-owned subways with power to increase fares and postpone recapture for municipal operation seems to compel us to construct a new system of independent

lines. It appears indisputable to me that the route of any new independent lines should be designed for service of the largest number of people, so that such route may be made self-sustaining in the shortest possible time. No subway can ever be self-supporting at a low rate of fare when the population is all on one side. The existing crosstown route all the way from the turn of Bedford Avenue and Wallabout Street to McCarren Park would have population only on one side, because there will be no residential development in the three or four blocks adjoining the river front.

3. The crosstown route can be designed that will give a subway to the populous central section of Brooklyn that can be self-sustaining at a five-cent fare, and that will be a logical part of an independent system passing through the Boroughs of Brooklyn and Manhattan. It seems to me that the new Board of Transportation should be given an opportunity to study the situation before your Board definitely adopts a policy. Otherwise the new Board will come into office on July 1st under conditions similar to those which prevented initiative in respect to the route by your recent Conference Committee. When the appropriating body that has constitutional control of the streets takes its position in regard to routes there remains nothing to be settled except details of construction.

4. I believe that before any construction contracts are authorized the New Board of Transportation and the Board of Estimate and Apportionment should adopt a plan to serve at least three of the boroughs. The cost of such a comprehensive plan should be estimated and the available funds should be equitably apportioned to each of the routes. The points at which construction should begin will be a consideration to be decided when

it is known what construction is to take place. Every borough would than have an interest in supporting a city plan to have subway bonds exempted from the debt limit by substituting them for water bonds or else all must face the necessity of providing funds for construction by local assessment. The alternative is to put all the available money into the Washington Heights Line and the Brooklyn Line and let the other boroughs wait. But I think we should consider the construction on an equitable basis.

5. I believe that a crosstown route through Central Brooklyn would be the line of greatest public benefit, but the Bedford Avenue Line would certainly be the line of least resistance. If you do not approve this contract you will be assailed with the charge that you are wilfully obstructing the progress of subway building. An organized group of property owners working to enhance the value of real estate in the vicinity of Bedford Avenue and Fulton Street at public expense will fight bitterly to keep the crosstown line on Bedford Avenue. Some of the loudest haters of this administration are in this group. Unless you build a new subway so as to pass through Bedford Avenue at Fulton Street you will not be deemed fit to hold public office. This group will be energetically supported by all the agitation that the elevated and surface railroads can arouse, because central Brooklyn is regarded as a private railroad preserve. You may expect hot denunciation from any quarters if you set up any competition to the Fulton Street or the Broadway elevated lines of the surface railroads. So put on your gas mask if you decide to reject this contract.

6. Your Board is not required by law to either adopt or reject this contract immediately. The only compel-

ling feature at all is that the contractor may withdraw his bid after the expiration of 45 days from the time it was tendered. As to the technical features the engineers certify that the contractor is responsible and that the price is reasonable under present conditions.

Respectfully submitted,

JOHN H. DELANEY,
Chairman, Committee of
Transportation Facilities."

EXHIBIT O

Objections To Determinations Of Costs

ITEMS WHICH HAVE BEEN SUBJECT TO REDETERMINATION

After each item is given the several Determinations as to which the objection to the item was filed.

Item	Determinations
1. *Interest on Amount of Debt Discount:*	
(a) on $40,000,000 of bonds issued April 4, 1923	12, 13, 14, 15, 16, 17, 18, 19
(b) on $20,000,000 of bonds issued November 4, 1915	12, 13, 14, 15, 16, 17, 18, 19
2. *Excessive rate of Interest*, being the difference between 5%, the rate of the bonds, and 6%	12, 13, 14, 15, 16, 17, 18, 19
3. *Salaries of Executives*, being the objection to the salary of T. S. Williams, President, at $25,000 per annum	12, 13, 14, 15, 16, 17, 18, 19
4. *Debt Expense*, being fee of $3,000 for listing of New York Municipal bonds on New York Stock Exchange	13
5. *Rental for Yards of South Brooklyn Railway Co.*	
(a) $14,625, representing quarterly rental for yard bounded by 37th and 39th Streets, 2nd and 3rd Avenues, Brooklyn	15, 16, 17, 18, 19
(b) $6,250 semi-annual rental of yard at 38th Street, West of 2nd Avenue, Brooklyn. This objection is discontinued as per previous report	16

The following is a further description of the items above listed:

1. *Interest on Amount of "Debt Discount."*

To provide the money required for Contract No. 4 and the Related Certificates, the Brooklyn Rapid Transit Co. sold its 5 per cent. notes on a 6 per cent. basis. With the proceeds from the sale of these notes, the Brooklyn Rapid Transit Co. bought the bonds of the New York Municipal Railway Corp. at 97 per cent. of par. The loss through the discount on the sale of the notes, was billed by the Brooklyn Rapid Transit Co. to the New York Municipal Railway Corp. on the theory that it was acting for the latter company, and this was allowed by the Public Service Commission by resolution adopted June 30, 1913 and thereafter included in the Prior Determination, see Page 40 thereof. On this same theory of agency the profit which the Brooklyn Rapid Transit Co. made by the transaction should be credited to the New York Municipal Railway Corp. The interest on the amount of the 3 per cent. discount, ($1,200,000 on $40,000,000 bonds issued April 4, 1913 and $600,000 on $20,000,000 bonds issued November 4, 1915) on the purchase by the Brooklyn Rapid Transit Co. of the New York Municipal Railway Corp. bonds, was a profit of this nature until the maturity of the notes when the amount of the 3 per cent. discount would be needed for retiring the notes.

This credit has not been made in the Determinations nor in the Redeterminations and may be submitted to arbitration or to the court.

2. *Excessive Rate of Interest*

The Chief Engineer has included in each of the Determinations mentioned, the following item:

"Additional interest accrued at 1 per cent. on $20,000,000 bonds issued November 4, 1915 to conform with intent of Contract 4 and Certificates that Company's interest charges during construction be figured at 6 per cent. per annum rather than 5 per cent. per annum, the rate borne by the bonds........................$50,000.00"

The purpose of this item was to make an allowance of 6 per cent., assumed to be the actual cost to the New York Municipal Railway Corp. through the sale by the Brooklyn Rapid Transit Company of its 5 per cent. notes on a 6 per cent. basis. This office would not have made this objection on its own initiative. The objection has been made acting upon the request of the Corporation Counsel. The allowance is for the same purpose as the allowance for prepaid interest on $40,000,000 of bonds, which item is now before the Supreme Court in an action by the City of New York to annul the Prior Determinations on this account. Acting Corporation Counsel, George P. Nicholson, in his letter to you of January 31, 1921 requests that, "written notice be given the Lessee that you require such Redetermination to be submitted to arbitration or to the Court as provided by Article XXX of Chapter VI of said contract."

3. *Salaries of Executives*

The particular objection being to the salary of T. S. Williams, as President, at the rate of $25,000.00 per annum.

It has been pointed out in previous reports that the salary of the President of the New York Municipal Railway Corp. and the associated companies was increased by $25,000.00 to $75,000.00 per annum at about the time Contract No. 4 was executed, and the increase charged to cost under Contract No. 4 and the related certificates. This was done without the approval of the Commission. Subsequent to the period covered by the determinations under discussion, the Chief Engineer has arranged with the Company for a reduction of the charge for the President, the difference being charged to other companies in the B. R. T. system.

4. *Debt Expense*

Being in particular a three thousand dollar fee for listing the $60,000,000 of the New York Municipal Railway Corp. bonds on the New York Stock Exchange. The facts are fully set forth on the Thirteenth Quarterly Determination, in which the writer called attention to the item but did not recommend objection.

5. *Rental for Yards of South Brooklyn Railway Company.*

Of two items, the objection to one has been discontinued, as heretofore reported. The remaining item is the following:

$14,625.00 quarterly rental paid under lease between the South Brooklyn Railway Corporation and New York Municipal Railway Corporation of the premises bounded by 37th Street and 39th Street, 2nd and 3rd Avenues, in the Borough of Brooklyn.

Two rentals are paid for this property. A quarterly rental of $14,625.00 is paid by the New York Municipal Railway Corporation and an annual rental of $20,000.00 by the Transit Development Company, which in turn recovers this rental from the New York Consolidated Railroad Company in its maintenance charges. Objection has been made to this rental on the ground that the condition required an adjustment of one or the other rental or both. The adjustments have not been made in the Determination and Redetermination and may be submitted to arbitration or the Court.

6. *Accrued Interest Receivable from the New York Consolidated Railroad Company on the Cost of Railroads in Operation.*

The basis for this objection is the practice of the New York Consolidated Railroad Company of making a deduction from operating revenue for interest on the difference between the company's expenditures as estimated by them, on account of the cost of construction and equipment and the cost as given in the latest available Determination but failing to credit the New York Municipal Railway Corporation with a corresponding amount in adjusting interest charges between the portions in operation and those not in operation. The failure to credit the New York Municipal Corporation is detrimental to the interests of the City, in that such failure affects the amount of bank balances of the New York Municipal Railway Corporation and consequently the amount of interest received on such bank balances. As Contract No. 4 provides that the cost for interest be reduced by the amount of interest received on bank balances, the effect of the practice now followed is to increase the capital cost of the railroad.

This credit has not been allowed in the Determinations or in the Redetermination and may be submitted to arbitration or the Court.

7. *Cost of Lawrence Street Station, Section* 3, *of Route* 33.

The Chief Engineer has excluded from the Determinations the cost of constructing the Lawrence Street Station, Section 3, of Route 33. The reason for excluding these costs is given in foot notes in the Determinations, which read as follows:

> "The Cost of constructing the Lawrence Street Station under an agreement modifying the contract is not included pending the consummation of an agreement modifying Contract No. 4, so as to provide for the construction of this station."

The fact that the station when completed will be an integral part of the railroad was the basis for objecting to the failure to include its cost in the Determinations. The cost has been excluded from the Determination and the Redetermination and may be submitted to arbitration or to the Court.

Objections to the 20th Quarterly Determination Interest on Company Money.

Objections should be filed as in the case of previous Determinations, to the following details of Interest on Company Money:

(1) $15,000.00 interest for the quarter year at 5 per cent. per annum on the 3 per cent. discount on $40,000,000 bonds issued April 4, 1913.

(2) $9,000.00 interest for the quarter year at 6 per cent. per annum on the 3 per cent. discount on $20,000,000.00 bonds issued November 4, 1915.

(3) $50,000.00 interest for the quarter year at 1 per

cent. per annum on $20,000,000.00 bonds issued November 4, 1915.

The reason for these objections has been set forth in reports on prevoius Determinations. The item of $50,000.00 is the one to which Mr. George P. Nicholson, Acting Corporation Counsel, in his letter to you of January 31, 1921, requests you to file objections on behalf of the City. The amounts objected to are included in the following items of the Determination among others:

Page 79—Interest on moneys provided by Company.

Interest accured during the months of January, February and March, 1918, on $40,000,000.00—5 per cent. bonds issued April 4, 1913	$500,000.00
Interest accured during the months of January, February and March, 1918, $20,000,000.00 — 5 per cent. bonds issued November 4, 1915	250,000.00
Additional interest accrued during the months of January, February and March, 1918, at 1 per cent. on $20,000,000.00 bonds issued November 4, 1915, to conform with intent of Contract 4 and Certificates that Company's Interest Charges during Construction be figured at 6 per cent. per annum rather than 5 per cent. per annum, the rate borne by the bonds . .	50,000.00
	$800,000.00

Also on page 4, Summary for Quarter Year Ended March 31, 1918, Undistributed Cost, $225,282.97; page 4, Summary of Total at March 31, 1918, Undistributed

Cost, $11,162,889.74; page 9, Summary of Expenditures by City and Company, Interest during construction, $229,945.07; pages 10 and 11, Summary of Expenditures by the Company Quarter Year Ended March 31, 1918, Interest during construction, $229,945.07.

Salaries of Executives.

Objection has been made in several of the previous Determinations to the allowance of $6,250 for the Quarterly salary of T. S. Williams, President of the Company. The amount of this charge for the 20th Quarter (ended March 31, 1918) is $1,250.00, or at the rate of $5,000.00 per annum. This is a reduction of $20,000.00 per annum from the rate previously charged. In the schedule to become effective on January 1, 1920, given in a letter from Mr. Turner to you dated March 30, 1920, no charge is to be included for the services of the President. The variation in this charge has been as follows:

To December 31, 1917........	$25,000.00 per annum.
January 1, 1918 to September 30, 1918..............	5,000.00 per annum.
October 1, 1918 to December 31, 1919	4,000.00 per annum.
Subsequent to January 1, 1920.	0.00

The Charge for the 20th quarter at the rate of $5,000.00 per annum does not seem to be unreasonable. Objections were made to this item in the 12th to 19th Quarterly Determinations inclusive.

Rental of South Brooklyn Railway Yards.

A quarterly rental of $14,625.00 is paid by the New York Municipal Railway Corporation, and an annual rental of $20,000.00 by the Transit Development Company for the premises bounded by 37th and 38th Streets,

2nd and 3rd Avenues, in the Borough of Brooklyn. The rental paid by the Transit Development Company is recovered by that Company in its maintenance charges to the New York Consolidated Railroad Company, operating assignee of the New York Municipal Railways Corporation. This situation seems to require the adjustment of one of the other rental or both; I recommend, therefore, that objection be filed to the item of $14,625.00 quarterly rental included in the 20th quarteerly determination. This item is included but not identified in the Summary on Page 4, Item Cost of Equipment of the Railroad for Initial Operation, $412,726.49, and in the summary Pages 10-11 Item Cost of Equipment, Broadway-Fourth Avenue Line Labor and Materials $316,185.41.

Accrued Interest on Interest Chargeable to Operation.

It is recommended that objection be made to the failure to include a credit, in an amount undetermined, or accrued interest receivable on the cumulative amount of interest chargeable to operations on the cost of the parts of the railroads in operation. This credit should have been allowed in connection with Interest on moneys provided by the Company as shown on page 79 of the Determination. The basis of this objection is the practice of the New York Consolidated Railroad Company of making a deduction from operating revenue for interest on the difference between the company's expenditures as estimated by them, on account of the cost of construction and equipment and the cost as given in the latest available determination, but failing to credit the New York Municipal Railway Corporation with a corresponding amount in the Journal Entries adjusting interest charges between the portions of the railroad in operation and those not in operation. The failure to credit the New York Municipal Corporation, is detrimental to the interests of the City in that such failure will affect the amount of the bank balances of the New York Municipal Railway Corporation and consequently the amount of interest received on such bank balances. As Contract No. 4 provides that the cost for interest be reduced by the amount of interest received on bank balances the effect of the practice now followed is to increase the capital cost of the railroad. This is one of the objections made to the 18th and 19th Quarterly Determinations as to which the Chief Engineer in his Redetermination states, "Upon a careful examination of the above objections the engineer is unable to find any grounds for altering his original conclusions."

Cost of Lawrence Street Station.

The following amounts paid on account of work done in constructing the Lawrence Street Station has been excluded from the amounts included in the statements on page 56 of the Determination Details of City's Cost for Labor and Materials, Quarter Year Ended March 31, 1918.

Route 33, *Section* 3:

Regular Estimate No. 34, January, 1918. $3,474.90
Regular Estimate No. 35, February, 1918. 1,239.30
Regular Estimate No. 36, March, 1918... 5,143.50

The reason for excluding these amounts is given in a foot note reading "The Cost of constructing the Lawrence Street Station under an agreement modifying the contract is not included pending the consummation of an agreement modifying Contract No. 4, so as to provide for the construction of this station." This station when completed will be an integral part of the railroad and objection should be made to the failure to include its cost in the City's Cost for Labor and Materials. This objection was also made in the 19th Quarterly Determination.

INDEX

References are to pages.

PAGES

PAGES

PAGES

PAGES

PAGES

PAGES

M. B. Brown Printing & Binding Co.,
37-41 Chambers Street, N. Y.

www.ingramcontent.com/pod-product-compliance
Lightning Source LLC
LaVergne TN
LVHW010543110826
845149LV00003B/547

* 9 7 8 1 4 1 8 1 8 7 8 2 8 *